SUN
TZU

SUN TZU

THE
NEW TRANSLATION

SUN-TZU
*Research and
Reinterpretation by*

J. H. Huang

QUILL
William Morrow
New York

Library of Congress Cataloging-in-Publication Data

Sun-tzu, 6th cent. B.C.E.
   [Sun-tzu ping fa. English]
   Sun-tzu / by Sun-tzu ; [translated and with a commentary by J. H.
   Huang].
     p. cm.
   Includes bibliographical references.
   ISBN 0-688-12400-3
   1. Military art and science—Early works to 1800.   I. Huang,
J. H. II. Title.
U101.S95   1993
355.02—dc20
                                      92-33951
                                        CIP

Printed in the United States of America

First Quill Edition

1 2 3 4 5 6 7 8 9 10

BOOK DESIGN BY MICHAEL MENDELSOHN OF MM DESIGN 2000, INC.

To all those who have suffered from war

Imperial officials come with the emperor's requests on the country's security.
Incessantly scribbling in the palace, only far into the night do I return.
Myriad homes and thousands of dwellings are all peacefully at rest.
Ah, under the moonlight there are but crystalline dewdrops sprinkling my court robe.

—PRIME MINISTER LI DEYU (787–849), Tang Dynasty

ACKNOWLEDGMENTS

This work would not have been possible without the generous help of many people over the past seven years, and to each and every one of them I owe a great deal.

My editor at Morrow, Thomas Darling, and the editor of Quill, Andrew Dutter, offered help at every turn, and their confidence in both me and this work made it all worthwhile.

Certain wonderful people encouraged me from the very beginning, when this was just the germ of an idea: Ambassador and Mrs. Everett Drumright, former Minister of Defense Dr. Yu Ta-wei and General Wei Ju-lin of the Republic of China, and Colonel Frederick Schweitzer (U.S. Army, Ret.) and his late wife, Susan. I also would like to thank Dr. Donald Abenheim of both the Hoover Institution and the Naval Postgraduate School, and Drs. Michael Handel and Arthur Waldron of the U.S. Naval War College for their support and ideas. For sharing both their experience and knowledge I want to express my particular gratitude to Colonel John Boyd (U.S. Air Force, Ret.); Dr. Paul Godwin of the National War College; Colonel Donald Boose (U.S. Army, Ret.), Professor Art Lykke, and Colonel George K. Osborn III (U.S. Army, Ret.) of the U.S. Army War College; Major D. J. Pollock and Colonel William Given of the U.S. Marine Corps Headquarters; Dr. Monte Bullard of the Monterey Institute of International Studies; Dr. William Snyder of the Air War College; and Dr. Cho-Yun Hsu of the University of Pittsburgh. A special note of thanks goes to Colonel William Darryl Henderson (U.S. Army, Ret., an author, company combat commander in Vietnam, and member of the President's Commission on the Assignment of Women in the Military), who provided me with much-needed inspiration.

For assistance with Japanese translation I must thank my friends Mrs. Shirley Cheng and Mrs. Fusako Honda. For helping locate research materials I would like to

9

express my gratitude to Dr. Raymond Tang and Byron Chang of the East Asian Library, University of California, Berkeley, and Mrs. Teresa Wang Chang of Taipei's National Central Library.

General Colin L. Powell, Chairman of the Joint Chiefs of Staff, was kind enough to read my manuscript and encourage me. Dr. Richard R. Kinney, former director of the University of Iowa Press and now at the Getty Trust, was enthusiastic and pointed me in the right direction.

To friends and family who were there throughout it all I will always be grateful. Special appreciation goes to my cousin, Mrs. Diane Hawes, for technical support. My father and mother, Colonel (R.O.C. Air Force, Ret.) L. C. and Mrs. Gloria Huang, as well as my daughter, Deborah, I thank for being there when I needed it the most. And finally I am in great debt to my wife, Carolyn, for all her help in writing this book.

CONTENTS

Introduction   15

Part 1: The Text of Sun-tzu   35

Book 1: Surveying   37

Book 2: Mobilizing for Armed Conflict   43

Book 3: Planning an Offense   48

Book 4: Control   53

Book 5: Combat Power   57

Book 6: Superiority and Inferiority   62

Book 7: Armed Contention   69

Book 8: The Nine Adaptations   75

Book 9: Troop Maneuvers   79

Book 10: Terrain   88

Book 11: The Nine Zones   94

Book 12: Attacks Using Fire   107

Book 13: Espionage   111

Part 2: Comments — 117

Book 1: Surveying — 119

Book 2: Mobilizing for Armed Conflict — 144

Book 3: Planning an Offense — 157

Book 4: Control — 163

Book 5: Combat Power — 171

Book 6: Superiority and Inferiority — 179

Book 7: Armed Contention — 188

Book 8: The Nine Adaptations — 200

Book 9: Troop Maneuvers — 205

Book 10: Terrain — 218

Book 11: The Nine Zones — 221

Book 12: Attacks Using Fire — 241

Book 13: Espionage — 248

Appendixes — 255

Appendix 1: The King of Wu's Queries — 257

Appendix 2: The Four Adaptations — 262

Appendix 3: The Yellow Emperor's Attack on the Red Emperor — 265

Appendix 4: Terrain II — 267

Appendix 5: An Audience with the King of Wu — 269

Appendix 6: Queries on the Nine Zones 274

Appendix 7: Dynastic Chronology of China 281

Bibliography 283

Index 289

N

Han Dynasty site of
Linyi City

—the Han site is 28.8 km north of
Linyi's present location—

Yingueshan

—burial site where
the Linyi's bamboo-
slat text of *Sun-tzu*
was found—

Jingueshan

PACIFIC
OCEAN

Present-day
location of
Shanding
and Linyi

INTRODUCTION

Sun-tzu[1] is the earliest extant strategic book in human history. It is also the most brilliant and widely applied strategic book ever written.

This timeless, invaluable classic has been handed down to us over approximately twenty-four hundred years.[2] Even its earliest existing version—the Linyi text—is about twenty-one hundred years old. Throughout these two millennia, *Sun-tzu*'s compact but rich text has been the authoritative guide for military affairs and political activities primarily in the Far East.

In more modern times, *Sun-tzu* was translated into French (in 1772)[3] and so gradually was introduced to the West. It also has come to be extensively adopted in all areas where problem solving, competition, or development require strategic guidance. Therefore, in addition to its traditional military and political uses, it has naturally become a part of international affairs, global trade, political campaigns, athletic competitions, the management of large or small businesses,[4] and even daily concerns for both profit and success. We therefore may say that *Sun-tzu* can address something as enormous as a country's existence and the achievement of its military goals, or as modest as a person's satisfaction in life.

THE AUTHOR, SUN WU

Sun-tzu is the book's title, and it also is the author's name; labeling a book after its author was customary in China during the pre-Qin period (before 211 B.C.). From historical records we know that Sun-tzu's given name was Sun Wu, that he was born into a noble clan initially surnamed Chen which lived in the state of Qi, and that he was a younger contemporary of Confucius.[5] Since the early Zhou Dynasty his ances-

15

tors had possessed feudal territory south of the Yellow River; theirs was a small state called Chen, which was later assimilated by the major power, Chu[6] (see the map in Appendix 1).

The state of Chen was filled with political intrigues. In 675 B.C. a political storm in which the heir apparent was murdered swept the state, and this persuaded the princeling Chen Wan to escape to the state of Qi. This princeling was the first generation of Sun Wu's clan to live in Qi.

When Chen Wan was still young, his father, the Lord of Chen, invited a *taishi* in charge of records and astronomy for the Zhou emperor's court to cast an oracle for his son; this oracle foretold that Chen Wan's descendants would possess a state outside of Chen. Later, when Chen Wan was betrothed, his fiancée's family had the bridal couple's fortunes read, and they were told that their descendants would begin to prosper in the fifth generation, and by the eighth generation they would be without peer.

The Power Struggles of Sun Wu's Ancestors

After the Chen clan immigrated to Qi, its members showed a marked ability for political advancement. The fifth-generation descendant of Chen Wan was named Chen Wuyu, and he ultimately achieved the paramount station of *daifu* (comparable to a proconsul); this coincided with what had been foretold at his great-great-grandmother's betrothal.

Since the Chen clan rose out of a dangerous environment awash with political machinations, it grew to be adept in cultivating exceptional strategic insight. So, at about the time Chen Wuyu became a *daifu*, he and his father, Chen Wenzi, sensitively took note of the increasingly serious dissension between the ruling Qing clan of Qi and the other nobles. The father said to his son, "Something is about to happen. . . . What can we gain from this?" Chen Wuyu obliquely replied, "On the main boulevard of the capital we will be able to secure a hundred carts of the Qing family's lumber." Chen Wenzi warned him to "guard them carefully." (This riddle meant that they would obtain the resources on which the Qing clan's political power was based.)

In the autumn of 545 B.C., the wielder of the Qing clan's political power, Qing Feng, went on a hunt with Chen Wuyu accompanying him as an attendant. Before they arrived at the hunting ground, Chen's father sent him the grievous news that Chen

Wuyu's mother was critically ill. Qing's men immediately had a tortoiseshell oracle cast and were given a forewarning of death. Tightly clasping the shell in both of his hands, Chen Wuyu wept, and Qing Feng therefore allowed him to return. On his way back, though, Chen Wuyu destroyed all of the boats and bridges, thereby cutting off Qing Feng's return route. And upon his arrival, the Chen clan instantly allied itself with the enemies of the Qing clan.

Before long, the Lord of Qi held the autumnal sacrifices. While the Qing clan still remaining in the capital guarded the shrine, the Chens and their allies sent in their own grooms to sing at the festivities. As the hours passed, the Qing men took off their armor, tethered their horses, drank wine, and enjoyed the entertainment. When the time was ripe, the Chens and their allies swiftly stole all of the armor and weapons, then slew the entire Qing family. The Chen clan thereupon began its climb to become the most politically influential in all of Qi.

Chen Wuyu had three sons: Kai, Qi, and Shu.[7] The surname Sun was conferred upon the third son, Chen Shu, because of his military accomplishments; he became Sun Wu's father.[8] The three sons of Chen Wuyu all gained considerable experience as battle commanders, in addition to their political seasoning.

The second son, Chen Qi, was the most adept of the three at political intrigue; he was the one his father and grandfather relied on for realizing their plans to seize power in Qi. Since ancient times those who have lusted after power typically have been ruthless—they have cared nothing for bonds or relationships—so we can imagine how fragile the family ties of these three Chen brothers must have been.

The Reason Sun Wu Left Qi for Wu

In 484 B.C., when Chen Shu and the Qi troops were about to go to battle against the allied armies of Wu and Lu, Chen Qi told his younger brother, "Upon your death, my prospects will brighten," a line that speaks volumes about their relationship.[9] After Chen Qi had allied with the other clans in removing the obstacle posed by the Qing clan, his ambition to seize power for himself burned fiercer.

This placed the family of Chen Shu in a precarious position and most likely was the reason Chen Shu's son, Sun Wu, left Qi for the state of Wu. Sun Wu's studies of military theory had already reached maturity, and Wu's military power was just on the verge of escalating.

The Meeting Between Sun Wu and the King of Wu, Helü

It is not known for certain when Sun Wu arrived in the state of Wu, but it would have been no later than 514 or 513 B.C., when Helü ascended the Wu throne.

Helü was not only a king, but also a very good and experienced commander with expansionary ambitions. After he initially met and spoke with Sun Wu, he immediately saw the value of Sun Wu's theories on military affairs; this definitely created the favorable environment that permitted *Sun-tzu's* knowledge to be handed down over the millennia.

To later generations, this meeting between Helü and Sun Wu was a momentous occasion, but at that time it was no more than a king interviewing a talented man. Therefore, few historical records could have existed about their meeting, and what remains extant is sparse indeed.[10]

Sun Wu's Career in the State of Wu

Nevertheless, after Sun Wu and the King of Wu met, Sun Wu was appointed both to be in charge of troop discipline and also to assist General Wu Zixu—who had escaped from the state of Chu—in designing their expansion strategy.[11] The most important collaboration between General Wu and Sun Wu brought about the weakening of Chu and finally led to the Wu state's massive invasion of it.

The Attack on Chu

At that time Chu was large and populous: the armies of this one superpower could withstand those of ten other states in central China. Facing this tough opponent, the King of Wu, General Wu, and Sun Wu deemed that their best strategy in dealing with Chu was to "split our armies into three divisions and conduct hit-and-runs against them. When one division approaches Chu, they all will have to emerge; when they emerge, we will withdraw, and when they withdraw, we will emerge. Chu will become frenzied on the road. We will then continue to overwhelmingly conduct this action until they are exhausted, doing whatever we can to make them err."[12]

The state of Wu actively pursued this strategic goal against Chu over five years, thereby completely tiring the Chu troops and dealing them great losses. At last, in the sixth year (506 B.C.), as soon as the time was ripe, the state of Wu launched a decisive assault. The attacks were so fierce that Wu swiftly won every one of the five battles and finally took Chu's capital, Ying. The Chu king, unable even to flee, "ordered his palace officers to set elephants' tails on fire and so make them rush the Wu troops"; he barely avoided capture by absconding from the country.[13] After that, the Wu state was able to work its way north toward the central part of China in its quest for superpower status.

The Death of Helü

In 496 B.C. the King of Wu, Helü, personally commanded a battle against the state of Yue, where he was mortally wounded in the foot. The heir apparent, Fucha, succeeded Helü, and three years later he saw that Wu was avenged on Yue.

After Fucha conquered Yue, he grew increasingly arrogant, while the governmental cliques also became more and more antagonistic to each other. Before long General Wu's inner circle was shunned by the new King of Wu, Fucha. In that age the loss of political power almost always resulted in massive bloodshed, so General Wu's group grew uneasy.

The Conclusion to Sun Wu's Story

The states of Wu and Lu became allies around 484 B.C. and were about to declare war on Qi. But before their swords were unsheathed, General Wu was sent as an envoy to Qi. He took this opportunity to spirit his son away to a powerful Qi minister's family for safekeeping. Upon his return, this was exposed by King Fucha, so General Wu was ordered to commit suicide.[14]

In the summer of 484 B.C., the allied armies of Wu and Lu conducted appalling field battles against Qi. The Qi soldiers had prepared themselves to fight to the death, but their lack of strength led to their defeat. Sun Wu's father, Shu, and many other commanders were taken as prisoners of the Wu state. Sun Wu learned this disastrous news immediately after his longtime colleague General Wu died, so he found himself plunged into days of isolation and enmity.

Details on Sun Wu after this cannot be found, except for a solitary entry in the book *Yuejueshu*,[15] which provides a modest epilogue to his life: "Outside of the city gate of Wu is a large tomb—the tomb of the King of Wu's foreign official, Sun Wu—which lies ten miles from the county. He was expert at military strategy."

During the last years of Sun Wu, the Chen clan in Qi finally grew strong enough to usurp the throne. For hundreds of years after that down to the end of the Warring States Period, all of the Qi lords were of the Chen clan. So, the fortune told to Chen Wan and his bride at last became fulfilled.

Century upon century passed; neither the tomb of Sun Wu nor the state of Qi any longer existed. The Chen clan continued ceaselessly to machinate and connive in Qi over many generations, deviously clutching and grabbing for power and fortune. They, too, eventually crumbled into the dust of history. Yet, exiled away in Wu, the man Sun Wu, who had never enjoyed a life of tranquility, left behind the sapient teachings that became the strategic classic *Sun-tzu*.

In the more than two thousand years since then, it is not known how many ages have owed their rise and fall to this classic, nor how many historical personages can trace their great achievements and exalted deeds to these teachings. Down through history until today, *Sun-tzu*'s influence has continued to grow and expand. This cannot help but make us feel how trivial the strivings by Sun Wu's ancestors actually were.

THE BOOK *SUN-TZU*

The greatness of *Sun-tzu* lies in its sweeping grasp of strategy's comprehensive truths, and with inspiring prose[16] it sophisticatedly forges these versatile principles into an uncomplicated but perfectly tangible system.

The Need for Prerequisite Studies in Understanding *Sun-tzu*

An exquisitely practical book such as this naturally is sought by all; it also is something that everyone should read. However, we must first remember that *Sun-tzu* is, after all, an ancient classic dating from two millennia ago. The meaning of the Chinese language and both the political and social systems had all markedly changed even as early as between the pre-Qin era (before 211 B.C.) and the late Eastern Han Dynasty (roughly A.D. 100), when Cao Cao first annotated *Sun-tzu*.[17] Needless to say, in the two thousand years between then and today, evolution in all of these areas has been beyond our imagination. Furthermore, in the transmission of this book over the years, facsimiles have been produced from earlier copies, resulting in numerous discrepancies among the versions.

For these reasons, a full comprehension of *Sun-tzu* requires much more than a simple translation. It is very clear that an encyclopedic grasp of *Sun-tzu* has as its necessary prerequisites pre-Qin research on related subjects and textual criticism.

The Discovery of the Linyi Bamboo-Slat Text of *Sun-tzu* and Its Significance

An enormous amount of material can be utilized for this, but the bamboo-slat text of *Sun-tzu* discovered twenty years ago in a Han tomb has been the most indispensable.[18]

This find occurred near the ancient Han site of Linyi in Shandong Province, which is about 28.8 kilometers (50 Chinese miles) north of present-day Linyi; for this reason we refer to this version of *Sun-tzu* as the Linyi text. In pre-Qin times, old Linyi was located in the state of Lu, and during the Western Han Dynasty it was situated in Dongjun (lit., "East County"). To the east of the ancient site is the Yi River, and to the south and southeast are two ancient tomb sites called respectively Yinqueshan (lit., "Mount Silver Sparrow") and Jinqueshan (lit., "Mount Gold Sparrow").

In April 1972, Chinese archaeologists unearthed in the Han tomb of Yinqueshan some unique burial objects, among them the remains of ancient books made up of 4,942 bamboo slats. After carefully sorting and studying these, they found that "more than two hundred slats containing twenty-four hundred characters"[19] were the remnants of an ancient version of *Sun-tzu* dating from between the Qin and Han periods (roughly twenty-one hundred years ago), as well as a wooden plate that recorded the content titles, and some pre-Qin materials related to *Sun-tzu* never heard of before (see Appendixes 1 to 5). This Linyi bamboo-slat version of *Sun-tzu* is to our understanding the closest approximation to the pre-Qin format for *Sun-tzu*.

Wherever discrepancies exist between the Linyi text's characters or sentences and those of the later versions, we have concluded that the Linyi text is nearly always more accurate. Many scholars have in fact long been aware of the great value of the Linyi text in the study of *Sun-tzu*, so the materials that have been released serially since the 1972 Linyi discovery have been mandatory sources for any *Sun-tzu* studies, either of its content or its language.

Sun-tzu's Structure

Historical records say that the earliest version of *Sun-tzu* had thirteen books. Every rendition of *Sun-tzu* we can see today has thirteen books, too. A distinct logic is evident in their structure, so we know that *Sun-tzu* was subjected to strict editing before it was completed; it was for this reason that the Qing Dynasty scholar Sun Xingyan (1753–1818) logically postulated that these thirteen books "were personally determined by Sun-tzu."[20] The main themes of these thirteen books are as noted below:

I. Strategic Deliberation

BOOK 1, "SURVEYING"

Overview of one's capability; also, discussion of basic rules for overcoming the enemy

BOOK 2, "MOBILIZING FOR ARMED CONFLICT"

Economic burdens in conflict operations and conservation methods

BOOK 3, "PLANNING AN OFFENSE"

Strategic options and five advantageous conditions for the conduct of armed conflict

II. Application of Force Capabilities

BOOK 4, "CONTROL"

The grasp of victory in conflict situations

BOOK 5, "COMBAT POWER"

Exercise of the dynamics of power

BOOK 6, "SUPERIORITY AND INFERIORITY"

Achievement of superiority in the balance of strength

III. The Conduct of Operations

BOOK 7, "ARMED CONTENTION"

Attainment of the initiative in operations

BOOK 8, "THE NINE ADAPTATIONS"

Strategic adjustments, the manipulation of allies, the need for setting protections, and commander character traits that may lead to failure

BOOK 9, "TROOP MANEUVERS"

Adaptation to the principal geographical areas and judgment of enemy conditions during conflict; also, how to establish leadership in armies

IV. Use of Geographical Factors

BOOK 10, "TERRAIN"

Discernment of the use of terrains and the six breakdowns in command; also, the choices between governmental orders and the proper conduct of battles, command in troop application, and the perception of victory

BOOK 11, "THE NINE ZONES"

Comprehension of the use of strategic zones, as well as adaptations and advantageous use of various situations for the conduct of offensive operations; also, ways forces are applied by superpowers, and coordination with the government

V. Supplementary Deliberation

BOOK 12, "ATTACKS USING FIRE"

The use of fire to assault the enemy; the different results of using either fire or water in assaults (The last part of this book constitutes the conclusion to *Sun-tzu* proper.)

VI. Additional Discussion

BOOK 13, "ESPIONAGE"

The importance and procedures of intelligence work

THE CARDINAL THOUGHTS OF *SUN-TZU*

Although *Sun-tzu* is composed of only about six thousand characters, its comprehensive essays offer limitless avenues for study. The purpose of our book is the correct rendering of *Sun-tzu*, so discussion of its theories is not relevant here; however, three points must be clarified for our readers:

First, throughout *Sun-tzu* there is no mention of defensive warfare. This demonstrates that in Sun Wu's opinion, strategy requires a dynamically assertive spirit. The Chinese ancients used to say, "When enemy strongholds crowd the borders, this is to the officials' shame."[21] Plunging one's own territory into battle is not what strategy is all about.

Second, *Sun-tzu*'s position, to our knowledge, is that the purpose of strategy is not conflict, but advantage; conflict serves as no more than one of the strategic tools. Therefore, conflict is a tactical choice rather than a certitude. That is why *Sun-tzu* says, "neutralize an adversary's military power, but not through battles" (p. 49), a theory with innumerable historical examples.

Third, generally, insofar as practical advantages are concerned, some armed conflicts do not necessarily end in victory and some victories are not necessarily advantageous. So, armed conflict should never be lightly initiated; it must have unequivocal strategic value. In other words, "not battling" is indeed a form of strategy. The decision not to conduct armed conflict often rises out of strategists' resourceful deliberations and ought not to be considered cowardice.

These three points are fundamental subjects seldom touched by *Sun-tzu* scholars. In raising them here we believe that they will serve to elucidate *Sun-tzu*. Of course, the optimum approach to *Sun-tzu* is a direct study of the text itself, as it will teach rational and effective ways for resolving the complicated problems of countries, armies, businesses, and even personal affairs to our greatest advantage.

J. H. HUANG
Santa Clara, California

Notes to the Introduction

1. *Sun-tzu* is the original title of this book (see p. 15), and it was renamed *Sunzi bingfa* (*bingfa* means "the principles for using forces") at a much later date. This is generally translated in English as "The Art of War," which actually is an emulation of the titles of books written by Machiavelli and Baron de Jomini.

   Sun-tzu in the pinyin system is spelled *Sunzi*, but *Sun-tzu* is the broadly accepted English rendering.

2. Regarding the thirteen books of *Sun-tzu*, three opinions exist as to how they were composed. The "Sunzi zhuan" (Biography of Sun-tzu) in the *Shiji* notes that Sun Wu first met with the King of Wu, Helü, after the book *Sun-tzu* had been written. If that is true, then we calculate that *Sun-tzu* would have been finished by around 514–13 B.C. (see note 5).

   However, every book of *Sun-tzu* begins with the line "Sun-tzu said," which suggests the second opinion that the text was actually recorded by Sun Wu's disciples after he had died; the distinct logic of this work, though, implies the third opinion that it "was personally determined by Sun-tzu" (as Sun Xingyan wrote in his preface to the *Sunzi shiyijia zhu*). If that is so, then we could assume that the entire work was concluded in the eleven years between 484 B.C., when his father was taken as a prisoner of war by the state of Wu (see p. 19), and 474 B.C., when the state of Wu was destroyed (see note 5).

   Although all of these conjectures still require concrete evidence, such early Warring States strategists as Sun Bin and Weiliao referred to the principles of *Sun-tzu* to a great extent; moreover, a great business tycoon of that time, Bo Gui, also employed Sun Wu's principles for using forces in his commercial affairs (see note 4). These facts show that the most reliable account of *Sun-tzu*'s completion would place it at about twenty-four hundred years ago.

3. Legend has it that Napoleon read *Sun-tzu* at one time. When the French edition

was first published, Napoleon was a student in military school; this story is therefore possible, but to our knowledge it has yet to be proved.

4. The *Shiji* records that in the waning years of the Spring and Autumn Period, the strategist Fan Li retired after assisting Yue in the destruction of the Wu state and amassed a great fortune from his business dealings. Also, in the early Warring States Period the business tycoon Bo Gui (c. fourth century B.C.) declared that he conducted his transactions as "Sun [Wu] and Wu [Qi] used forces" (vol. 129, "Huozhi liezhuan," pp. 1188–89). These are the earliest explicit records of strategic concepts being successfully applied to business.

5. We hypothesize that the year of Sun Wu's birth was probably no later than 534 B.C. and that he passed away after the state of Wu was destroyed in 473 B.C. Sun Wu also possibly saw with his own eyes the annihilation of the Zhi clan in the state of Jin (453 B.C.; see Appendix 1, "The King of Wu's Queries").

These views are based mainly on the fact described later in the Introduction that between the time that Sun Wu met the King of Wu, Helü (around 514–13 B.C.), and the time that Sun Wu's father, Chen Shu, was taken by Wu as a prisoner of war (484 B.C.), there is an interval of around thirty years.

The *Liji* records, "Seventy is considered aged, and family duties are [then] conveyed [to others]." It also says, "When a *daifu* is seventy, his duties revert" ("Quli" [*Shisanjing*, pp. 2662–63]). So, seventy was the upper age limit for a man to bear duties. In ancient times, there were occasional exceptions to this rule, but they remained very rare. The *Liji* also notes, "At twenty, one is *ruoguan* [lit., 'young with a man's hat']" ("Quli" [*Shisanjing*, p. 2662]). Therefore, the age of twenty was considered the beginning of a man's adulthood.

Using this framework, we can surmise that if Sun Wu met the King of Wu when he was twenty or so, his father, Chen Shu, would have been seventy when he became a prisoner of war. Ascribing dates other than these to their lives makes it impossible to account correctly for all of the important dates in Sun Wu's and his father's lives.

From these dates we can also deduce, using the year that Sun Wu was born, that he was sixty-one in 473 B.C. when Wu was annihilated. So, by the time that the Zhi family was eradicated in Jin, he would have been over eighty, also making it possible for him to have seen this happen. Based on these dates, then, we have formulated the following chronology for the life of Sun Wu:

Year	Chen Shu	Sun Wu	Important Occasions
534 B.C.	20*	born	
523	31	11	Because of Chen Shu's accomplishments in the attack on Ju, Lord Jing confers upon him the surname Sun.
514–13	40–41	20–21*	Sun Wu meets the King of Wu, Helü.
496	58	38	The King of Wu, Helü, dies; his son, Fucha, succeeds him.
484	70	50	Chen Shu is taken by Wu as a prisoner of war.
479	(year of Chen Shu's death unknown)	56	Confucius dies at age 72 or 73.
473		61	The state of Wu is annihilated by Yue.
453		81	The Zhi clan is eradicated in Jin.
		(year of Sun Wu's death unknown)	

*It is quite possible that Chen Shu was twenty when he fathered Sun Wu, and that Sun Wu in turn was twenty when he first met the King of Wu, Helü. One example of this early maturity was shown by their ancestor, Chen Wan. It is known for certain that Chen Wan was born in 706 B.C. and that he escaped to Qi in 672, where he met Lord Huan and became his palace chief of staff (*gongzheng*); at that time Chen Wan was no older than twenty-four and already married.

Also, *Mozi* states, "The sage kings established a rule saying, 'When men are the age of twenty, none may be unmarried; when women are the age of fifteen, none may be unwed; this is the sage kings' rule'" (vol. 6, "Jieyong" *shang*, p. 100). So this was the ancient tradition. This is also shown in the saying a man "is to be wed at age thirty," as noted by the *Liji* (vol. 1, "Quli," and vol. 28, "Neize" [*Shisanjing*, pp. 2662 and 3184]), as well as in the *Zhouli* (vol. 14, "Meishi" [*Shisanjing*, p. 1578]) and the *Guliang zhuan* (vol. 11, "Wengong shiernian" [*Shisanjing*, p. 5226]). We are afraid, however, that this was not necessarily the pre-Qin reality.

Thus, Sun Wu was a slightly younger contemporary of Confucius. The other ages given above for Chen Shu and Sun Wu are educated guesses on our part to fill in gaps both in their lives and in history, but further historical proofs are still needed to confirm them.

6. Chen was obliterated by the Chu state in 478 B.C. The *Shiji* says, "In the twenty-fourth year of the Mingong reign, King Hui of Chu returned to his country and used forces to invade the north, killing Lord Min of Chen, thereby annihilating Chen and assimilating it" (vol. 36, "Chen shijia," p. 506).

7. The fact that Chen Wuyu had three sons can be seen in Takezoe Kokou's *Sashi kaishen* (vol. 25, "Zhaogong ershiliunian," p. 46, note) and Yang Bojun's *Chunqiu Zuozhuan zhu* ("Zhaogong ershiliunian," p. 1473, note). But Yang also pointed out, "Shu was surnamed Sun, and Sun Wu was his offspring," so he ascertained the stance of Sun Xingyan (*Sunzi shijia zhu*, preface).

8. No records exist in the *Shiji* (vol. 65, "Sunzi zhuan"; see note 10) regarding Sun Wu's ancestors. Instead, the most forthright records can be found in the *Xin Tang shu* (vol. 73 *xia*, "Zaixiang shixibiao" [Genealogical tables of the prime ministers], p. 722, and "Sunshi zaixian" [Prime ministers of the Sun clan]). What this source suggests is the following primitive family tree:

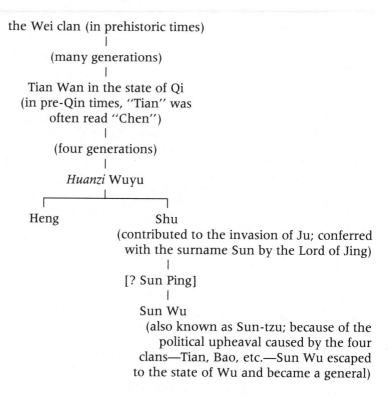

the Wei clan (in prehistoric times)
|
(many generations)
|
Tian Wan in the state of Qi
(in pre-Qin times, "Tian" was
often read "Chen")
|
(four generations)
|
Huanzi Wuyu
|

Heng   Shu
(contributed to the invasion of Ju; conferred
with the surname Sun by the Lord of Jing)
|
[? Sun Ping]
|
Sun Wu
(also known as Sun-tzu; because of the
political upheaval caused by the four
clans—Tian, Bao, etc.—Sun Wu escaped
to the state of Wu and became a general)

The *Xin Tang shu* was written by (Song) Ouyang Xiu et al., so this should be considered the product of Song scholars' research. Also, the records of (Song) Deng Mingshi in the *Gujin xingshishu bian* gives the same background for Sun Wu as does the *Xin Tang shu*. (This author has not personally seen Deng's book, but bases this finding on quotes from Deng's book in the *History of Wars in China* [vol. 2, p. 36].)

Their views ought to have referred to the *Zuozhuan*, yet one area remains unclear: The political struggles conducted by the Tians, Baos, and other clans lasted for a considerable period of time, so it is uncertain in both matter and date when they addressed "the political upheaval caused by the four clans—Tian, Bao, etc."

In addition, there are two errors in their genealogical table. First, Chen Wuyu had three sons, not two (see note 7). Also, Chen Heng should have been the grandson of Chen Wuyu, who assumed political power in Qi, so he was not Chen Wuyu's son.

Second, neither Tian Ping, Chen Ping, nor Sun Ping can be found in the *Zuozhuan*. If we calculate the time, we find that it would have been impossible for Sun Wu to be the grandson of Chen Shu (that is, Sun Shu), but rather was his son. Sun Xingyan noted, "Sun-tzu should have been Shu's offspring," and "Sima Qian did not thoroughly research this [in the *Shiji*]" (*Sunzi shijia zhu*, preface). Yang Bojun also maintains this position (*Chunqiu Zuozhuan zhu*, "Zhaogong ershiliunian," p. 1473, annotation).

That Chen Wan was Sun Wu's ancestor is certain. It is also irrefutable that their family tree can be traced back to the feudal state of Chen, as well as to prehistoric times when they had the surname Wei and were descended from the emperor Yuxun.

For our development of Sun Wu's chronology, we referred to related records in the *Zuozhuan* ("Zhuanggong ershiernian," "Xiangong ershibanian," "Zhaogong shijiunian," and "Zhaogong ershiliunian," among others) and then expanded them into a complete description.

9. "Aigong shiyinian" *xia*, *Zuozhuan* (*Shisanjing*, p. 4703).

10. When scholars discuss Sun Wu, they often refer to the "Sunzi zhuan" (Biography of Sun-tzu) in the *Shiji* (vol. 65, p. 735), the text of which is as follows:

Sun-tzu, [named] Wu, was a native of Qi and presented "the principles for using forces" to the king of the Wu state, Helu [note: the *Zuozhuan* gives his name as Helü, which we follow in our translation of *Sun-tzu*].

Helu said, "I have read all thirteen books of yours. Could we try a bit of it in training forces?"

[Sun-tzu] replied, "We can."

Helu asked, "Could you try it with women?"

[Sun-tzu] replied, "I can."

Therefore, permission was granted and the lovely ladies sent out of the palace totaled 180. Sun-tzu divided them into two arrays and appointed as leaders the king's two beloved concubines. He made them all hold halberds, asking them, "Do you know where your heart, your left and right hands, and your back are?"

The ladies said, "We know."

Sun-tzu said, "Advance by following the heart; turn left by following the left hand; turn right by following the right hand; retreat by following the back."

The ladies said, "Yes, sir."

As soon as the rules had been announced, they set up the headsman's ax, then thrice repeated the orders and explained them five times. Thereupon the drums were rolled for a right turn. The ladies laughed.

Sun-tzu said, "When an announcement is unclear and an order's explanation is not completely understood, this is the commander's fault." Again, they thrice repeated the orders, explained them five times, and the drums were rolled for a left turn. Again, the ladies laughed.

Sun-tzu said, "When an announcement is unclear and an order's explanation is not completely understood, this is the commander's fault. When they already are clear and the rules are not followed, this is the officers' fault." He then went to execute the leaders of the left and right arrays.

From his belvedere, the King of Wu was shocked at seeing that his two beloved concubines were about to be executed, and he immediately sent a messenger to relay his order: "I already know you are adept at using forces. But without these two concubines even food would lose its taste. Please cancel the execution."

Sun-tzu replied, "Since I have been appointed commander, when commanders are commissioned an army, some lords' orders need not necessarily be accepted." Thus he had the two leaders executed to expiate their faults and promoted the next ranks to leaders. Then, the drums again were rolled. The ladies' performance in turning left and right, advancing and withdrawing, kneeling down and standing up all were in accordance with the regulations and none dared make a sound.

Sun-tzu then sent a messenger to report to the king: "The forces are ready, Your Majesty. Please come to view them. They can be used as Your Majesty wishes. Even if driven into a flood or flame, they will not falter."

The King of Wu said, "The general must be tired and may return to the guest house. I do not desire to see them."

Sun-tzu said, "The king is one who talks but does not act on his words." Helu then knew that Sun-tzu was adept at using forces and at last appointed him as a general.

They destroyed mighty Chu to the west and entered [the capital] Ying, threatened Qi and Jin to the north, and built up their position among the other lords; in this Sun-tzu made contributions.

In this record the most important points are that (1) *Sun-tzu* is made up of thirteen books, (2) Sun Wu met with Helü to discuss military affairs and was later appointed a general, and (3) Sun Wu made beneficial contributions to the Wu state's strategies for expansion.

However, these are not the main subjects of this biography. In addition to Ye Shi's (Song, 1150–1223) question, "What type of formation divides 180 people into two arrays?" (*Xixue jiyan*, vol. 46, "Sunzi," p. 675), this story should not only be seen as simply absurd, but also as absolutely countering the text of *Sun-tzu* (see Appendix 5). By the Qing Dynasty, scholars had already pointed out that "this was an anecdote handed down by the Seven States [i.e., Warring States] people" (see Ling Yangzao, *Lishuobian*, vol. 20, p. 330).

Obviously, this story could not have come from the pen of such a great and highly disciplined historian as Sima Qian, the author of the *Shiji*. After the death of Sima, portions of the *Shiji* were either lost or damaged, and so Han scholars amended these losses in later years. Thus, the mythical story placed in the "Sunzi zhuan" very possibly might have originated with them.

11. The *Shiji* says, "Wu appointed Sun Wu to straighten out military discipline and to ensure that rewards and punishments were according to regulations; [Wu] finally surpassed all the lords and enveloped their territory" (vol. 25, "Lüshu," p. 332).

    The *Shiji* also records that Wu "destroyed mighty Chu. . . . Sun-tzu contributed to this" (see note 10). Later it notes:

Helu ruled three years and raised troops . . . because he wanted to reach Ying. General Sun Wu said, "The people are fatigued and cannot do so; we should wait on this [note: this line can also be found in vol. 31, "Wu Taibo shijia"] and then return." . . . In the ninth year the King of Wu, Helu, said to [Wu] Zixu and Sun Wu, "Previously you declared we could not yet invade [Chu]; what is your opinion now?" The two replied, "... Your Majesty, if you wish to make a decisive attack, then you must gain first [the states of] Tang and Cai, and you will be able to succeed." (vol. 66, "Wu Zixu zhuan," pp. 740–41)

It also says, "[The state of] Wu applied the strategies of Wu Zixu and Sun Wu to destroy mighty Chu in the west." Based on these comments we are able to assert that Sun Wu indeed contributed to Wu's strategies against Chu at that time.

However, it is also clear that Sun Wu was not the main person responsible for these duties, as the "Wu Zixu zhuan" twice mentions Wu Zixu first and then Sun Wu (see above). That Wu Zixu was Sun Wu's superior is very obvious. Since Sun Wu was the subordinate, any generalizations made in the history books would not have mentioned him. The *Shiji* notes, "King of Wu, Helu; Wu Zixu; Bopi; [and the states of] Tang and Cai together attacked Chu. Chu was overwhelmingly defeated and the Wu [state] thereby entered Ying" (vol. 40, "Chu shijia," p. 554). Wu Zixu was the field marshal and Bopi was the prime minister, so this account emphasizes only the main people involved and ignores ancillary-level persons such as Sun Wu.

"Qinggong sinian," *Zuozhuan*, records that the state of Wu invaded Ying (*Shisanjing*, p. 4636); the absence in it of any mention of Sun Wu would be for the same reason.

12. "Zhaogong sanshinian dong eryue," *Zuozhuan* (*Shisanjing*, p. 4615). From a strategic standpoint, the precursors of modern Chinese guerrilla warfare are much more ancient than most people realize. "Hit-and-runs" reads *si* in the Chinese text; we follow Yang Bojun's annotations here (*Chunqiu Zuozhuan zhu*, p. 1509).

Historians have indicated that this strategy emulates the lore handed down from the Jin state's General Xun Ying, since they reorganized four armies into three, to exhaust Chu; however, Wu's tactics far exceeded those of Xun Ying (*History of Wars in China*, vol. 2, pp. 40 and 49).

The Wu state's use of this as its strategic goal correlates with what is discussed in Book 1, "Surveying," of *Sun-tzu.*

13. "Dinggong sinian dong shiyiyue," *Zuozhuan* (*Shisanjing*, p. 4637).

14. "Aigong shiyinian," *Zuozhuan* (*Shisanjing*, p. 4704). Also see the *Shiji*, vol. 66, "Wu Zixu zhuan," p. 742.

15. Vol. 2, "Wudi zhuan," p. 38.

16. During the Liang Dynasty the great literary critic Liu Xie (b. 465) commented, "The phrasing of Sun Wu's strategic classic is like pearls and jade" (*Wenxin diaolong*, vol. 10, "Chengqi," p. 71). *Sun-tzu*'s writing indeed has a graceful and simple power.

17. If this was not the case, why did every classic from the pre-Qin period require the early annotations of such Eastern Han scholars as Jia Kui, Kong Anguo, Mao Heng, Zheng Xuan, and so on?

18. See "Shandong, Linyi, Xi Han mu faxian 'Sunzi bingfa' " and " 'Sun Bin bingfa' deng zhujian de jianbao," *Kaogu*, no. 2 (1974), pp. 15–35. Also, "Shandong Linyi Jinqueshan jiuhao Hanmu fajue," *Wenshi jilin*, fifth cumulative vol., p. 172; "Linyi feixian," *Zhongguo lishi ditu*, pp. 9–10, map H-4, and pp. 15–16, map H-3; and "Sanshinian lai Shandongsheng wenwu kaogu gongzuo," *Wenwu kaogu gongzuo sanshinian, 1949–1979*, p. 193.

19. Zhan Libo, "Luetan Yinqueshan Hanmu zhujian 'Sunzi bingfa,' " *Yinqueshan Hanmu zhujian "Sunzi bingfa,"* p. 1.

20. *Sunzi shijia zhu*, preface. Also see note 2.

21. *Liji*, the line "*sijiao duolei, ci qin daifu zhi chi,*" vol. 3, "Quli" *shang* (*Shisanjing*, p. 2704).

PART 1

THE
TEXT
OF
SUN
TZU

BOOK 1
SURVEYING*[1]

THE PREMISES:

a. a country must have sufficient military capability

b. a country must have a comprehensive security strategy

TWO TOPICS OF DISCUSSION DEVELOPED FROM THE PREMISES—THE ESTABLISHMENT OF MILITARY CAPABILITY AND THE SURVEYING OF EITHER A COUNTRY'S SECURITY OR THE POSSIBILITIES FOR VICTORY:

a. the establishment of military capability—five spheres should be dealt with by one's government:

SUN-TZU SAID,

Military affairs are a country's vital political concerns.[2]

The lands that are lethal or safe and the ways that cause existence or destruction must never be taken lightly.

Then, they are based on these five[3] and are verified through surveys[4] to assess their status:
the first is leadership,[5]
the second are cyclic natural occurrences,[6]

*Note numbers in Part 1 refer to the comments in Part 2 beginning on p. 117.

the third are geographical factors,[7]
the fourth is commandership,[8]
and the fifth are rules.

1. leadership—political requirements from the perspective of a country's security

Leadership causes people to follow their superiors willingly; therefore, following them in death and in life, the people will not betray them.[9]

2. the components of cyclic natural occurrences

Cyclic natural occurrences include yin and yang,* cold and heat, and the seasons and lunar periods.[10]

3. physical features of the land

Geographical factors are the high and the low,[11] the wide and the narrow, the far and the near, the difficult and the easy, the lethal and the safe.

4. commander cultivation

Commandership requires wisdom, credibility, benevolence, courage, and discipline.

5. the functions of rules

The rules are in regulations for mobilization, official duties, and the management of matériel.[12]

b. an overview of the conditions for a country's security:

All generals have to learn these five in their entirety.[13]

Those who know them will be victorious.
Those who do not know them will not be victorious.

Then, they are verified through surveys to assess their status.

*"Yin and yang" here means day and night and the hours, as well as unusual changes in the weather; see comment 10.

These are:

1. the ability of political authorities	Which lord has better leadership?
2. commander talent*	Which side has more capable commanders?[14]
3. adaptations to cyclic natural occurrences and physical features of the land	Which side takes better advantage of the cyclic natural occurrences and geographical factors?
4. capability in military systems:	
i) officer ability and internalized troop discipline	Which side carries out rules and orders more thoroughly?
ii) quality of weapons and people	Which side has stronger weapons and people?[15]
iii) training quality	Which side's warriors and soldiers[16] are better trained?
iv) effectiveness in creating soldiers' self-motivation	Which side has clearer rewards and punishments?

From these we are fully able to perceive victory and failure.[17]

---

*Note that the subject "commanders" is moved here directly after "leadership" and before the others, which differs from the order of the preceding "five spheres"; Sun Wu thereby indicates that this is either a security procedure or preparation for armed conflict.

ON THE CONDUCT OF ARMED CONFLICT:

a. commander appointment—the duty of a commander is to carry out his country's strategy for victory

When commanders heed our surveys and are appointed, victory is assured; retain them.

When commanders do not heed our surveys and are appointed, defeat is assured; dismiss them.[18]

b. the achievement of victory:

1. establish superiority:

    i) first according to the strategic intention

    Survey advantages that are heeded, and then accordingly create combat power to support outland missions;[19]

    ii) then by adapting to the conflict situation

    combat power comes from weighting the balances to our advantage.

2. weaken the enemy—the exercise of unconventional means:

    And, military operations entail unconventional means.*[20]

    Therefore,

    i) through deception:

        —hiding one's capability

        have a capability, but appear not to;

        —hiding one's application

        make use, but appear not to;

---

*"Unconventional means" is different from today's "unconventional warfare"; see "unconventional means" in comment 20, pp. 136–37.

	—hiding one's distance	be near but appear far, or be far but appear near;
ii)	through enticement:	
	—with advantages	show gains to lure them;
	—with disarray	show disorder to make them take a chance;[21]
iii)	through the use of defense	where superior, set protections against them;
iv)	through the use of evasion	when strong, avoid them;
v)	through discouragement	if of high morale, depress them;[22]
vi)	through delusion	seem humble to fill them with conceit.[23]
vii)	through fatigue	If at ease, exhaust them.[24]
viii)	through disunity	If united, separate them.

3. issue a decisive attack:

i)	strike enemy inferiorities:	
	—in their strength	Attack their weaknesses;
	—in their minds	emerge to their surprise:[25]
ii)	objectively judge the most advantageous moment for a strike	such victories of strategists never can be prematurely self-determined.[26]

CONCLUSION:

the success of strategy relies on the promise of victory beforehand

Before armed conflict, the court's reckonings predict victory when more positive answers are gained.[27]
Before armed conflict, the court's reckonings predict no victory when fewer positive answers are gained.

More positive answers lead to victory and fewer positive answers lead to no victory, least [of all] when there are no positive answers at all.

In this way we observe it; victory or failure is completely clear![28]

BOOK 2

MOBILIZING FOR ARMED CONFLICT[1]

IN DESIGNING STRATEGY ONE MUST CONSIDER:

a. the heavy logistical costs

SUN-TZU SAID,

Generally, fundamentals in using forces are:
a thousand swift chariots, a thousand leather-armored chariots, a hundred thousand laced corselets, and drayage of provisions through a thousand miles,* in addition to outland and domestic expenses, envoy and foreign advisory services, and adhesive and varnishing materials, as well as vehicle and armor supplies[2]
—expend thousands of pounds of gold[3] per day; only then are a hundred thousand troops raised.

And, they will be capable of waging armed conflict.[4]

*Throughout *Sun-tzu*, the original Chinese units of measure have been given familiar English equivalents to simplify the understanding of *Sun-tzu*, but they will not obstruct his teachings.

b. the hazards caused by military actions if they do not proceed smoothly:

1. damage to a country's capacity

With protraction, weapons will dull and keenness will dampen; with the besieging of a city, strength will be exhausted; with long troop exposure, the country's resources will become insufficient.

2. the tempting of another country into a challenge

When weapons are dulled, keenness is dampened, strength is exhausted, and goods are depleted, then other lords will take advantage of these complications and rise up; even if there were an ingenious man,[5] he would not be able to rectify the aftermath.

c. the elimination of hazards and the obtainment of advantages:

1. military operations should be effective and brief

Thus, regarding forces we might hear of methodical swiftness, but we should never see cleverness cause protraction.[6] For forces to protract and yet benefit the country would be without precedent.[7]

2. the avoidance of hazards must be thoroughly deliberated before operations

So, by not fully knowing the hazards of using forces, one cannot fully know the benefits of using forces.[8]

3. lessen burdens by shifting them to the enemy

Those sophisticated at using forces neither draft additional conscripts nor thrice[9] requisition provisions; they equip themselves in the country and take advantage of the enemy's provisions.

Thus, their army's food is sufficient.

IN THE CONDUCT OF OPERATIONS ONE MUST KNOW:

a. the country's inevitable financial hardship during conflict:

A country can be impoverished by its troops: when they are far away, there is distant drayage.

1. the people's losses

When they are far away and there is distant drayage, then the citizenry will become impoverished.

Places near markets will post high prices; high prices will then dry up the citizenry's finances.

Once finances are dried up, there will be a dire need for heavier conscription and taxes.[10]

When the labor pool is exhausted in the heartland,* all homes[11] will lie bare —and seven tenths[12] of the citizenry's property will be lost.

*"The heartland" in early China was delineated by the Yangtze River to the south, Mongolia and Manchuria to the north, Shaanxi Province to the west, and Shandong Province to the east. This area was often the battlefield in conflicts between lords.

2. the public's losses

Regarding the public's property —damaged chariots, worn-out horses, armor, helmets, arrows, bows, bills, infantry shields, spears, large protective shields, draft oxen, and transport carts[13] —six tenths of them will be lost.

b. how to eliminate hazards and obtain advantages:

1. by benefiting oneself and setting back the enemy, a double loss is dealt to one's opponent

So, wise commanders actively[14] consume the enemy's supplies, for consuming one unit of the enemy's rations equals twenty times our own, and one measure of their fodder equals twenty times our own.

2. by effectively motivating troops:

i) with morale

So, trounce the enemy[15] by means of high morale

ii) with rewards

and snatch the enemy's advantages by means of valuable goods.

3. gain strength through victory

So, in chariot battles when chariots are captured, the ten-chariot unit commander will reward the first to capture them[16] and will switch their battle standards and flags;* their chariots are mixed

---

*Battle standards were used in combat to control direction, while flags were employed in combining the troops.

with ours and driven; their soldiers are
treated kindly when given care:[17]
this is conquest for aggrandizement.

CONCLUSIONS:

a. from the standpoint of strategy—
short and effective military operations are necessary

Therefore, forces prize victory, not
protraction.

b. from the standpoint of conducting
operations—the correct realization
of a commander's duty is necessary

Therefore, a commander who knows
forces is the Guardian of the people's
lives and the ruler of the entire country's
security.[18]

BOOK 3

PLANNING AN OFFENSE

ON OFFENSIVE STRATEGY:

SUN-TZU SAID,

a. the principles of security:

1. the primary deliberation in strategy is, what is the safest option?

Generally, fundamentals in using forces are that:
annexing an entire country is best, destroying it is second best; annexing an entire army is best, destroying it is second best; annexing an entire battalion is best, destroying it is second best; annexing an entire company is best, destroying it is second best; annexing an entire squad is best, destroying it is second best.[1]

2. when victory can be effectively obtained in other ways, battles should be avoided

Then, achieving victory in every battle is not absolute perfection: neutralizing an adversary's forces without battle is absolute perfection.

b. four stages in conforming to conflict situations:

1. their intentions

So, the best military strategy is to crush their plans,[2]

2. their supports

following this is to crush their diplomatic relations,

3. their battle capabilities

and following this is to crush their forces;

4. their strongest line of defense

worst of all is to besiege their city fortifications.[3]

(rigid attack brings calamity)

Besiege city fortifications only when no other option is left.[4]

The building of large protective shields and armored carriers and the preparation of siege equipment require three months.
A city blockade[5] requires another three months.

When commanders cannot rein in their rage but order the scaling of city fortifications, one third of their warriors will be sacrificed, yet the city shall not be occupied: this is the tragedy of siege.

c. conclusion — when conducting conflict, do not rely mainly on physical and material power, but on mental power

So, those sophisticated at using forces neutralize an adversary's military power, but not through battles; occupy an adversary's cities, but not through siege; and destroy an adversary's country, but not through protraction.

By ensuring perfect contention in the world, their blades are not dulled while their advantages are fully gained:
these are fundamentals for planning an offense.

ON THE CONDUCT OF STRATEGY:

a. the employment of different force sizes:

So, the fundamentals in using forces are:

1. larger

ten to one, beset them;
five to one, attack them;
double, divide them;

2. equivalent

equal, be able to battle against them;[6]

3. smaller

fewer, be able to evade them;
weaker, be able to avoid them.[7]

Thus, with a smaller force against them, conduct dynamic actions;
with a larger force against them, conduct ensnaring actions.[8]

b. the interference of political authorities:

1. discouraging commander loyalty

Commanders are the supports of the country; with their close support the country will definitely be strong.

With gaps in their support the country will definitely be weak.

2. damaging army cohesion:

So, a lord may harm the armies[9] in three ways:

    i)   by causing hindrance

By not knowing that the armies cannot make an advance but ordering them to do so, or by not knowing that the armies cannot make a withdrawal but ordering them to do so
—this is called entangling the armies.

    ii)   by causing confusion

By not knowing the armies' affairs yet interfering[10] with the armies' policies; the armies' warriors will be leery.

    iii) by causing undermined trust

By not knowing the armies' estimations yet interfering with the armies' work; the armies' warriors will be suspicious.

When the armies are both leery and suspicious, calamities caused by other lords will follow
—this is called disrupting the armies and surrendering victory.[11]

c. the five conditions that determine victory in actions beforehand:

So, victory can be perceived with these five:

1. correct judgment

By perceiving possibilities and then conducting battles, there is victory.

2. flexibility in troop use

By knowing how to apply many and few, there is victory.

3. cohesion

By unifying will among the high and low ranks, there is victory.

4. surprise actions

By awaiting unpreparedness with preparedness, there is victory.

5. freedom from political interference

By having commanders who are capable and a lord who does not intervene, there is victory.

These five are the ways of perceiving victory.

d. conclusion—victory relies on outstanding intelligence work and a full grasp of one's situation before actions are launched

Therefore, regarding forces:[12]

By perceiving[13] the enemy and perceiving ourselves, there will be no unforeseen risk in any battle.[14]

By not perceiving the enemy yet perceiving ourselves, there will be partial victory and partial loss.

By not perceiving the enemy and not perceiving ourselves, every battle will be an unforeseen risk.

BOOK 4

CONTROL[1]

CONTROL IN STRATEGY:

SUN-TZU SAID,

a. understand the nature of victory:

    1. it exists in preparedness and in opportunity

    Long ago, those sophisticated at strategy first created undefeatability and then awaited the enemy's defeatability.[2]

    2. it exists in the enemy's failure

Undefeatability lies with ourselves. Defeatability lies with the enemy.

Thus, those sophisticated at strategy are able to create undefeatability but are unable to make the enemy defeatable.

    3. it is never determined by only one side

So we say, victory can be perceived, but it cannot be created.

b. understanding defense and offense:

    1. the functions of defense and offense

    For undefeatability, defend; with defeatability, attack.[3]

2. the conduct of defense or offense is determined by the balance of strengths

Defense is for sufficiency; attack is for deficiency.[4]

3. the key to designing defense or offense is impenetrability

Long ago, those sophisticated at a defense were as if concealed in the deepest bowels of the earth, and those sophisticated at attack were as if moving in the highest reaches of the heavens.

They were thus able to secure themselves and achieve complete victory.[5]

CONTROL IN OPERATIONS:

a. on the control of victory:

1. if the plan for—and the realization of—victory cannot surpass general conceptions, it will certainly not surpass those of the enemy, so chance is an element in victory

Visualization of victory which does not extend beyond common concepts is not absolute perfection.

Gaining victory in battle to the whole world's acclaim is not absolute perfection.[6]

2. a secured victory hinges on an impotent enemy

For,[7] lifting autumn down does not concern great strength, seeing the sun and the moon does not concern sharp eyes, and hearing thunder does not concern sensitive ears.

Those known as sophisticated at strategy vanquish those who are easily vanquished.

3. seize victory through prearrangements

So, the battles of those sophisticated at strategy do not have unorthodox victories,[8] are not known for genius, are not acknowledged for valor
—because their victories contain no miscalculations.[9]

"No miscalculations" means their arrangements are victorious, achieving victory over those who have already lost.

b. on control in conflict:

1. every conflict's situations for victory or defeat are unique; how to secure oneself and defeat the enemy should be discerned beforehand

Those sophisticated at strategy[10] occupy undefeatable positions and never overlook the enemy's losses.

2. victory is determined before, not just during, battle

Therefore, victorious forces first achieve victory and then conduct battle;[11] losing forces first conduct battle and then seek victory.

3. good leadership and effective rules always are the foundations for victory—they should never be underestimated

Those sophisticated at strategy cultivate leadership and sustain rules so that they can be the controllers of victory and of defeat.[12]

ON THE CONTROL OF SUPERIORITY IN THE THEATER OF WAR:

a. the five factors through which commanders control victory in the theater of war—from the perspective of deploying battle arrays

There is a rule:[13]
first, assessment;
second, quantity;
third, numbers;
fourth, weighing;
and fifth, victory.

b. the progression of these five factors—a decisive attack can thereby be visualized

Theater engenders assessment, assessment engenders quantity, quantity engenders numbers, numbers engender weighing, and weighing engenders victory.

c. victory results from the contrast of our superiority with the enemy's inferiority

Victorious forces are like weighing a hundred pounds against an ounce; defeated forces are like weighing an ounce against a hundred pounds.

d. conclusion: a good commander must know how to control his irresistible power against the enemy's weakest points in the theater of war

Those who weigh victory engage their people in battle just as if they had released the floodgates on an extremely deep gorge[14]
—that is control.

```
┌─────────────────────────┐
│                         │
│       BOOK 5            │
│      ─────────          │
│   COMBAT POWER¹         │
│                         │
└─────────────────────────┘
```

PREREQUISITES FOR THE EXERCISE OF COMBAT POWER:

SUN-TZU SAID,

a. on troops—the establishment of capability:

1. competent organization and training

Generally, handling many can be like handling few
—through organization and squad training.[2]

2. effectual command systems

Launching many into combat can be like launching few
—through signals and designations.[3]

3. the ability to exercise flexible actions in combat

The armies' legions can be sent to fully[4] engage the enemy and will never be defeated
—through irregular and regular actions.

4. the capacity to conduct decisive strikes against the enemy's weaknesses

Where forces overwhelm can be like a hard rock cast onto eggs
—through contrasts in strength.[5]

57

b. on tactics—the use of irregular and regular actions:

1. the functions of irregular and regular actions

Generally, in battle apply regular actions to initiate combat and apply irregular actions to defeat them.[6]

2. on flexible command in troop actions

So, to those sophisticated at creating irregular actions[7] these are as endless as the heavens and the earth, and as inexhaustible as the rivers and the seas.[8]

At their cessation they are renewed, as are the sun and the moon. At their death they are reborn, as are the four seasons.

3. the successfulness of tactics depends on the steadfast mutual support of irregular and regular actions

The tones are but five; variations in the five tones are limitless to the ear.
The colors are but five; variations in the five colors are limitless to the eye.
The tastes are but five; variations in the five tastes are limitless to the tongue.[9]

Combat power in battle is but the exercise of irregular and regular actions; variations in irregular and regular actions can never be limited.

Irregular and regular perpetually engender each other like a ring without a breach[10]—who can limit them?

COMBAT POWER AND A RESTRAINED RELEASE OF FORCE:

a. the creation of superior combat power
—a decisive charge of mass

The strength of a cataclysmic flood which would even be able to float rocks shows combat power.[11]

b. the function of a restrained release of force
—a bursting, precise strike

The strike of raptors which would even be able to produce destruction shows a restrained release of force.[12]

c. the principles for applying combat power and a restrained release of force

Therefore, those sophisticated at battle have combat power that is irresistible and a restrained release of force that is instantaneous.[13]

d. the sequence in an operation for exercising combat power and a restrained release of force

Combat power is as if setting a crossbow; a restrained release of force is as if pulling the trigger.

REQUIREMENTS FOR THE CREATION OF VICTORIOUS COMBAT POWER IN BATTLE:

a. flexible and strong troop capabilities

Turbulence and ferment: while fighting amid chaos, we may not be confused.

b. skillful and forceful command in the movements of battle arrays

Rolling and tumbling: while controlling within gyrations, we may not be defeated.

c. tactical capabilities for entrapping the enemy:

1. on deception—the display of disorder, cowardice, and weakness

Disorder appears out of discipline, cowardice appears out of courage, and weakness appears out of strength.

Disorder by way of discipline concerns squad training,
cowardice by way of courage concerns combat power,
and weakness by way of strength concerns control.

2. on dominating the enemy's actions

So, those sophisticated at actuating the enemy contain them, and the enemy will surely follow; leave opportunities, and the enemy will surely take a chance; manipulate them through stillness[14]
—and lie in wait for them with soldiers.[15]

ON THE RELATIONSHIPS AMONG COMBAT POWER, TROOP CAPABILITY, AND SITUATION:

a. select capability to fit a need—combat power cannot be realized by forcing one's subordinates

So, those sophisticated at battle strive for combat power but do not compel their men, and thus are able to select their men for the exercise of combat power.

b. take advantage of situations by adapting to the best uses of one's troops

Those who exercise combat power engage their men in battle like rolling logs and rocks: the nature of logs and rocks is that they are still when on a level place, move when on a steep place, stop when they are squared, and roll when they are rounded.

c. conclusion: flexibility is the key to properly exercising combat power in conflict

So, the combat power of those sophisticated at launching their men into battle is like the rolling of a round rock down from a mile-high peak
—that is combat power.

BOOK 6

SUPERIORITY AND INFERIORITY[1]

ON THE OCCURRENCE OF SUPERIORITY AND INFERIORITY:

SUN-TZU SAID,

a. strategic principles for the occurrence of superiority:

1. manipulate the enemy:

i) through preparedness

Generally,[2] those who first position themselves on the battlefield and await battle[3] are at ease; those who later position themselves on the battlefield and rush into battle are fatigued. So, those sophisticated at battle dominate the adversary but are not dominated by the adversary.

ii) through psychology

Be able to make enemies[4] approach of their own accord by laying advantages; be able to make enemies not approach by laying hazards.

iii) through actions

So, when enemies are at ease, be able to exhaust them; when full, be able to

62

starve them; (when steady, be able to move them):[5]
emerge where they have to rush over, and rush over to their surprise.[6]

2. take advantage of enemy vulnerability:

  i) act beyond enemy abilities:

      —in maneuvers

March over a thousand miles without threat[7] by going where there are no adversaries.

      —in attack

Attack and be certain of occupation by attacking what they cannot defend.

      —in defense

Defend and be certain of safety by defending what they cannot attack.[8]

  ii) act beyond enemy understanding:

      —in an offense

So, against those sophisticated at attack, enemies will be unsure of how to defend;

      —in a defense

against those sophisticated at defense, enemies will be unsure of how to attack.

3. partial conclusion: absolute impenetrability assures absolute superiority

Subtly, subtly, they become invisible; wondrously, wondrously, they become soundless
—they are thus able to be their enemies' Fates.[9]

b. the occurrence of superiority in operations:

    1. on advance and withdrawal

        Achieve an advance that cannot be withstood by rushing their weak sectors; achieve a withdrawal that cannot be entrapped by departing with unsurpassable rapidity.[10]

    2. on attack

        So, once we want to conduct battle, even if enemies hide themselves behind high fortresses with deep moats, they cannot but engage us, by attacking what they must rescue.

    3. on defense

        Once we do not want to conduct battle, even if defense is a line drawn on the ground, the enemy will be unable to engage us, by positioning where they are deceived into not going.

    4. on the domination of enemy strength

        So, those who are sophisticated at command contain the adversary but are free of containment:[11] we are then combined and the enemies are divided.

        We combine into one and the enemies divide into ten; that is, ten is applied to strike one.

    5. appended discussion—using the few to attack the many:

i) contain enemy actions

We are the few and the enemies are the many: be able to use few in striking the many when those who battle against us are confined.[12]

ii) make enemies unaware of their situation

Where we will battle against them cannot be anticipated; when it is not anticipated, the enemies will lay many passive protections.

When passive protections are many, those who battle against us will be few.

c. the occurrence of inferiority:

1. causes for shortcomings in strength

With the frontline passively protected, the rear will have few; with the rear passively protected, the frontline will have few; with the left passively protected, the right will have few; with the right passively protected, the left will have few; with every sector passively protected, every sector will have few.

2. the causes for "many" and "few" in military operations

"Few" means setting passive protections against the adversary; "many" means compelling the adversary to set passive protections against us.

d. perception of a conflict situation produces superiority or inferiority:

1. correct judgment creates superiority

By perceiving where battlefields will lie and by perceiving when battles will happen,[13] battles can be launched over a thousand miles.

2. lack of correct judgment leads to inferiority

By not knowing where battlefields will lie and by not knowing when battles will happen, the front cannot support the rear, the rear cannot support the front, the left cannot support the right, and the right cannot support the left[14]
—needless to say, when their range is as far as several tens of miles or as close as a few miles.

e. partial conclusion: superiority comes from domination of the enemy; it is not necessarily decided by a larger number of troops

In my judgment, though Yue's* troops are many, how could this promote their victory?

So it is said, victory can be grasped.[15]

Though the enemies are numerous, they can be made unable to engage in combat.

ON DOMINATING SUPERIORITY IN CONFLICT:

a. the four requisites for combat commanders:

Therefore,

1. with regard to planning

plan, but know the calculation of gains and losses;[16]

*Sun Wu was the guest of the King of Wu, and the state of Yue was their deadly enemy.

2. with regard to initiating actions	mobilize, but know the causes for action and inaction;
3. with regard to control	control, but know lethal and safe terrains;
4. with regard to conflict	and fight, but know where there are sufficiencies and deficiencies.
b. on flexibility in control:	When the control of forces approaches its zenith, evolve into imperceptible control.
1. in handling enemies	With imperceptible control, no deeply hidden agents can penetrate and no ingenious men can scheme.
2. in employing troops:	Adapt control in arranging victory for our legions, yet our legions are incapable of knowing.
i) beyond common concepts	Everyone may know the control through which we are able to achieve victory, but cannot know the control through which we are able to determine[17] victory.
ii) beyond set patterns	So, our victories in battles will not be repeated and our responsive control will be unlimited.
c. on flexibility in tactics:	
1. using water as an illustration:	Thus, the control of forces is like water:

i) do not fight rigid battles

Water's movement avoids the high and runs downward.[18]

A force's victory avoids superiority and strikes inferiority.[19]

So, water conforms to terrain in determining movement,[20] and forces conform to the enemy in determining victory.

ii) do not conduct rigid tactics

Forces do not have immutable combat power, nor do they have unchangeable control.[21]

2. using nature as an illustration— always make the best adaptations to variable situations

Those who are able to adapt to changes in the enemy and achieve victory are considered supreme[22]
—just as none of the five universal elements has unvarying superiority, as the four seasons are not static, as the sun has short and long spans, and as the moon has death and rebirth.[23]

BOOK 7

ARMED CONTENTION

SUN-TZU SAID,

Generally, fundamentals in using forces are:
the commander receives orders from the lord, summons the armies, musters the legions, and sets up bases in coordination with the order of battle.[1]

ON ADVANTAGES AND DISADVANTAGES IN ARMED CONTENTION:

a. on the design of an action—trade disadvantages for advantages

Nothing is more difficult than armed contention.

The difficulties in armed contention are: turning the circuitous into the direct and turning disadvantage into advantage.

Plan to circuit our routes and lure them with advantages; set forth after the adversary but arrive before the adversary —that is the knowing of "circuitous as direct calculations."

69

b. on risks in the operation to gain advantages:

Armed contention has advantages; armed contention has risks.[2]

1. caused by camps

By bringing the camp[3] while contending for advantages, we would fall behind; by laying the camp aside while contending for advantages, we would lose our supplies.

2. caused by actions:

   i)   over a hundred miles away

So, by rolling up armor, rushing forward without stopping day and night, and conducting a forced march over a hundred miles while contending for advantages, all of the armies' commanders could be ensnared:[4] the strong ones would be in the front and the weaker ones would be in the rear
—as a rule, only one tenth would arrive.

   ii) over fifty miles away

By contending for advantages over fifty miles, the spearhead force's commander[5] might be thwarted
—as a rule, only one half would arrive.

   iii) over thirty miles away

By contending for advantages over thirty miles, only two thirds would arrive.

3. caused by loss of matériel and supplies

So, armies cannot survive without supplies, cannot survive without provisions, cannot survive without stockpiled materials.

c. some other requirements for contending with the enemy—allies, topography, and terrain

By not knowing other lords' minds, one cannot secure allies;[6] by not knowing the topography of mountain forests, obstacles, and swamps, one cannot conduct maneuvers; and by not having experienced scouts, one cannot obtain the terrain's advantages.

ON THE CONDUCT OF ARMED CONTENTION:

a. the operation:

1. basic principles

Forces achieve missions with unexpectation,[7] take action to fit the advantages, and create diversity through scattering and regrouping.

2. the requirements:

i)   for taking action

Thus, they act as swiftly as the wind;
they march as steadily as forests;
invading like fire,
standing firm like mountains,

ii) for preparing and attacking

as unpredictable as rain clouds,
striking like thunder and lightning.[8]

b. the occupation of enemy territory:

1. domination over their people and the terrain's advantages

Invade a countryside and rule the people; expand one's land and rule the advantageous points;[9] weigh situations and then take action.

2. readiness for surprise actions

Those who perceive beforehand "the means of circuitous as direct"[10] are victorious
—this is a fundamental in armed contention.

c. the signal orders used in combat for unified command:

1. the need for signal orders

Junzheng* reads, "When voice cannot be clearly heard, drums and gongs are used; when eyesight cannot clearly observe, battle standards and flags are used."

2. signal use must fit the circumstances

Therefore, in day battles emphasize battle standards and flags; in night battles emphasize drums and gongs.

3. the effect of signal orders on command

These drums, gongs, battle standards, and flags are used to unify the ears and eyes of the people.
The people are then united; thus, the courageous ones will not be allowed to charge forward alone, and the cowardly ones will not be allowed to retreat alone, either.

These are fundamentals in employing legions.[11]

*It is said that this was an ancient military book.

d. the achievement of supremacy against the enemy in battles:

1. basic tactical doctrine:

The morale of the armies can be dampened, and the sense for commanding battle arrays can be dampened.[12]

   i) handling their morale

Therefore, in the beginning morale is high, then slackens, and at last dissipates.[13]

So, those sophisticated at using forces avoid their high morale and strike them when it has slackened or dissipated
—this is how to handle morale.

   ii) handling their sense

Await disorder with discipline; await clamor with calmness
—this is how to handle sense.

2. on arrayed battles:

   i) handling their strength

Await a distant enemy with proximity to the battlefield; await fatigue with ease; await hunger with repletion
—this is how to handle strength.

   ii) handling their variations

Do not engage those with well-ordered flags; do not strike those with imposing arrays
—this is how to handle their diversity.

APPENDED DISCUSSION— BE AWARE OF THE ENEMY'S POTENTIAL FOR HARMING US WHEN CONDUCTING COMBAT:

Then, fundamentals in using forces are:

a. with regard to terrain

with high buttes, do not fight toward them; with the enemy backed by a mound, do not issue a frontal attack;[14]

b. with regard to enemy subterfuge

with a deceptive retreat, do not hunt for them; with elite soldiers, do not attack them; with baited forces, do not devour them;[15]

c. with regard to a defeated enemy

with surrounded organized troops, leave a gap; with orderly retreating troops, do not block them;[16] with desperate foes, do not exceedingly push them[17]
—these are fundamentals in using forces.[18]

BOOK 8

THE NINE ADAPTATIONS[1]

SUN-TZU SAID,

Generally, fundamentals in using forces are:
the commander receives orders from the lord, summons the armies, and musters the legions.

ON THE CONDUCT OF STRATEGIC ADAPTATIONS:

a. in five specific zones

Never camp in compartmentalized zones,[2] unite allies[3] in key traffic zones, and never linger in severable zones.
With surrounded zones, plan stratagems; with lethal zones, conduct battles.[4]

b. in the execution of plans

Some routes need not necessarily be taken, some armies need not necessarily be struck, some cities need not necessarily be besieged, some land need not necessarily be contended, and some lords' orders need not necessarily be accepted.[5]

c. on the aptitude of commanders for strategic adaptations:

1. with regard to strategy

So, commanders who comprehend the advantages in the nine adaptations[6] know the use of forces.

2. with regard to terrain

Commanders who do not comprehend the advantages in the nine adaptations—even while knowing a terrain—cannot gain the land's advantages.

3. with regard to troop employment

Those who command forces but do not know how to practice the nine adaptations—even while knowing the five advantages*—cannot gain the use of their men.

THE NECESSITY FOR STRATEGIC ADAPTATIONS:

a. their occurrence—through perceiving advantage and disadvantage

Therefore, the deliberations of the ingenious ones must refer to both the advantageous and the disadvantageous.

b. their value—to gain advantage and to avoid disadvantage

By referring to the advantageous, tasks can be fulfilled.[7]
By referring to the disadvantageous, calamities can be removed.

---

*This, according to Cao Cao (Eastern Han, 155–220), indicates the preceding list beginning with, "Some routes need not necessarily be taken"; see page 75.

APPENDED DISCUSSION—OTHER IMPORTANT CONCERNS IN STRATEGIC ADAPTATIONS:

a. on handling allies:

1. how to make them acquiesce

Therefore, make other lords yield through disadvantages;

2. how to win their cooperation

make other lords work on our behalf through successes;[8]

3. how to urge them to act quickly

make other lords rapidly take action[9] through advantages.

b. on our own groundwork—the sole matter we can unreservedly depend on in a conflict

Fundamentals in using forces are:
do not rely on their not approaching, but rely on our readiness against them;
do not rely on their not attacking, but rely on our readiness which cannot be attacked.

c. on characteristics in our commanders' personalities which the enemy might use against them

Commanders can have five pitfalls:
in having a death wish, they can be killed;
in having self-preservation, they can be captured;
in having short tempers, they can be humiliated;
in having moral sensibility, they can be insulted;
in having fondness for the people, they can be worried.

All of these five are commanders' flaws and are disastrous during the employment of forces.

An army's failure and a commander's extermination are definitely due to these five pitfalls.

These must never be taken lightly.

BOOK 9

TROOP MANEUVERS

ON POSITIONING ARMIES:

SUN-TZU SAID,

Generally, when positioning armies and studying[1] the enemy:

a. the four main regions and the uses of their terrains:

1. in mountains

Cross mountains and cling to valleys; observe the safe and position on heights;[2] when battling against a high position,[3] do not fight uphill
—these are how armies are positioned in mountain regions.

2. near a river

After crossing rivers, be sure to distance ourselves from the rivers; if opponents come over by crossing a river, do not meet them mid-river: induce a partial crossing and strike them
—this is advantageous.

If battle is desired, do not locate near rivers when encountering opponents; ob-

serve the safe and position on heights;
do not face down-flowing water*
—these are how armies are positioned
in riverian regions.

3. near a swamp

After crossing swamps, unconditionally
strive to leave and do not linger; when
engaging armies in a swamp, cling[4] to
reeds and be backed by brush†
—these are how armies are positioned
in swampy regions.

4. on a plain

On level ground, position in the peripheral sites[5] with the right flank backed by
height, the lethal to the front, and the
safe to the rear
—these are how armies are positioned
on level ground.

The advantages in all these four army
positionings were used by the Yellow
Emperor to achieve victory over all of
his enemies.[6]

b. gaining the terrain's advantages:

1. with regard to height

Generally, armies prefer the high to
the low

2. with regard to direction

and prize southerly sites over northerly
sites.[7]

*This means that one should not situate downstream from the enemy.
†Reeds and brush denote areas of solid ground in a swamp.

3. with regard to positioning

Occupy the safe[8] and position where there is solidity
—these ensure victories, and the armies may avoid disease.[9]

c. the use of hills and banks

Regarding hills or banks, be positioned[10] on a southerly site and with the right flank backed by them
—these are advantageous to forces and are terrains' reinforcements.

d. caution with floods

When rainwater rises and currents approach, halt crossing until it has subsided.[11]

e. extremely hazardous obstacles:

1. the types

Generally, if terrain consists of severed ravines, gigantic pits, gigantic prisons, gigantic coops, gigantic traps, and gigantic rifts,[12] one must strive to skirt them and never go near.

2. how to gain advantages from them

When we distance ourselves from them, the enemy will be near them; when we move to face them, the enemy will be backed by them.

f. searching and guarding

In army maneuvers, where obstacles, flooded lowlands, tall reeds, mountain forests, or thick vegetation lie and could be used for hiding, carefully reconnoiter and search them

—hidden enemies might be positioned there.[13]

ON STUDYING THE ENEMY:

a. judging enemy reactions in encounters:

   1. when they have gained the most advantageous sites

Enemies are near but calm: they are supported by their barriers.

   2. when they use tactical tricks

Enemies are distant but challenging: they are drawing adversaries into an advance.

   3. when they act against common sense

Where they situate is on level ground: this indicates possible advantages.[14]

b. judging the enemy's irregular actions:

   1. clandestine advance

When the woods move, this indicates approach.

   2. enigmatic actions

When grasses are massed into many embankments, this indicates a smoke screen.

   3. hidden foes

Scattering birds indicate ambush.

   4. surprise flank attacks

Startled beasts indicate a pincer movement.[15]

c. judging enemy actions from the dust they raise:

    1. chariot movement

        When dust is towering and peaked, chariots approach.

    2. infantry action

        When low and vast, infantry approach.

    3. collection of firewood

        When streaked and scattered, firewood is being cut and collected.[16]

    4. bivouacking of troops

        When sparse and fluttering, camp is being set.[17]

d. judging the enemy's attempts:

    1. inference from comparing their speech and behavior:

        i) the desire to advance

        When speech is humble and protections increase, this indicates an advance.

        ii) the desire to retreat

        When speech is threatening and forward actions are taken, this indicates a retreat.

    2. inference from their activities:

        i) preparation for battle

        When light chariots first emerge and situate on the flanks, this indicates deployed arrays.

        ii) the contrivance of shams

        When without prior arrangements a ceasefire is requested, this indicates a scheme.

iii) preparation for strategic actions

When running about and arraying forces, this indicates a joint operation.[18]

iv) decoy actions

When partially advancing, this indicates a lure.[19]

e. judging the enemy in inferior situations:

1. distress:

i) starvation

When propping themselves upright, this indicates hunger.

ii) dehydration

When water details[20] drink first, this indicates thirst.

iii) fatigue

When gains are seen but not pursued, this indicates exhaustion.[21]

2. camp conditions:

i) clandestine withdrawal

When birds gather, this indicates evacuation.

ii) terror

When they shout at night, this indicates fright.

3. command:

i) lack of leadership

When armies are unsettled, this indicates commanders lack authority.

ii)	loss of discipline	When battle standards and flags wobble, this indicates turbulence.
iii)	psychological burnout	When officers are enraged, this indicates mental weariness.
iv)	crises	When horses are fed grain, meat is eaten, and the army no longer has water jars or returns to its encampment, this indicates desperate foes.[22]
v)	forfeiture of their men's obedience	When disorderly and shirking, but words are spoken guardedly,[23] this indicates loss of the legions' compliance.
vi)	quandary	When rewards are continuous, this indicates a dilemma.
vii)	loss of morale	When punishments are continuous, this indicates demoralization.
viii)	injudiciousness	When first violent and then fearful of their legions, this indicates extreme imprudence.

f. additional cases:

1.	a longing for rest from battle	When a humble compromise is offered, this indicates a desire to pause.
2.	ambiguous situations—scrutinize them	When forces approach with high morale, but for a long time they neither battle nor depart, be certain to regard this cautiously.[24]

CONCLUSION:

to conduct armed conflict is to achieve victory cautiously and effectively

With forces, many are not necessarily ideal; just do not advance boldly, be able to concentrate strength decisively, anticipate the enemy, and annihilate the adversary—that is all.

Only those who deliberate carelessly and lightly view their enemies will be ensnared by the adversary.

APPENDED DISCUSSION—ON LEADERSHIP IN AN ARMY:

a. the establishment of disciplinary authority:

1. discipline must be based on loyalty

When there is no bond with the soldiers but punishments are meted out, they will be disobedient; if disobedient, they will be difficult to use.

When there is a bond with the soldiers but punishments cannot be meted out, they still will be useless.[25]

2. build up troop discipline by combining kindness with toughness

So, unite them through benevolence and regulate them through strictness—these ensure internalized discipline.[26]

b. the establishment of leadership:

1. leadership is grounded in the people's habituation

Establish the ingrained execution of orders[27] in training one's people, and then the people will follow.

Fail to establish the ingrained execution of orders in training one's people, and then the people will not follow.

2. the people's obedience is secured by winning their compliance

The ingrained execution of orders comes from being in accord with the legions.

BOOK 10

TERRAIN

ON THE TERRAINS THAT WARRANT SPECIAL ATTENTION:

SUN-TZU SAID,

a. the six types

Terrain can be passable, barbed,[1] stalemated, gorge path, obstacled, and remote.

b. the characteristics and adaptations of these terrains:

1. passable

Where we can go through and they can come over is called passable.

With passable terrain, first situate in southerly sites of the heights and secure supply routes: battles in this way are advantageous.

2. barbed

Where advance is possible but return is inexpedient is called barbed.

With barbed terrain, if the enemy is unprepared, emerge to defeat them.

88

When the enemy is prepared and emergence cannot be victorious, return will be difficult
—this is disadvantageous.

3. stalemated

Where our emergence is disadvantageous and their emergence is disadvantageous is called stalemated.

With stalemated terrain, even though the enemy acts to our advantage, do not emerge.

Conduct a withdrawal: induce the enemy into a partial emergence and strike them
—this is advantageous.

4. gorge path

With gorge path terrain, if we first situate in it, be ready at the gorge mouth to await the enemy.[2]

If the enemy first situates in it and is ready at the gorge mouth, do not hunt for them; if not, hunt for them.[3]

5. obstacled

With obstacled terrain, if we first situate in it, situate on the southerly sites of the heights to await the enemy.

If the enemy first situates in it, conduct a withdrawal; do not hunt for them.

6. remote

With remote terrain, combat power is balanced and challenges are difficult to issue; battles would be disadvantageous.

All of these six are the principles for terrains and are the commanders' express duties.

These must never be taken lightly.

ON THE SIX DETRIMENTS IN OPERATIONS:

a. the types

In forces there can be desertion, laxity, paralysis, collapse, turbulence, and downfall.

All of these six are not calamities caused by heaven or the terrains,[4] but by the commanders' errors.

b. the causes:

    1. for desertion

When combat power is balanced and one is employed to strike ten, there is desertion.

    2. for laxity

When soldiers are tough but officers are weak, there is laxity.

    3. for paralysis

When officers are tough but soldiers are weak, there is paralysis.

    4. for collapse

When high-ranking officers are irate and insubordinate, and when encountering the enemy are belligerent and battle uncooperatively, yet the commanders are unaware of what they might do,[5] there is collapse.

5. for turbulence

When commanders are weak and lenient, conduct ineffective training, have unregulated officers and soldiers, and have haphazardly arrayed forces, there is turbulence.

6. for downfall

When commanders cannot anticipate the enemy, launch the few against the many, employ the weak to strike the strong, and the forces have no spearhead, there is downfall.

These six all are reasons for defeat.

These are the commanders' express duties.

These must never be taken lightly.

APPENDED DISCUSSION—ON A COMMANDER'S DUTY IN CONDUCTING BATTLE:

a. the duty of the spearhead force's commander

The terrains act as reinforcements for the forces.

Anticipation of the enemy, the determination of victory, and the calculation of obstacles and distances are the duties of the spearhead force's commander.[6]

Those who perceive these and then operate battles have definite victory; those who do not perceive these and then operate battles have definite defeat.

b. on the choice between the government's orders and the conduct of battle—the duty of a commander is victory

So, when the ways for battle are definitely victorious, even if the lord orders no battle, the battle may still be waged; when the ways for battle are not victorious, even if the lord orders a battle, the battle may still not be waged.

c. a commander's ethic—the selfless fulfillment of one's duty

So, a commander[7] who advances not for glory, withdraws not to evade guilt, and cares for only the people's security along with the lord's interests is the country's treasure.

d. the art of command:

  1. be compassionate

View soldiers as infants and thus be able to lead them into ravines.

View soldiers as beloved sons and thus be able to lead them unto death.

  2. but never overindulge subordinates

Soldiers who are treated kindly but cannot be ordered, cared for but cannot be employed,[8] and unruly but cannot be disciplined are like spoiled children; they are useless.

e. on victory—one must perceive both our own and the enemy's strengths, as well as the use of terrain

Perceiving our soldiers being used in a strike, but not perceiving that the enemy cannot be struck, leads to partial victory.

Perceiving the enemy being struck, but not perceiving that our soldiers cannot be used in a strike, leads to partial victory.

Perceiving the enemy being struck and perceiving our soldiers being used in a strike, but not perceiving that the terrain cannot be used for battle, leads to partial victory.

f. conclusions:

1. on action

So, those who know forces make movements without confusion and take action without limitation.

2. on the perception of victory

Therefore we say:

By perceiving the enemy and perceiving ourselves, victory thereby has no unseen risks.

By perceiving the geographical factors and perceiving the cyclic natural occurrences, victory thereby is complete.[9]

BOOK 11

THE NINE ZONES

OFFENSIVE STRATEGY— A GENERAL DISCUSSION:

a. the nine types of strategic zones:

1. the types

2. their definitions:

i)   separated zones

ii) susceptible zones

iii) contended zones

iv) dually traversable zones

SUN-TZU SAID,

The fundamentals in using forces are:

separated zones, susceptible zones, contended zones, dually traversable zones, key traffic zones, dominant zones, compartmentalized zones, surrounded zones, and lethal zones.[1]

Where a lord conducts battles in his individual sector is separated.[2]

Where the adversary's land is shallowly penetrated is susceptible.

Where either our occupation is advantageous or their occupation is advantageous is contended.

Where we can go through and they can come over is dually traversable.

v) key traffic zones	Where a lord's land converges with many places[3] and if reached first will win major support among all the countries is key traffic.
vi) dominant zones	Where the adversary's land is deeply penetrated and behind us are many cities and towns is dominant.
vii) compartmentalized zones	Where there is a maneuverable mountain, forest, obstacle, or swamp and the passes are difficult to forge is compartmentalized.[4]
viii) surrounded zones	Where the entrance is narrow, the exit path is circuitous, and few of them can strike many of us is surrounded.
ix) lethal zones	Where fierce combat leads to survival but lack of fierce combat leads to destruction is lethal.[5]
3. fundaments for action in the nine strategic zones	Therefore, with separated zones, do not battle; with susceptible zones, do not halt; with contended zones, do not attack; with dually traversable zones, do not leave gaps;[6] with key traffic zones, strengthen diplomacy;[7] with dominant zones, conduct appropriations; with compartmentalized zones, depart;

with surrounded zones, plan stratagems; and with lethal zones, conduct battles.

b. the principles for conducting offensive strategy:

Those who long ago were known as sophisticated at battle could make adversaries in conflict:[8]

1. cut off their mutual support

sever mutual contact between the front and the rear, sever mutual dependence between the many and the few, sever mutual succor between the noble and the humble, sever mutual protection between the high and the low ranks,

2. obstruct the exercise of their combat power

have soldiers disperse and not regroup, and have forces engage in battle and not synchronize.

3. take action wholly in accordance with the advantages

Act when advantageous; halt when not advantageous.

4. how to handle a well-prepared enemy

Question: If the enemy is numerous and is advancing in well-ordered arrays,[9] how are they handled?

Answer: First seize what they care about, and they will do as wished.

c. conclusion to general discussion— outstanding offensive strategy should be conducted with:

1. speed

The nature of forces[10] is predominantly swiftness: it takes advantage of the adversary's delay

2. surprise and exploitation of their weaknesses

and follows unexpected routes to attack where they are unaware.

THE CONDUCT OF AN OFFENSE:

a. on operations:

Generally, the ways of being invaders are:

1. deep penetration:

    i)   the purpose for deep penetration—the creation of superiority

with deep penetration comes consolidation
—defenders will not prevail;[11]

    ii) follow-up actions:

       —collect provisions

with appropriation of productive land, the armies will have sufficient food;

       —strengthen forces and conduct stratagems

provide proportionate care, avoid overexertion, unite courage, build up strength, dispatch forces, calculate plans, and take actions in unpredictable ways.

    iii) exhort forces into fully expressing their strength—use their desperation

Launch them into inextricable positions: unto death they will not desert. And with death, how can our warriors' perseverance not be had?[12]

2. troop psychology in battle

Warriors when irretrievably trapped will be fearless, in inextricable positions will be resolute, when deeply penetrated will consolidate, and without other alternatives will fight.[13]

3. troop preparation for combat needs:

i)   internalized obedience

Therefore, the forces without being disciplined[14] are highly aware, without being required are devoted, without being exhorted are united, without being ordered are diligent.

ii)   removal of qualms

Forbid superstition, dismiss apprehension,[15] and then unto death they will not desert.[16]

iii) psychological readiness for facing death

Our warriors will have no affluence not for despising property and risk numerous deaths[17] not for despising longevity.

On the day orders are given, the seated warriors' tears[18] moisten their collars, and the prostrate ones' tears streak down their cheeks.

And when they are launched into inextricable positions, the valor of great heroes[19] will arise.

4. on battle arrays:

i)   victorious armies always have close mutual support

Those sophisticated at commanding battle arrays[20] are like a *shuairan.*

The *shuairan* was a serpent at Mount Heng[21]: when its head was struck, the tail came; when its tail was struck, the head came; and when the middle of its body[22] was struck, both the head and tail came.

ii) the viability of such support is created by the proper design of anticipated psychological reactions

Question: Can forces be modeled after a *shuairan?*

Answer: Yes.

The people of Yue and Wu hated each other; however, while navigating the same boat,[23] they helped one another like left and right hands.

5. the employment of forces in offensive actions requires:

Therefore, joining horses and embedding cartwheels[24] are not at all dependable.

i) the full expression of strength

Uniting valor as one is the way of command;

ii) the advantages of the terrain

gaining both rigidity and suppleness is the principle for terrain.[25]

iii) cohesion in actions

So, those sophisticated at operating battle arrays make them work hand in hand as one without other alternatives.

6. on commanding troops in offensive actions:

Concerns in commanding armies are:[26]

i) the skill of command:

—basic principles

scheming in impenetrability[27] and being impartial in supervision;

having the capability to subjugate the eyes and ears of warriors and soldiers, making them suppress their senses;[28]

—in maneuvering

modifying their assignments and adapting their plans, making the people suppress their judgment;[29]

modifying their campsites and winding their routes, making the people unable to think;

—in campaigns

leading them on joint operations as if climbing to a high spot and removing their ladder;

leading them in deep penetration of other lords' lands and pulling their trigger;[30]

ii) the duty of command:

—completely rule the minds and actions of one's forces

herding them as a flock of sheep, being herded to and fro without ascertaining the destination;

—properly send forces into jeopardy

concentrating all the armies' legions and launching them into danger
—these are concerns in commanding armies.

iii) the requisite capabilities for command

Adaptations to the nine zones, advantages in either compliance or aggressiveness, and psychological reactions must never be taken lightly.

b. on forces in penetrated positions and the actions to be taken in strategic zones:

1. forces' reactions when influenced by the range of penetration

Generally, the ways of being invaders are:
with deep positions come consolidation and with shallow positions come dispersion.

2. on the six varieties of strategic zones that warrant special attention:

i) severable zones

(Where away from the country, at a distance from the border, and troops are set is a severable zone.

ii) key traffic zones

Where many places converge is a key traffic zone.

iii) dominant zones

Where deeply penetrated is a dominant zone.

iv) susceptible zones

Where shallowly penetrated is a susceptible zone.

v) surrounded zones

Where the rear is blocked and the front is narrow is a surrounded zone.

vi) lethal zones)

Where inextricable positions lie is a lethal zone).[31]

3. actions for strategic zones:

i) separated zones

Therefore, with separated zones we will unify our intent,

ii) susceptible zones

with susceptible zones we will urge them to advance swiftly,[32]

iii) contended zones

with contended zones we will rapidly approach them from their rear,[33]

iv) dually traversable zones

with dually traversable zones we will fortify their junctures,[34]

v) key traffic zones

with key traffic zones we will be diplomatic in our alliances,[35]

vi) dominant zones

with dominant zones we will maintain our food supply,

vii) compartmentalized zones

with compartmentalized zones we will proceed to their exit routes,

viii) surrounded zones

with surrounded zones we will blockade their openings,

ix) lethal zones

and with lethal zones we will have the troops face mortality.

c. conclusions—to conduct an offense one must know:

1. the forces' proper responses to diverse situations

The nature of forces is: when within range, defend; when without other alternatives, fight; and when superior, hunt for them.[36]

2. how to win allied support

Then, by not knowing other lords' minds, one cannot secure allies;

3. how to exercise advantageous maneuvers

by not knowing the topography of mountain, forests, obstacles, and swamps, one cannot conduct maneuvers;

4. the use of scouts

and by not having experienced scouts, one cannot obtain the terrain's advantages.

APPENDED DISCUSSIONS:

a. on superior powers:

1. what a superior power should comprehend

Of these several things, if a single one is not known, an overlord's forces cannot be realized.[37]

2. the exercise of a superior power's strength:

i) the attack of enemy forces

Once this overlord's forces invade a large country, its legions will be incapable of assembly;

ii) the destruction of enemy allied support

when his omnipotence engulfs the enemies, their alliances will be incapable of forming.

3. the coordination between a superior power's political activities and its military strength

By competing for worldwide alliances and developing worldwide influence,[38] an overlord will thereby give rein to his ambitions, and his omnipotence can engulf the enemies:
thus, their city may be occupied and their country toppled.[39]

b. on forceful command while launching campaigns:

1. adapt rewards and orders to fit the need of situations

Transcend rules when conferring rewards; transcend policy when issuing orders.[40]

2. strictly employ forces using:

i) synchronization without exception

Direct[41] all the armies' legions as if exercising authority over one person.

ii) orders without reasons

Direct them onto missions without explanation.

iii) soldiers' will to fight without hesitation

Direct them into hazardous situations without revealing other prospects.[42]

3. boldly conduct decisive actions

Launched into annihilative places, they will then survive.

Trapped in lethal places, they will then live.

Only troops perilously caught will have for victory sought.

4. partial conclusion—principles for the effective achievement of a mission

So, the concerns in conducting operations are:
warily scrutinizing the enemy's intent, concentrating against the enemy toward one goal, and trouncing their commanders over a thousand miles[43]
—this is called adeptly achieving a mission.[44]

c. on government coordination of an offense:

1. strictly guard the borders and sever relations with the enemy country

Therefore, on the day when the policy is enacted, bolt the border gates, sunder the passes,[45] and refuse their envoys.

2. governmental activities

Take effective actions in the court departments to manage their duties.[46]

3. invasion

As soon as the adversary in conflict has a breach,[47] swiftly infiltrate.

4. the enemy's defeat

Occupy first what they care about; secretly take actions toward joint operations.[48]

Follow the enemy as a carpenter's chalk[49] to resolve the concerns of armed conflict.

5. conclusion—a successful offense should be done with surprise

So, at the start we act like reticent maidens.

Once the adversary in conflict opens the door, burst through like a fleeing hare.

The enemy will fail to resist in time.

BOOK 12

ATTACKS USING FIRE[1]

THE OBJECTS OF ATTACK FIRES:

SUN-TZU SAID,

Generally, there are five attack fires:[2]

a. their men

first, the burning of adversaries;

b. their matériel and food

second, the burning of stockpiles;

c. their weapons and equipment

third, the burning of arsenals;

d. their mobile armaments and conveyances

fourth, the burning of vehicle pools;

e. their supply and evacuation lines

and fifth, the burning of transport lines.[3]

THE REQUIREMENTS FOR ATTACK FIRES:

a. existing proper conditions

The operation of fires requires proper conditions, and these conditions must exist beforehand.[4]

b. climatic requisites:

Starting a fire requires specific times; setting a fire requires specific days.

1. aridity	"Specific times" are when the weather is dry.
2. high wind	"Specific days" are when the moon is aligned with the constellations Qi, Bi, Yi, and Zhen;* these four[5] are the days that gales blow.

ON ATTACKS COORDINATED WITH FIRE:

a. different objects of a strike require different tactics	Generally, attacks using fire must reflect the five fires' diversity and respond accordingly.
b. preparedness is necessary prior to using fire	When fire is set from within, synchronize earlier on the outside.
c. during an operation be continually wary of the enemy's reactions	When fire is set and their forces are calm, cancel the attack.[6]
d. the effectiveness of an attack depends on correct judgment	Let the fire inflict the severest damage; hunt for them when huntable; halt when not huntable.[7]

ON ADAPTABILITY IN ATTACK FIRES:

a. be flexible to actual needs rather than adhere to tactical rules	When fire can be set outside, do not wait for it to be started from within; take advantage of the specific time in setting it.

*The constellation Qi is in Sagittarius, Bi is in Andromeda, Yi is in Crater, and Zhen is in Corvus.

b. avoid carelessly harming oneself when attacking the enemy

When fire is set upwind, do not attack downwind.

c. while conducting battle, notice changes in the coordinating environmental factors—wind is just an example

Diurnal winds are forceful; nocturnal winds are gentle.[8]

d. be wary of the enemy doing likewise

All armies must know the diversities of the five fires and take defensive measures against them.[9]

DIFFERENCES IN THE EFFECTS OF ATTACKS AIDED BY FIRE AND BY WATER:

Attack supported by fire is indefensible.[10]

Attack supported by water is powerful.

Water can be used for isolating but cannot be used for plundering.

APPENDED CONCLUSION— A SUMMING UP OF ALL THE MILITARY OPERATIONS DISCUSSED ABOVE:

a. a military victory is to provide effective support for the political establishment; it is not only an arena for destruction

When battles gain victories and attacks achieve occupations, yet these successes are not followed up, it is disastrous.
This is known as "persisting turmoil."[11]

b. the planning of military operations is based on the political strategy's projected victory; a failed political strategy cannot create successful military operations

So we say, an enlightened lord considers these and distinguished commanders follow them.

c. one's strategy must be fully rational

Without advantages, do not act; without gain, do not utilize; without crises, do not battle.

d. Sun Wu's candid advice to political authorities and commanders—a war must never be initiated lightly

Lords must not raise armies[12] out of rage; commanders must not launch battles out of fury.

Act when advantageous;
halt when not advantageous.[13]

(once armed conflict has begun, no one can ever redress its losses in any way)

For, those enraged may be happy again, and those infuriated may be cheerful again, but annihilated countries may never exist again, nor may the dead ever live again.[14]

Therefore, enlightened lords: be vigilant with these;
distinguished commanders: be alert to these
—this is the way of safeguarding the country and securing the army.

BOOK 13

ESPIONAGE

**ON THE NECESSITY OF
INTELLIGENCE WORK:**

SUN-TZU SAID,

a. the tremendously heavy costs of a
country's military operations:

1. financial costs

Generally, when raising a hundred
thousand troops and advancing out of
the country for conflict over thousands
of miles,[1] the citizenry's outlay and public financing are thousands of pounds of
gold per day.

2. physical costs

When there is internal and external un-
rest and exhaustion on the roads, daily
tasks are abandoned in seven hundred
thousand homes.

3. durational costs

Both sides stalk each other over several
years[2] to contend for victory in a single
day.

b. commanders are thus entrusted by their country with seeking victory, so they should never let concerns for personal gain cloud their duty to perceive the enemy

To be parsimonious[3] with positions, compensations, or hundreds of pounds of gold, and thereby blind to the enemy's status, is to be extraordinarily inhumane: such a man can never be his people's commander, can never be his lord's aide, and can never be the ruler of victory.

c. moreover, a successful mission is based on comprehension prior to action

So, as for enlightened lords or distinguished commanders, the reason they can overcome the adversary when action is taken and achieve unparalleled success is prescience.

d. of all the information sources, men are the most reliable

Prescience cannot be gained from ghosts or gods, cannot be augured through signs, and cannot be proved through conjectures.

It must be gained from what is learned by men.[4]

ON AGENTS:

a. the types

So, in espionage are these five: agents-in-place, moles, turned agents,[5] hidden provocation agents, and mobile informants.

b. their applications

Once these five agents all take action, none can penetrate their ways
—this is covert mastery,[6] a sovereign's treasure.

c. definitions of the five types of agents:

    1. agents-in-place

For agents-in-place,[7] look to their local personnel and utilize them.

    2. moles

For moles, look to their officials and utilize them.

    3. turned agents

For turned agents, look to enemy agents and utilize them.

    4. hidden provocation agents

Hidden provocation agents, when a sham is constructed externally, then apprise our agents and disseminate it among the enemy.[8]

    5. mobile informants

Mobile informants are those who return with reports.

d. the nature of agent activities

Of those close to the armies, none are closer than agents;[9]
no rewards are heavier than those granted to agents;
no activities are observed more than those of agents.

e. the requisites for conducting agent activities:

    1. the need for wisdom

No one but a sage can utilize espionage;

    2. the need for morality

except with humanity,[10] one cannot deploy agents;

3. the need for keen scrutiny

except with thorough observation,[11] one cannot gain truth from agents.

f. areas where agents may be used

Observe, observe![12]
There are no events where agents are not utilized.

g. the handling of intelligence leaks

Before an agent's activity is under way, if it is leaked, none of the agents nor those informed may live.[13]

h. agents must obtain highly detailed information prior to each military action

When an army is intended to be struck, a city is intended to be besieged, or an adversary is intended to be killed, be certain to first learn the names of their defending commander, his aides, his couriers, his gate guards, and his administrative officers
—order our agents to ferret these out without fail.

ON TURNED AGENTS:

a. the acquisition of turned agents

Be certain to ferret out the enemy agents who come to spy on us.[14]
Then find chances to ply them with advantages; instruct and release them so turned agents can be held and utilized.

b. turned-agent operations are the key to espionage:

1. along with agents-in-place and moles

When perceived in this way, agents-in-place and moles can be held and deployed.

2. along with hidden provocation agents

When perceived in this way, hidden provocation agents, if a sham is constructed externally, can be sent to inform the enemy.

3. along with mobile informants

When perceived in this way, mobile informants can be sent in accordance with the scheduled plan.

c. without turned agents, reliable espionage is difficult

Regarding the five agents' activities, the lord must know them.[15] Knowledge of these must come from turned agents, so turned agents cannot be treated lightly.

CONCLUSION:

the achievement of military concerns is deeply influenced by intelligence work and agent quality

Long ago, the rise of the Shang sovereign was due to Yizhi in the Xia court; the rise of the Zhou sovereign was due to Lüya in the Shang court.*[16]

Only when enlightened lords and distinguished commanders are able to use highly intelligent men as their agents will they certainly have great success.

These are the precepts for military affairs and are the guides for the armies' operations.[17]

---

*The Shang sovereign was victorious over the Xia lord because Yizhi once served in the Xia and relayed their secrets to the Shang (prior to 1766 B.C.). The Zhou sovereign was victorious over the Shang lord because Lüya once served in the Shang and relayed their secrets to the Zhou (prior to 1122 B.C.).

PART 2

COM-
MENTS

COMMENTS ON BOOK 1

SURVEYING

1. "Surveying" in the Chinese text reads *ji* and follows the Linyi text.[1]

Du Mu (Tang, 803–52) indicated in his annotation to the line "they are verified through *ji*"[2] (p. 37) that the *ji* in this line is the same as the one in the title. Sun Xingyan (Qing, 1753–1818) and (Qing) Wu Renji wrote in their critical notes under the same textual line, "This book's discussion of military affairs [*bing*] places its emphasis on *ji*," so they agreed with Du's opinion.[3] When written as "they are verified through *ji*," this provides the correct understanding of *ji* as used by Sun Wu.

In this phrase we understand that *ji* must be the method or activity for examining the tangibility of a matter. Since the premise uses a government's position to grasp the political situations or security conditions in either its own or the enemy's country, the character *ji* here naturally becomes the equivalent of today's "surveying."

[1]The *Wujing qishu* version of *Sun-tzu* (hereafter referred to as the *Wujing*) gives the title of the first book as "Shiji" (beginning with *ji*). Both the *Shiyijia zhu* version of *Sun-tzu* (hereafter referred to as the *Shiyijia*) and the *Shijia zhu* version (hereafter referred to as the *Shijia*) record this title as "Jipian" (*ji* chapter). The Sakurada version found in Japan gives the title as "Jipian diyi" (*ji* chapter, the first). The bamboo-slat text of *Sun-tzu* discovered in the Han tomb at Linyi, Shandong Province (hereafter referred to as the Linyi text), suffered damage in this section, but from the examples provided by the other book titles in this text, which do not have the character *pian* (chapter) or numbers for the books, we know that this should simply read "Ji."

Note: For convenience, throughout our discussion "the later versions" will collectively refer to the *Wujing*, *Shiyijia*, and Sakurada versions. Also, in the comments, whenever the opinions of the eleven annotators in the *Shiyijia* (i.e., Cao Cao, Mengshi, Du You, Li Quan, Du Mu, Chen Hao, Jia Lin, Mei Yaochen, Wang Xi, He Yanxi, and Zhang Yu) are quoted, the *Shiyijia* will not be specifically cited.

[2]See comment 4.

[3]*Shijia*, vol. 1, p. 2a. The criticisms of this line by Sun Xingyan and Wu Renji are correct, but there is one other problem; see footnote 18.

During the pre-Qin period (about 500 to 211 B.C.), the examination of a matter's status could be called *ji*.[4] So, when political authorities thoroughly viewed an administrative condition or achievement, this was also referred to as *ji*;[5] the first book of *Sun-tzu*'s use of the character *ji* adopts this latter concept.[6]

Some modern scholars have tried to use "estimate" to express the meaning of *ji*; their sources for this interpretation are unknown.[7]

[4]Usually, the pre-Qin period is used to mean around 475 to 221 B.C., but we use it more loosely to indicate from about 500 to 211 B.C. in order to include the time when the book *Sun-tzu* possibly came into being.

As for *ji*, *Guanzi* records, "Hard and soft, light and heavy, large and small, sufficiency and deficiency, far and near, many and few, are all called *ji shu* [the analysis of numbers]" (vol. 2, "Qifa," pp. 28–29). (Tang) Yin Zhizhang noted, "All of these twelve things must be *ji* to know their *shu*." This tells us that *ji* (to analyze) is used to evaluate an activity or sequence; *shu* (lit., "number") is the achieved result.

[5]E.g., the *Zhouli* has the line "every three years a great *ji* is held of all the officials' work" (vol. 7, "Tianguan: Sishu" [*Shisanjing*, p. 1467]). Also in the same book it records that "the eighth is the official *ji*" (vol. 2, "Taizai zhi zhi" [*Shisanjing*, p. 1389]). Zheng Xuan (Han, 127–200) noted, "Official *ji* . . . were used to judge all of the officials' work."

The Han Dynasty book *Chunqiu fanlu* says, "Before and after are three reviews, and then demotions and promotions are granted; this is called *ji*" (vol. 7, "Kaogongming diershiyi," p. 1b). So, even as late as the Han, the ancient meaning of *ji* had not been lost.

[6]*Ji* had three definitions in ancient times:

(i) "Overviewing," "surveying," "figuring out," or "analyzing" (*ji* 稽; the examples in footnote 5 use this definition). In addition to the instances cited in footnote 5, another can be found in the *Zhouli*: "*ji* 稽 the grading of their merits" ("Tianguan: Gongzheng" [*Shisanjing*, p. 1412]). Zheng Xuan noted, "*ji* is as if saying *kao* [to figure out thoroughly] or *ji* 計." We therefore know that these two *ji* could be interchangeable. Moreover, the *Shiji* records, "[Taishigong said, 'Emperor] Yu met all of the feudal lords to the south of the Yangtze, *ji* their merits, passed away, and was buried there, so it was named *Kuaiji* [the Assembly for Ji].' This Kuaiji 會稽 was Kuaiji 會計" (vol. 2, "Xiabenji," p. 31). Similar records can be found in two other sources: One edition of the *Yuejueshu* reads this *ji* as 計 (vol. 8, "Jidizhuan" [*Zengding Han Wei congshu*, p. 973]), while the Tieruyiguan manuscript edition of the *Yuejueshu* reads this *ji* as 稽 (p. 110). These all prove the *Shiji*'s explanation that these two *ji* were interchangeable.

(ii) "To plan" or "to deliberate" (*mou*) ([Tang monk] Xuanying's *Yiqiejing yinyi*, vol. 13, p. 7b, the line "*buji*," which quotes Jia Kui's [Han, 30–101] *Guoyu zhu*).

(iii) "Reckoning" or "calculations" (*suan*) (*Shuowen*, 3 *shang*, p. 94; see comment 27c).

The character *ji* as used in *Sun-tzu* here has "surveying" as its meaning; however, since ancient times this definition has been found only in the classics. The commonly known meanings have been "reckoning" or "calculations," especially in dictionaries; for this reason it is easily misinterpreted. Cao Cao (Han, 155–220) felt that *ji* meant the activities in the court's reckonings (see p. 41). Although Du Mu correctly pointed out that the title "Ji" was the same as the *ji* in "verified through *ji*," he was still hampered by its definition as "reckoning" and so was unable to obtain a comprehensive understanding.

[7]Insofar as character meaning is concerned, "estimate" up until the Han Dynasty was generally written as *gu*, and later this was modified to the terms *guji*; the meaning of all such phrases, though, lies in the character *gu*, not *ji*, so their interpretations cannot be used.

2. "Military affairs are a country's vital political concerns" in the Chinese text reads *"bing zhe, guo zhi dashi ye"* and follows both the Linyi text and the Sakurada version.[8]

2a. "Military affairs" in the Chinese text reads *"bing."* Since *bing* is modified by "a country's vital political concerns" (see comment 2c), we thus know its meaning here is "military affairs."[9] This character *bing* has not been defined over the centuries; it has only been in present times that many interpreters of *Sun-tzu* have tried to define *bing* as "war" (*zhanzheng*); their source for this definition is unknown.[10]

---

[8]The *Wujing* and *Shiyijia* read this line as flowing into the next line without a full stop indicated by the character *ye*.
Note: The sentence pattern "A, B *ye*" generally has as its translation format "A + to be + B." Some people have thought that the translation format is the equivalent of its grammatical form, which is a serious misconception. In fact, this format in many instances cannot interpret a Chinese sentence's correct meaning. Wang Li once wrote, "In the exercise of language we will run across some statement sentences where the relationship between the subject and predicate cannot be analyzed according to the needs of the format's logic. In modern Chinese this is true, and in ancient Chinese this also was true. . . . With regard to these types of statement sentences with condensed content, we should not ruin their meaning because of the written format" (*Gu Hanyu tonglun*, 10, "Panduanju [Statement sentences]: Ye zi," pp. 93–94); this is a highly valuable guideline worth utilizing.

[9]*Bing* (see comment 15, footnote 49) as a part of "the affairs of a government" has been discussed considerably since ancient times. One example can be found in the *Lunyu*, where Zigong asked Confucius about governing; Confucius answered that it was "sufficient food and sufficient *bing*" (vol. 12, "Yanyuan" [*Shisanjing*, p. 5435]).
Following *bing* is the character *zhe*, which indicates a pause; see Wang Yinzhi's (Qing, 1766–1834) *Jingzhuan shici* (p. 196) and Yang Shuda's (1885–1956) *Ciquan* (vol. 5, p. 19, the third definition).

[10]The *Ciyuan* incorrectly gives "war" as the third definition of *bing* (rev. ed., p. 315). The sources it cites are two lines from the *Zuozhuan*: "[Jixiu] was beloved and liked *bing*. The lord did not restrain [him]" (vol.3, "Yingong sannian" [*Shisanjing*, p. 3739]). This line has never been interpreted, but by expanding on this text, the character *bing* here should more likely indicate the activities of "driving a war chariot and practicing with sharp weapons." Forcing the definition of "war" on the character *bing* here goes way beyond its original meaning. Yang Bojun more correctly notes in his *Chunqiu Zuozhuan zhu* (p. 31) that the character *bing* here indicates martial activities (*wushi*).
More recently, some scholars have quoted *Sun Bin bingfa* in an attempt to prove that *bing* is defined as "war" ("Jian Weiwang," the line "raise *bing* to align them"), but this is problematic. Because war is an action involving mutual conflict (see comment 27a), how could one side alone rouse both sides' activities? The term in question, "to raise *bing*," from this line in *Sun Bin bingfa*, is still properly interpreted as "to raise forces."
Cihai has "military affairs" (*junshi*) as its third definition of *bing* (1989 rev. ed., p. 745); its cited source expressly is *Sun-tzu*, "Surveying," the line "military affairs are a country's vital political concerns" (*"bing-zhe, guo zhi dashi ye"*), which is identical to our findings.

2b. "Country" in the Chinese text reads "*guo.*" We are using a more general concept in our interpretation[11] to aid in the understanding of modern readers.

2c. "Vital political concerns" in the Chinese text reads "*dashi.*" *Dashi* was normally a special term in the pre-Qin period. It is inappropriate to consider it as having the meaning of "vital importance," a definition assigned to it by some later scholars. Examples of this pre-Qin term can be found in the *Zuozhuan, Zhouli, Xunzi,* and so forth.[12]

Based on our own studies, *dashi* was another way of saying "political concerns" in pre-Qin times.[13] However, it concerned not everyday political affairs, but the extremely important activities directly under a lord's authority which involved the entire country. We therefore added "vital" to convey this meaning.

3. "Then, they are based on these five" in the Chinese text reads "*gu, jing zhi yi wu.*"

---

[11]According to Jiao Xun (Qing, 1763–1820), "With regard to all of China, every feudal appointment constituted a *guo*" (*Qunjing gongshitu,* "Chengtu" 7 [*Huang Qing jingjie xubian,* "Zhujing zongyi," p. 14854]).

Guo had "walled city" as its basic meaning (*Zhouli,* "Tianguan: Zhongzai," the line "set the *guo's* layout and regulate the outlying areas"; (Tang) Jia Gongyan's note (*Shisanjing,* p. 1373). See also Jiao Xun's second explanation (above); Du Zhengsheng's *Zhoudai chengbang,* p. 9; and Cho-Yun Hsu's *Xi Zhou shi,* p. 288).

The ancient concept of *guo* was that it constituted a political, economic, and military base; this later developed into the modern concept of "country."

Ma Rong (Han, 79–166) believed that the character *guo* in this line meant "a feudal state." Jia Gongyan proved in the *Zhouli* that Ma's explanation was incorrect; in the *Zhouli, guo* could mean the emperor's territory, while feudal states were actually referred to as *bangguo,* not *guo,* as Jia mentioned (*Shisanjing,* p. 1374).

[12]E.g., the *Zhouli* has the line "with *dashi* [lit., 'big affairs'], then follow one's superior; with *xiaoshi* [lit., 'small affairs'], then carry it out by one's self," using *dashi* and *xiaoshi* as contrasting terms ("Tianguan: Xiaozai" [*Shisanjing,* p. 1404]). The *Zuozhuan* records, "When *dashi* go against righteousness, critical disasters will certainly result" (vol. 54, "Dinggong yuannian" [*Shisanjing,* p. 4626]). Moreover, *Xunzi* has the line "if so, then *dashi* will be spoiled because they are uncontrollable, and *xiaoshi* will be spoiled for being disregarded," which also uses *dashi* and *xiaoshi* as contrasting terms (vol. 5, "Wangzhi," p. 1b; also, Jijie edition, p. 95). All of these prove that *dashi* in ancient times indeed was a special term.

[13]Yang Bojun and Xu Ti have for the seventh definition of *dashi* "the political concerns of a country" (*Chunqiu Zuozhuan cidian,* p. 38), which is identical to our own findings.

3a. "They are based on" in the Chinese text reads *"jing zhi."* Because the subject here is not specified, we may understand it as acting in the passive voice.[14] The basic meaning of *jing* is "the warp,"[15] which is fundamental to the weave. So, we interpret *jing* here as "to be based on."[16] *Zhi* ("they" in the passive voice) indicates "military affairs."

3b. "These five" in the Chinese text reads *"wu"* and follows the Linyi text.[17]

4. "Are verified through surveys" in the Chinese text reads *"xiao zhi yi ji"* and follows the Linyi text.[18]

For *ji,* see comment 1.

[14]In ancient Chinese, the passive voice was shown with the active voice; see *Wang Li wenji*, vol. 1, "Zhongguo yufa lilun," p. 25, and Zhou Fagao's *Zhongguo gudai yufa*, "Zao ju bian" *shang*, p. 96.

[15]*Shuowen*, 13 *shang*, p. 650. Clarifications can be found in other sources as well. (Song) Dai Tong noted, "Whenever cloth or silk is made, the warp is first set, and then the weft" (*Liushugu*, vol. 30, "Jing"). See also the line *"jing shi lingtai"* in the *Shijing* ("Daya: Wen Wang series: Lingtai" [*Shisanjing*, pp. 1,129–30]); Kong Yingda's (Tang, 574–648) annotation for this is "to measure the beginning for setting a belvedere's foundation." This demonstrates that "to set the foundation" for a belvedere was a meaning of *jing*, which precisely complements the character meaning of *jing* as "the warp" or "to set the warp."

[16]E.g., the *Erya* has the lines " 'to be the foundation of' [*ji*] means *jing*" and " 'to be the foundation of' means *she* [to establish]" (vol. 3, "Shiyan" 3 [*Shisanjing*, p. 5,612]); Xing Bing (Song, 932–1010) noted, "*Ji* means the earth under a wall. Also defined as 'beginning'; when conducting an affair, first make a plan that must 'set in fundamental order.' "

Jing in ancient times also was commonly defined as "to regulate," "to manage," or "to administrate," and sometimes even "to govern" (e.g., "Yingong shiyinian," *Zuozhuan*, the line *"jing* the country" [vol. 4, *Shisanjing*, p. 3,767]); Kong Yingda's notes. But because a lord's leadership may not be "governed" (see p.2), we know therefore that this interpretation is inapplicable.

[17]The later versions all write this, though, as *wushi* (five *shi*), which is incorrect; Sun Xingyan and Wu Renji discussed this in their *Shijia* (vol. 1, p. 2a). They pointed out that *"wu"* became *"wushi"* when later writers' annotations were used to "amend" the text of *Sun-tzu*. This line in the Linyi text does not in fact have the character *shi*. (Although Sun and Wu were accurate here, they mistakenly read this line as connected to the preceding text, thus *"jing zhi yi wu xiao zhi ji."* Later in this first book of *Sun-tzu* [p. 3], this line is repeated as *"xiao zhi yi ji, yi suo qi qing"* [they are verified through surveys to assess their status], which is clear proof.)

[18]*Xiao* 效 in the later versions of *Sun-tzu* is written as 校 (also read *jiao*), and these two characters were interchangeable in ancient times (i.e., *Guanzi* has the line "the people will then *shangxiao*" [vol. 1, "Mumin," p. 1], Yin Zhizhang's note). *Xiao* in this line of *Sun-tzu* meant "to be verified" (*yan*) (*Guangya*, "Shiyan," vol. 5 *xia*, p. 25a, Wang Niansun's [Qing, 1744–1832] note; it also could also mean "to make clear" [*Xunzi*, vol. 12, "Zhengiun," p. 2b, the line "using this to *xiao* it," (Tang) Yang Jing's notes]).

Some previous annotations of *Sun-tzu* follow the later versions to read this character as *jiao*, meaning

5. "Leadership" in the Chinese text reads *"dao"* (lit., "the way"). This is a special term of Sun Wu's that is self-defined one line later as something that "causes people to follow their superiors willingly" (p. 37).

In the past, some annotations have defined *dao* as "benevolence," along with "justice" or "morality."[19] A few have even lent *dao* a more abstract, philosophical meaning.[20] Neither of these, though, are appropriate for interpreting the text of *Sun-tzu*.

6. "Cyclic natural occurrences" in the Chinese text reads *"tian"* (lit., "sky" or "heaven"). In ancient times this character was also used to indicate what we today know as "nature."[21] *Sun-tzu* explains that *"tian"* embraces "yin and yang

---

bijiao (to compare), which is not proper. *Jiao* written as a shorthand form of *bijiao* is a modern development, but in pre-Qin times it was never seen as meaning "to compare." This character in ancient times was generally used to mean "to view" or "to examine" *(kao)* (e.g., the *Wenxuan* has the line "xiao the warriors by using swift birds" [vol. 9, "Changyangfu," p. 174], where Li Shan's [Tang, d. 689] annotation quotes Jia Kui's notes in the *Guoyu zhu*).

The modern term *bijiao* acquired its definition because *bi* means "to put into order" (*Shuowen*, 8 *shang*, p. 390), while *jiao* (or, *xiao*) means "to examine," so "to examine and put into order" was expanded to mean "to compare."

An example of *bijiao* as used in the pre-Qin era can be found in the *Guoyu*, the line *"bijiao* the people with better cultivation" (vol. 6, "Qiyu," p. 2b); Wei Zhao (Three Kingdoms, 204–73) noted, *"Bi* means 'to compare'; *jiao* means 'to review the grade of.' " Also, *Zhuangzi* has the line *"bi* and scrutinize the *xing* and *ming*" (vol. 4, "Tiandao," Jijie edition, p. 81), about which the *Jingdian shiwen* says, *"Bi* means 'to compare' " ("Zhuangzi yinyi" *Zhong*, p. 382). Therefore, the phrase "to compare" in ancient times took its meaning from the character *bi*, not from *jiao (xiao)*.

[19]The book *Xunzi* notes that "such benevolence and justice is used to rectify political affairs" (vol. 10, "Yibing," Jijie edition, p. 186), so benevolence and justice are actually aspects of leadership. Du Mu's annotation also used this line from *Xunzi* in an attempt to prove that *dao* meant "benevolence" (*ren*) and "justice" (*yi*).

However, benevolence and justice are two ethical traits, and if they are not put into practice politically, how can they "cause people to follow their superiors willingly"? If, on the other hand, benevolence and justice are practiced in dealing with the people, this is leadership, and that is expressly what is meant by this passage from *Xunzi*. Du Mu's opinion is therefore not acceptable from the position of contemporary understanding.

[20]Mencius said, "The *dao* is like a great road" ("Gaozi" *xia* [*Shisanjing*, p. 5990]). Qian Daxin (Qing, 1744–1813) asked regarding this, "How, then, can one search into abstraction to obtain *dao?*" (*Yangxinlu*, vol. 18, p. 417). Our question therefore is, in what way can abstraction be applied to governing? As Qian noted, "Having abstraction as the *dao* is sufficient to annihilate a country" (Qian quoting from Zhang Wugou).

[21]*Zhuangzi* has the line "first comprehend *tian* and then virtue" (vol. 5, "Tiandao," p. 15a; [Jin] Guo Xiang's note).

[see comment 10a], cold and heat, and the seasons and lunar periods [see comment 10b]"; all of these are cyclically changing factors in nature, so we interpret it accordingly.[22]

7. "Geographical factors" in the Chinese text reads "*di*" (lit., "the earth" or "land"). *Sun-tzu*'s own definition can be clearly obtained later in the text as "the high and the low, the wide and the narrow, the far and the near, the difficult and the easy, the lethal and the safe" (p. 38). Some scholars have interpreted *di* here as "terrain," which is problematic.[23]

8. "Commandership" in the Chinese text reads "*jiang*." Cao Cao, later in the text, where Sun Wu provides his own definition, pointed out, "*Jiang* should have five cultivations," which is absolutely correct. So, we follow Cao Cao's explanation here to understand that what Sun Wu lists ("wisdom, credibility, benevolence, courage, and discipline") are the requisites for the cultivation of commander ability.

9. "Leadership causes people to follow their superiors willingly; therefore, following them in death and in life, the people will not betray them" in the Chinese text reads "*dao zhe: ling min yu shang tongyi ye; gu ke yuzhi si, ke yuzhi sheng, min fogui ye.*"

[22]Some have translated *"tian"* as "the climatic condition" or "weather," neither of which evince a comprehensive understanding; "the heavens," though still obscure, would have been a safer interpretation.

[23]In the pre-Qin era, China's economy was primarily agrarian, so a government's existence and a people's livelihood depended on the land; naturally, this was also the foundation for military strength.
The classics contain many discussions of this, but none is as brief and clear as that in *Guanzi*: "The protection of the land [*di*] lies with the city fortifications; the protection of the city fortifications lies with the forces; the protection of the forces lies with the men; the protection of the men lies with grain. So, if the land is not developed, the city fortifications will not be secure" (vol. 1, "Quanxiu," p. 7). His belief that "the protection of the land lies with the city fortifications" came from a comprehensive strategic outlook; "the protection of the men lies with grain" came from an agrarian economic outlook. "If the land is not developed, the city fortifications will not be secure" came from the relationship between an agrarian economy and national defense. In other words, he was discussing the main premises for military affairs at that time, which also had to have been Sun Wu's viewpoint. We therefore know that what is being referred to as *di* here cannot be simply referred to as the terrain of a battlefield, as some scholars have supposed.

9a. "Superiors" in the Chinese text reads "*shang.*" In the pre-Qin period, *shang* (lit., "up" or "best") could be used to describe "ones superior to the people."[24] In later years this *shang* was used exclusively to indicate a lord, which was of course different from pre-Qin use.

9b. "The people will not betray them" in the Chinese text reads "*min fogui ye*" and follows the Linyi text.[25]

Gui in ancient times had as its basic definition "to go against" or "to be the opposite of" (*wei*),[26] and this was developed into "to oppose" or "to

---

[24]The *Zuozhuan* notes that "the *shang* and inferiors have no enmity" (vol. 49, "Zhaogong ershinian" [*Shisanjing*, p. 4543]); Kong Yingda noted, "There is no enmity between the *shang* and inferiors, which are officials and the people."

The *Lüshi Chunqiu* says that "when a lord is capable, a country is administrated well, so the talented ones are in *shang*" (vol. 16, "Xianshilan: Guanshi," p. 4a); (Han) Gao You noted that "*shang* is a superior position."

The *Xiaojing* has the line "loyalty and obedience are retained in serving their *shang*" ("Shizhang" [*Shisanjing*, p. 5536]); the Tang emperor Xuanzong noted, "[This is] the ability to achieve loyalty and obedience in serving a lord and superiors."

[25]The later versions are both different from this and erroneous. The *Wujing* records this line as "*er buwei* [fear] *wei* [danger] *ye*," the *Shiyijia* and Sakurada versions record it as "*er buwei wei*," and the *Shijia* lists it as "*er min buwei wei ye*." Yu Yue (Qing, 1821–1906) wrote, "Later versions have the character *wei* [fear], which was a subsequent addition" (*Zhuzi pingyi bulu*, vol. 3, "Sunzi," p. 6).

Also, the *Shiyijia* quotes (Liang) Mengshi as saying that during his time there were two different versions of this line, one reading "*ren buyi*" and the other "*ren buwei[gui]*," which proves that Yu's view was correct. (We know that the character *wei* in the second quote had the ancient definition of "to suspect" (*yi*), which Cao Cao also noted, so *wei* [lit., "danger"] here has been clearly shown to read *gui* and does not mean "danger," as we commonly define it today. Moreover, the character *ren* was used in both places to avoid the taboo character *min* from the Tang Taizong reign.)

All of the later versions miss the difference between the characters *fo* and *bu* at the beginning of this line. Ding Shengshu once pointed out that following *fo* there must be a transitive verb and the object is omitted, while after *bu* there can be an adverb, intransitive verb, or transitive verb, and the object can be either omitted or included (see Qi Peirong's *Xunguxue gailun*, p. 66).

[26]E.g., *Wenxuan*, the line "the outer gate and courtyard are *gui* and different" (vol. 2, "Xijing fu," p. 48); Li Shan's note, which quotes the *Shuowen*. (The *Shuowen* available today, however, defines *gui* as "request" [*ze*], and this has been disputed over the years. We follow Ma Xulun's determination that its definition as "request" was a Han Dynasty usage and not a pre-Qin practice [*Shuowen jiezi liushu shuzheng*, vol. 5, pp. 4675–76].)

Gui's meaning was also developed into "different" (*yi*) (e.g., *Wenxuan*, the line "*gui* color and distinguished sound" [vol. 12, "Hai fu," p. 233], Li Shan's note; and *Xunzi*, the line "changing *gui* and depressed" [vol. 13, "Lilun," p. 14b], Yang Jing's note), as well as "to trick" (*bianzha*), "cunning" (*jue*), and "to deceive" (*qi*) (e.g., Xuanying's *Yiqiejing yinyi*, the line "*guiyu*" [vol. 14, "Sifenlu section 49," p. 14a], which quotes the *Sancang* and *Guangya*), among other meanings.

betray" (*fan*).[27] *Gui* in this instance indicates a defiling of the people's willingness to "follow" their superiors, so we interpret it as "to betray."[28]

10. "Cyclic natural occurrences include yin and yang, cold and heat, and the seasons and lunar periods" in the Chinese text reads "*tian zhe: yinyang, hanshu, shizhi ye.*"

10a. "Yin and yang" in ancient Chinese concepts are two reciprocating, opposing natural forces. These rhythmical fluctuations create the earth's times, seasons, and aberrations in the weather.[29] Since "seasons" in the text of *Sun-tzu* are categorized as *shi* (see comment 10b), they were not meant to be included under the category of "yin and yang."

10b. "The seasons and lunar periods" in the Chinese text reads "*shizhi.*" Because the two preceding terms—*yinyang* and *hanshu*—are related word pairs, *shizhi* should be considered as having the same form. In pre-Qin

[27]*Wenxuan*, the line "changes like these that *gui* each other" (vol. 14, Ban Gu's [Han, 32–92] "Youtong fu," p. 269); Li Shan's note, which quotes (Han) Cao Dagu's interpretation.

[28]Mengshi's annotation defines *gui* as "disloyalty" *(erzhi)*, and Du You (Tang, 735–812) used the term "betrayal" *(panyixin)*. Their descriptions complement our definitions for *wei* as meaning "to go against" and *fan* as meaning "to betray."

[29]*Guanzi*'s description of these is that "spring, summer, autumn, and winter are due to the movements of yin and yang; the length of the day is due to the applications of yin and yang; changes from day to night are due to progressions in the yin and yang" (vol. 1, "Chengma," p. 13). It also says, "the day has morning and evening; the night has dawn and dusk" (vol. 4, "Yuhe," p. 63). Thus, with the exception of the seasons, *Guanzi*'s descriptions of the ancient concept of yin and yang show that they indicate "the hours, night and day, and morning and evening."
Also, the *Yijing* has the line "the meanings of yin and yang match the sun and moon" ("Xici" *shang* [*Shisanjing*, p. 162]). *Guanzi* noted, "The sun is in charge of yang, and the moon is in charge of yin" (vol. 14, "Sishi," p. 241). So, we know that the changes in yin and yang could be expressed in the sun's and moon's revolutions, as well as in aberrations in the weather.
The *Shujing* says, "When the moon is aligned with constellations, then there is wind and rain" (vol. 12, "Hungfan" [*Shisanjing*, p. 408]), which Kong Yingda explained, "If the sun and moon stray from the regular paths, then the weather will be affected and change." Kong also said that Zheng Xuan quoted from the *Chunqiuwei*, "When the moon is aligned with Qi, the wind whips the sand." (A similar prediction is noted in *Sun-tzu*; see "Attacks Using Fire," p. 108.)
The belief that the moon's alignment with constellations could cause rain can also be seen in the *Shijing*: "When the moon is aligned with Bi, the rain falls in torrents" (vol. 15, "Xiaoya: Yuzao series: Jianjianzhishi" [*Shisanjing*, p. 1075]). So, we can say that with regard to weather, yin and yang directly indicate its aberrations. The regular changes in the weather are considered part of "the seasons and lunar periods" (see comment 10b, footnote 31).

times, the character *shi* basically indicated "the seasons."[30] In order for *zhi* to complement *shi*, we know that this must indicate *jieqi*, or "the lunar periods."[31]

11. "The high and the low" in the Chinese text reads "*gaoxia*" and follows the Linyi text.[32]

12. "The rules are in regulations for mobilization, official duties, and the management of matériel" in the Chinese text reads "*fa zhe: quzhi, guanshou* [generally read *guandao*; see 12b], *zhuyong ye*."[33] Cao Cao's note says, "[*Fa*] means the system of *buqu* [army systems in the Han Dynasty; see 12a], banners, and signal gongs and drums; *guan* means the ranks of officers; *dao* means a supply route; *zhuyong* means the administration of military supplies and outlays." Ensuing scholars all made amendments within Cao's framework, but in fact, this explanation has at least three points which are imprecise: (i) his explanation uses the term "*buqu*," which was a Han system that did not yet exist during the pre-Qin period; (ii) *quzhi* was therefore a term that Cao misread as "*qu* and *zhi*"; and (iii) this line from *Sun-tzu* describes a peacetime situation, but Cao mistakenly believed this to be in wartime.[34]

[30]*Shuowen*, 7 *shang*, p. 305.

[31]This explication was first suggested by Yu Yue in his *Zhuzi pingyi bulu* (vol. 3, pp. 6–7).
The "lunar periods" *(jieqi)* are a traditional Chinese concept in which the changes in the entire year's weather, temperature, the length of days and nights, and animal activities are divided according to the moon's phases into twenty-four distinct periods. About every fifteen days there is an apparent change, and people's lives are scheduled to harmonize with these lunar periods. (Detailed references to these can be found in the *Liji* ["Yueling"], the *Lüshi Chunqiu*, and *Huainanzi* ["Shize"].)
Following this line the Linyi text says, "In going with or against them lies the forces' victory" *(shunni bingsheng ye)*. Most scholars do not believe that this is part of the original text of *Sun-tzu*. The factors in natural changes have been highly regarded in Chinese politics and military affairs ever since ancient times. We therefore understand that these can influence "the forces' victory." However, what is meant by "going with or against them" is not completely clear; it perhaps reflects old superstitions that disagree with Sun Wu's doctrine (see p. 112) and so cannot be used.

[32]None of the later versions includes this phrase. Book 9, "Troop Maneuvers," in *Sun-tzu* says, "Generally, armies prefer the high to the low" (p. 80), so we know that the Linyi text is more accurate here.

[33]"*Guanshou, zhuyong*" in *Heguanzi* is quoted as "*guanbei zhuyong*" (the officials are prepared for service to the lord). (This follows the reading of Lu Dian [Song, 1042–1102]; *shang*, p. 9a.) The text of *Sun-tzu* was modified here to fit Legalist theory.

[34]We know that Cao believed this line from *Sun-tzu* to be a description of wartime because he interpreted *dao* (lit., "way") as a supply route. If he had not supposed that was wartime, no discussion of

12a. First we will discuss Cao's use of *buqu*. This term was employed in the Han Dynasty to describe either of two situations: a type of army organization[35] or a formation for battle arrays.[36] Han scholars sometimes used Han circumstances to explain pre-Qin systems,[37] which is why Cao used *buqu* in his explanation.

In fact, *Sun-tzu* illustrates elsewhere the actual army system of his time: Book 3, "Planning an Offense," says, "Annexing an entire country . . . army . . . battalion . . . company . . . squad is best" (p. 48). This paragraph as a matter of course indicates the organization of "country" (*guo*), "army" (*jun*), "battalion" (*lü*), "company" (*zu*), and "squad" (*wu*), and it completely coincides with the system described in other pre-Qin books,[38] so this has absolutely nothing to do with *buqu*.

It is precisely because Cao was not aware of *quzhi*'s correct meaning that he was compelled to break the term into "*qu*" and "*zhi*." Sun Wu was a native of Qi (now located in eastern China in the area of Shandong Province). During the pre-Qin period, the book *Guanzi* was written in the Qi area, and it uncoincidentally has the term *quzhi* in it:

---

supply routes would have been necessary. See the margin notes on pp. 38–39, which demonstrate Cao's error.

[35]The *Wenxuan* has the lines "*buqu* had their positions" (vol. 1, "Xidu fu," p. 30) and "combine *buqu*, regulate arrays and squads" (vol. 2, "Xijing fu," p. 53); both of Li Shan's notes quote from (Jin) Sima Biao's *Xu Han shu*: "Generals all possess *bu*. Marshals' garrisons are divided into five *bu* each, and every *bu* has one person with the rank of *jiaowei*. Below the *bu* are *qu*, with each *qu* having one person with the rank of *junhou*."

[36]In the *Han shu* it is recorded, "When [Li] Guang maneuvered, [he] had no *buqu* arrays," and "[General] Cheng Bushi was strict about *buqu* formations and arrays" (vol. 54, "Li Guang zhuan," pp. 680–81).

[37]For example, the *Zhouli* says, "With massive conscriptions, he led laborers from among the people and arrived; [he] was in charge of both its policy and orders" ("Diguan: Xiangshi" [*Shisanjing*, p. 1536]). Zheng Xuan noted, " 'And arrived' means the initiation of *buqu*."
Chen Li (Qing, 1810–89) once noted, "Zheng [Xuan's] annotations to the three *Li* [i.e., the *Zhouli*, *Yili*, and *Liji*] use Han systems to describe Zhou systems" (*Dongshu dushuji*, vol. 7, "Zhouli" [*Huang Qing jingjie xubian*, vol. 951, p. 16250]). Zheng Xuan was a great explicator of the classics during the late Eastern Han Dynasty and also was a contemporary of Cao. His method of interpreting pre-Qin books, then, definitely is representative of the practices at that time.

[38]E.g., *Zhouli*, vol. 28, "Xiaguan: Zhijun" (*Shisanjing*, p. 1791).

When *quzhi* is needed and called, do not neglect its appropriate time or waste the use of lands. The acquirement of the condition of its measures had to originate in surveying.³⁹ So, such surveying in the conduct of armed conflict generally had to first reach an internal conclusion, and then forces could emerge from the border.

From this we can clearly see that *quzhi* concerned the raising of forces. Today, we refer to this as "regulations for mobilization."⁴⁰

12b. As for the *shou* in *guanshou* (normally known as *dao*), this follows the viewpoint of Wang Niansun.⁴¹

12c. Also, the *zhu* in *zhuyong* possessed the same ancient meaning as *shou* (in charge of),⁴² so we interpret *zhu* as "management." *Yong* means "that

---

³⁹"Surveying" here in *Guanzi* reads "*ji*," following the *Guanzi jijiao*, p. 90. The other versions of *Guanzi* read the original *ji* as *jishu* (see "*ji*" in comment 1). This passage comes from vol. 2, "Qifa Xuanzhen," p. 31.

⁴⁰The difficulty in interpreting the term *quzhi* lies in the character *qu*. *Qu* obtained its basic definition from "a vessel bent to hold things" (*Shuowen*, vol. 12 *xia*, p. 643, and Duan Yucai's [Qing, 1735–1815] notes). Therefore, because *qu* is "bent" and "sloped toward one end," these qualities led it to be developed into meaning *xiaoshi*, or "individual and detailed matters or affairs." (An explanation of *xiaoshi* [lit., "small affairs"] can be found in Wang Niansun, *Dushu zazhi*, IV-4, pp. 12b–13a, the line "*qu wei zhi fan.*" Previous scholars have used *da* [lit., "big"] to indicate "general" or "in principle," while *xiao* [lit., "small"] was used to indicate "individual" or "detailed.") Then, *qu* can mean "to flexibly deal with the individual needs of details" (*Liji*, the line "*qu er sha,*" Zheng Xuan's note, and the line "*jingli sanbai, quli sanqian,*" Kong Yingda's annotation; both in vol. 23, "Liqi" [*Shisanjing*, p. 3105]).

Therefore, *qu* came to mean "to put all details under control" (*Xunzi*, vol. 9, "Chendao," p. 1b, the line "*qu cheng zhi xiang,*" Yang Jing's note; also, *Xunzi*, "Zhengming," the line "*chengsu quqi*" [*Xunzi jianshi* (Selected Interpretations of *Xunzi*), p. 311, or *Xunzi jianshi* (Simplified Interpretations of *Xunzi*), p. 309], Liang Qixiong's note, which quotes Liu Nianqin's interpretation of *qu*; *Laozi* has the line "*qu ze quan*" [to be flexible is to be whole] [ch. 22, (Jin) Wang Bi's edition] takes the same standpoint).

Quzhi therefore should literally mean "detailed regulations," but we modify it to fit *Guanzi*'s description of its function in interpreting it as "regulations for mobilization."

Cao's interpretation of *quzhi* was erroneous. However, some later scholars who studied *Guanzi* did not realize Cao's serious mistake and went back to apply his interpretation to *Guanzi*. We must not lightly overlook this.

⁴¹Wang said, "The character *dao* is read to be *shou*, so this has the same meaning as *shou* [duties]" (*Dushu zazhi*, the line "this subordinate has *shou*" ["Zhiyu: Zhuangzi," p. 30b]).

Thus, *guandao* reads *guanshou*. *Mengzi* has the line "when talent and position do not match in one who has *guanshou*, he should be dismissed" (vol. 4 *shang*, "Gongsun chou" *xia* [*Shisanjing*, p. 5856]); (Han) Zhao Qi noted, "*Guanshou* is the one with an official position who conducts his duties." We therefore interpret this term as "official duties."

This type of explanation can also be seen in Yu Yue's *Zhuzi pingyi* under the line "whoever discerns that being, vanity, death, and life are but a single *dao* [*shou*], I would be his friend" (vol. 19, "Zhuangzi" 3, p. 215).

⁴²*Guangya*, "Shigu," *3 xia*, p. 5b.

which can be used"; modifying this to complement the subject of military affairs, we know that *yong* here means "army matériel."

13. "All generals have to learn these five in their entirety" in the Chinese text reads "*fan ci wuzhe, jiang mo buwen.*"

13a. "Generals" in the Chinese text reads "*jiang.*" The head of the army is referred to as a *jiang*.[43] In the pre-Qin era, *jiang* had such official positions as civilian governors or district chiefs.[44] So, at that time *jiang* were civilian administrators of both people and military affairs. In peacetime they would administrate the people, and when war erupted they would lead the people under their administration into battle. *Jiang*, at least in Sun Wu's time, were of a high position similar to that of proconsuls during the Roman Empire; there is no exact English equivalent for *jiang*, so we loosely interpret it as "generals."

Sun-tzu's discussion here is still from the vantage point of peacetime, so *jiang* does not indicate "commanders" in this instance.[45] "Commanders" during the Zhou were called *junjiang*, not the *jiangjun* of later Chinese.[46] Succeeding generations were not aware of the difference between *jiangjun* and *junjiang*, so the content and meaning of pre-Qin books were often confused as a result.

Throughout *Sun-tzu*, no matter whether *jiangjun* or *junjiang* is meant,

[43](Tang) Huilin, *Yiqiuejing yinyi*, under the term "*jiangbao*," which quotes the *Wenzi jilue* (vol. 4, p. 2b).

[44]In *Xunzi* under the line "[it] is the duty of a *jiangshuai*" (note: equivalent to a *jiang*) ("Fuguo," p. 119), Yu Yue's note is quoted in Wang Xianqian's (Qing, 1842–1917) Jijie edition. Sun Yirang (Qing, 1848–1908) also pointed out that in the pre-Qin era, "[The military positions of] *jiang, shuai, zhang,* and *sima* were [the people's] administrators" (*Zhouli zhengyi*, p. 2237).

[45]The *Zhanguoce* records that in the Qu state the Queen of Nan "sent a messenger to Zhang Zi [Zhang Yi] to tell him, 'We have heard the *jiangjun* is going to the Jin state'" ("Quce" 3, the passage "Zhang Yi arrived in Chu and was impoverished" [p. 300]). Zhang Yi was the *qin* (minister) of the Qin state (see "Qince" 1; the passage "King Hui of the Qin told Hanquanzi," pp. 53–54). On that occasion Zhang Yi had never led troops into battle, yet the Queen of Nan referred to him as a *jiangjun*, which is sufficient proof that this merely was a position title.

[46]Proof of this can be seen in the *Zhouli*: "The emperor has six armies, a large country has three armies, a secondary country has two armies, and a small country has one army. *Junjiang* [commanders] all are royally appointed [the position of] *qin*" ("Xiaguan: Sima: Xuguan" [*Shisanjing*, p. 1791]); see footnote 45.

both are represented by the single character *jiang* (except when later scholars mistakenly rewrote them as *jiangjun*). However, if we are careful of the conditions surrounding the descriptions, we can still easily distinguish between the two.

13b. "In their entirety" in the Chinese text reads *"fan"* and originally appeared at the beginning of this line. This interpretation follows the *Shuowen* definition.[47]

14. Of the two lines "Which lord has better leadership?" and "Which side has more capable commanders?" the Linyi text has extant "_____ *shu neng?*" so it has only the end of the second line. This is different from the later versions' *"you neng."*[48]

15. "Which side has stronger weapons and people?" in the Chinese text reads *"bing zhong shu qiang?"* *"Bing zhong"* indicates "weapons[49] and people." Some scholars have mistakenly believed that *"bing zhong"* indicates "troops."[50]

---

[47]Vol. 13 *xia*, p. 688; Duan Yucai's note. A similar definition can also be seen in the *Guangya*: "*Fan* means 'all' " ("Shigu," 3 *xia*, p. 5b).

[48]*Huananzi* has the queries, *"zhu shu xian?"* (which side's lord is better?) and *"jiang shu neng?"* (which side's commanders are more capable?) (vol. 15, "Binglue," p. 258); the last two characters in the second line have the same pattern as that in the Linyi text.

[49]*Shuowen*, 3 *shang*, "Bing," p. 105; Duan Yucai's note. In pre-Qin times, *bing* was also used to mean "armed soldiers" or "forces" (*Zuozhuan* has the line *"jian shangguo zhi bing"* [to review the west country's forces]; vol. 47, "Zhaogong shisinian" [*Shisanjing*, p. 4506]; Kong Yingda's annotation). In *Sun-tzu*, in addition to meaning "military affairs" (see Book 1, comment 2a), *bing* was also used to indicate concerns in the area of using forces, which we translate as "military strategy," "military operations," etc., to fit the sentence's context.

[50]This explanation has three areas that are incorrect.
First, from the preceding text's question, "Which side takes better advantage of the cyclic natural occurrences and geographical factors?" (p. 39) until the last question, each query lists a pair of related items. If *"bing zhong"* is believed to be a single thing, then this is a misreading.
Second, the subsequent query is, "Which side's warriors and foot soldiers are better trained?" (p. 39). Well-trained troops are understood to be strong, so if *"bing zhong"* is explained in terms of troop strength, then what does the subsequent query mean?
The third is that in ancient times *bing* and *zhong* were never combined into a single term, so making *bing zhong* the equivalent of "troops" is a forced interpretation. We know, then, that *bing* and *zhong* indicate two matters and so interpret them accordingly.

16. "Warriors and soldiers" in the Chinese text reads "*shi zu.*" *Shi* in military terms indicates "warriors." Pre-Qin *shi* primarily conducted chariot battles.[51] *Zu* indicated the "foot soldiers" or "infantry" who mainly conducted infantry battles.[52]

17. "From these we are fully able to perceive victory and failure" in the Chinese text reads "*wu yi ci zhi shengfu yi.*" The final character *yi* here is a mood indicator suggesting "already" or "completely" *(yiran),*[53] so "fully" is used here to interpret it.

    For "perceive," see Book 3, Comment 13.

18. "When commanders heed our surveys and are appointed, victory is assured; retain them. When commanders do not heed our surveys and are appointed, defeat is assured; dismiss them" in the Chinese text reads "*jiang ting wuji, yongzhi, bisheng, liuzhi; jiang buting wuji, yongzhi, bibai, quzhi.*" Ever since Cao Cao, this line has been given numerous confusing explanations. The problem mainly lies in exactly who is meant by the characters *jiang* (lit., "general") and *wu* (lit., "I" or "we"). Generally, over the centuries these opinions have aligned into four major categories:

    (i) The explanation does not touch on the characters *jiang* and *wu.*[54]

---

[51]E.g., *Liji,* "Wangzhi": "Train *shi* with chariots and armor" (*Shisanjing,* p. 2905); *Dadai Liji* has a description that is almost identical (vol. 9, "Qiancheng 68," p. 4b).

[52]E.g., the *Zuozhuan* has the line "prepare *zu* and chariots" (vol. 2, "Yinggong yuannian" [*Shisanjing,* p. 3722]), about which Du Yu (Jin, 222–84) noted, "*Bu* [infantry] are called *zu*"; also, Lu Deming's (Tang, 556–627) *Jingdian shiwen* says: "*Zu* . . . are *bubing* [infantry soldiers]" ("Chunqiu Zuozhuan yinyi" *zhiyi,* p. 226).
Moreover, the *Zhouli* records, "In difficult wilderness emphasize men [i.e., foot soldiers] and in flat wilderness emphasize chariots" ("Xiaguan: Dasima" [*Shisanjing,* p. 1809]), so we more or less can see the deployment of *shi* and *zu* in the battles of that time.

[53]Yang Shuda, *Ciquan,* vol. 7, "Yi," third and fourth definitions, p. 22.

[54]For example, Cao Cao noted, "If *ji* cannot be determined, then withdraw and leave" (note: Cao perhaps intended for *ji* to mean "consideration"). Du Mu followed Cao's interpretation and also quoted from the *Chunqiu zhuan* to support Cao's explanation: "Under the proper situation, then one should return." (Note: this quote actually is from "Xigong ershibanian," *Zuozhuan* [vol. 16, *Shisanjing,* p. 3957]. Du Mu's quote of it here was inappropriate; a better choice would have been the succeeding line in the *Zuozhuan:* "When difficulty is perceived, withdraw." It also is possible that a woodblock printing dropped this line from Du's version.)

(ii)   *Jiang* is interpreted as meaning *pijiang* (middle and low-ranking commanders under a marshal), and *wu* remains unexplained.[55]

(iii) *Wu* is explained as indicating Sun Wu himself.[56]

(iv)   *Jiang* is translated as "marshal," while *wu* is not clearly interpreted; the reader, though, may surmise that this probably indicates "lord."[57]

Of the above four categories, (iv) is comparatively logical, but the other three are problematic, as explained below:

The suggestion in (i) is valuable; when facing insurmountable crises on the battlefield, an early withdrawal is practical. However, such an announcement is simply not related to this line in *Sun-tzu* (see footnote 54).

If the assumption in (ii) is that *jiang* means *pijiang*, then *wu* naturally indicates a "marshal." However, how can a marshal fully take responsibility for military affairs that "are a country's vital political concerns," surveys of a country's strength, and considerations on whether to declare war?[58]

[55]Mengshi noted, "*Jiang* meant *pijiang:* '[If they] obey my plan and are victorious, keep them; [if they] disobey my plan and fail, dismiss them.' " During the Ming Dynasty, Liu Ying (*Wujing qishu zhijie, shang,* pp. 6a–b) and Zhao Benxue (*Sunzi shu jiaojie yinlei, shang,* pp. 13a–b) both emulated this opinion, and He Shoufa's views (*Yinzhu,* vol. 1, pp. 12a–b) also belong in this category. However, He particularly pointed out that "the character *jiang* in the preceding *jiangzhe* [i.e., the 'generals' in comment 14] means *dajiang* [marshals]"; other than this, He's descriptions belong in both categories (ii) and (iv).

[56]For example, (Tang) Chen Hao wrote, "Sun Wu used his book to seek [opportunities] from [the King of Wu] Helü by saying, 'Listen to my plan, then [you] will assuredly overcome the enemy, and I will stay and not leave. If my plans are not listened to, then [you] certainly will fail, and I will go and not remain.' "
Those who support this interpretation have suggested that *jiang* means different things. Chen Hao also explained that because Helü (the King of Wu) often "acted as commander, he was not referred to as 'lord,' but as 'commander.' " Mei Yaochen (Song, 1002–60) noted that *jiang* actually meant *wang jiang,* so that *jiang* should be interpreted as "going to," and personally added the subject of *wang* (your majesty). (Song) Wang Xi wrote, "*Jiang* meant *xing* [to carry out]" and that *yong* meant *yongbing* (to employ forces). Moreover, (Song) Zhang Yu added, "*Jiang* is a mood word."

[57]Qi Jiguang (Ming, 1528–87) wrote in *Daxue jingjie,* "*Jiang* is the one who commands the commanders, not the *jiang* who commands troops." He also wrote, "*Qu* [to dismiss] and *liu* [to retain] are from the lord's viewpoint" (note: we thus know that he intended for *wu* to be interpreted as "lord"; Qi's interpretation was cited in Yang Bingan's *Sunzi huijian,* p. 11).
In addition, Chen Jiuxue of the early Republic noted, "This *jiang* includes both marshals and *pijiang*"; the character *wu*, we therefore may infer, meant "lord" (in which case *jiang* meant "marshal") or "marshal" (in which case *jiang* meant *pijiang;* see Chen Jiuxue's *Qizi bingfa;* note: Chen's explanation actually emulates one of the descriptions noted in passing by He Shoufa).

[58]Moreover, Guo Huaruo noted that if *jiang* indicates *pijiang*, then this just indicates a question of discipline in obedience between upper and lower ranks, and is not a matter of personally leaving or staying (*Sunzi jinyi,* p. 20). This opinion is similar to that in Li Riyu's *Sunzi bingfa xinyanjiu,* p. 17.

In (iii), if one who wanted to be a commander submitted his plan and it was rejected by the lord, even if he did not want to leave, he probably wouldn't be allowed to stay—this is just common sense. Moreover, if this paragraph has Sun Wu speaking directly to Helü, then Sun Wu's words are posed as a threat to that lord, which would not have been wise. In any case, under no circumstance would Sun Wu have acted so petulantly.

Thus, the views propounded in (i), (ii), and (iii) are unacceptable. This paragraph in *Sun-tzu* actually discusses the candidate for carrying out the government's decisions regarding armed conflict, so *jiang* must be a "commander."

In regard to the *wu* in "wuji," this should indicate the lord and high-ranking generals who participate in the surveying of military affairs.[59] But, the ultimate power lies with the lord, so in Book 7, "Armed Contention," *Sun-tzu* says, "the commander receives orders from the lord" (p. 69).

19. "And then accordingly create combat power to support outland missions" in the Chinese text reads *"nai wei zhi shi, yi zuo qiwai."*

19a. "Combat power" in the Chinese text reads *"shi."*[60] *Shi* in the pre-Qin era was defined as "power."[61] Sun Wu said in Book 5 that "the strength of a cataclysmic flood which would even be able to float rocks shows *shi*" (p. 59) and that *"shi* is as if setting a crossbow" (p. 59). We therefore understand this to mean "combat power."[62]

19b. "The support of outland missions" in the Chinese text reads *"yi zuo qiwai."* What is worth our discussion here mainly is the phrase *qiwai*. Cao Cao

---

[59]See comment 13a.

[60]Today its form is 勢, but in ancient texts its form was 埶, as can be seen in the Linyi text.

[61]The *Shuowen* defines *shi* as "great strength or power" (Chen Changzhi woodblock edition, 13 *xia*, *xinfu*, p. 20a). The *Yijing* says "the *shi* of earth is *kun*" ("Kun diagram: Xiang"); Sun Xingyan's note quotes Yu Fan (Three Kingdoms, 164–233) that *"shi* is power" (note: this quotation was mistakenly located after the ensuing line). Also, the *Guoyu* says, "Do not measure the *shi* of lords" (vol. 8, "Jinyu" 2, p. 6b); Wei Zhao explained that this was "the *shi* of strength or weakness." *Xunzi* has the line "coerce them with *shi*" (vol. 10, "Yibing," Jijie edition, p. 181); Wang Xianqian annotated, "[This] means using power to compel them."

[62]*Sun Bin bingfa* records, "[Sun Bin said,] '*Shi* is that which makes warriors have to fight' " ("Weiwang wen," p. 42), which fully supports our viewpoint on this line.

indicated that it meant "exceeding ordinary methods." Many later scholars have emulated this interpretation. However, the preceding text of *Sun-tzu* discusses nothing more than surveying the possibilities for winning armed conflict and the principles for appointing commanders. There is absolutely nothing here connected to "ordinary methods." Zhang Yu's explanation of this section was, "To support its activities on the outside."[63] This has proven to be the pre-Qin reality.

The character *qi* (its) in *qiwai* is not identified in the preceding text, but since the topic of discussion in *Sun-tzu* is military affairs, we know that *qi* denotes "military affairs." Military affairs located outside the country are "missions," so we have interpreted *qiwai* as "outland missions."

20. "Military operations entail unconventional means" in the Chinese text reads "*bingzhe, guidao ye.*" From the development of the discussion on military affairs in the preceding text of *Sun-tzu*, we know that this is a dialogue on the undertaking of expeditionary missions, so the subject *bing* in this line indicates its "operations."

With regard to *guidao*, Cao Cao's interpretation is, "*Bing* has no unchangeable format; [it] is conducted through *guizha*." (Tang) Li Quan then annotated this, "Armies do not belittle deception [*zha*]."[64] Later scholars thus have emulated this interpretation of *gui* as deception. However, Huang Zhen (Song, 1213–80) asserted that the character *gui* in ancient times indicated the skill of using forces, and that when the word *gui* was used its meaning was ethical and did not connote deception.[65]

---

[63] Pre-Qin concepts were that a city delineated *nei* (internal) and *wai* (external). (The *Liji* has the line "external activities are held on hard days" [vol. 3, "Quli" (*Shisanjing,* pp. 2705–6)]; Zheng Xuan's and Kong Yingda's annotations.)

This concept also was used with regard to a country. E.g., Book 2, "Mobilizing for Armed Conflict," has the line "outland [*wai*] and domestic [*nei*] expenses" (p. 43); Wang Xi indicated, "*Nei* means inside the country, and *wai* means where the army was located."

[64] The source for Li's annotation was *Hanfeizi*, where the Qin official Jiufan said, "In battle arrays, deception [*zha*] is not belittled" ("Nan: Yi," p. 263). Therefore, one cannot say that Li's definition of *gui* concurs with that of *Sun-tzu*.

In Cao's interpretation we find that he did not directly equate *gui* with deception, but modified the description that "it is conducted through *guizha*" with "*bing* has no unchangeable format." Another look at his words shows that he emphasized "unpredictable flexibility" rather than just deception.

[65] *Huangshi richao*, vol. 58, "Du zhuzi: Sunzi," p. 666.

In fact, to understand what Sun Wu meant by *gui* here, we must also consider the succeeding twelve examples listed in the text, starting with "have a capability, but appear not to" (p. 40). And, we therefore know that deception is only one of these methods, not all of them.[66] From this we can see that if *zha* (deception) is defined as *gui*, lapses are unavoidable. Moreover, because Book 11, "The Nine Zones," has the line "so, the concerns in conducting operations are: warily scrutinizing the enemy's intent" (p. 105),[67] we know that the method for handling the enemy does not lie in a single specific concept or method that would lead to success; this is what is meant by having the cure fit the illness. Both Cao's and Li's explanations therefore did not fully illuminate Sun Wu's meaning, and to simply cling to "deception" as the interpretation of *gui* is to take *Sun-tzu* too lightly.

The character definition of *gui* has already been examined in comment 9b, so we will follow that discussion on *gui* as *wei* (to go against) or *yi* (different) to interpret it as "unconventional."[68] Insofar as *dao* (lit., "way") is concerned, in ancient times whatever was referred to using the character *dao* could not be unorthodox, so its modification here with "unconventional" shows that this actually was a substitute character for *shu* (means; methods).[69] Thus, *guidao* should properly be interpreted as "unconventional means." However, *guidao* are not equated with military operations but are the necessary procedures for achieving missions, so the verb we employ is "entail."

21. "Show disorder to make them take a chance" in the Chinese text reads *"luan er qu zhi."* This has been generally interpreted in one of two ways:

The first is much like Li Quan's annotation: "An enemy that is greedy for advantage certainly will be disorderly." This means that we can inflict disorder on the enemy. Zhang Yu then wrote, "Deceptively show disorder; lure and take them." The second follows Du Mu's annotation: "When the enemy is confused and in turmoil, we can seize this advantage and take them." This means that the

---

[66]See the margin notes on pp. 40–41.

[67]See Book 11, comment 43a.

[68]Kanetani Osamu interpreted *guidao* as "unusual methods" (*Sonshi*, p. 24), which is identical to our own standpoint.

[69]E.g., the *Zuozhuan*, the line "we yet know Wu's *dao*" (vol. 55, "Dinggong wunian" [*Shisanjing*, p. 4644]); Du Yu noted, *"Dao* is as if *fashu* [means] is intended."

enemy's turmoil is not due to our efforts; rather, all we have to do is grasp the opportunity.

Both of these interpretations are useful in defeating the enemy. But if this is the case, what is the difference between these interpretations and the line later in the text, "Attack their weaknesses; emerge to their surprise" (p. 41)? Also, preceding this line are five different means and following it are six other means, but not one of these issues offensive action, so why would this single line disrupt the pattern in these rules? We therefore know that these previous interpretations of *Sun-tzu* are misunderstandings.

The problem in comprehending this line lies in the phrase *qu zhi*, which actually was intended to mean "to make them *qu* [lit., 'to take']."[70] The character *luan* indicates "our disorder." This signifies that our side is purposely appearing chaotic to the enemy, and this in turn will cause the enemy to take a chance. The means described in both this and the preceding line ("show gains to lure them") discuss how to motivate the enemy to react in an expected way; the previous one shows gains, while here disorder is shown.

22. "High morale" in the Chinese text reads "*nu*." In modern Chinese this character means only "rage," "anger," or "ferocity," but as an ancient military term it had a completely different interpretation.

In Book 2, "Mobilizing for Armed Conflict," after the line "trounce the enemy by means of *nu*" (p. 46), Cao Cao pointed out that *nu* means *weinu*, and Li Quan noted that it meant *junwei*. In modern terminology both *weinu* and *junwei* indicate "high morale."

23. In the Linyi text, the section between "show disorder to make them take a chance" and "if of high morale, depress them" is damaged. This space though, could have contained only eight characters. The phrase "if of high morale, depress them" is then directly followed by "attack their weaknesses," so it is very possible that the Linyi text did not include the three lines from here through "if united, separate them."[71]

---

[70]The expression of "to make [or cause] someone to do something" in the pre-Qin dialect sometimes was done using a statement pattern; e.g., the *Zuozhuan* has the line "Hua Yuan at night entered the Chu camp, got on Zifan's bed, *qi zhi* [made him get up], and said, 'My lord has sent me to report our critical condition'" (vol. 24, "Xuangong shiwunian" [*Shisanjing*, p. 4094]).

[71]This standpoint follows the *Yinqueshan Hanmu zhujian "Sunzi bingfa,"* p. 32.

24. "If at ease, exhaust them" in the Chinese text reads "*yi er lao zhi*" and follows the *Wujing* and Sakurada versions. The *Shiyijia* reads "*yin er lao zhi*";[72] in pre-Qin usage, *yi* (to be at ease) and *yin* (lit., "to guide"; "to pull") were interchangeable.[73] Book 6, "Superiority and Inferiority," says, "when enemies are at ease [*yi*], be able to exhaust them" (p. 26), so we do not use *yin* here.

25. "Attack their weaknesses; emerge to their surprise" in the Chinese text reads "*gong qi wubei, chu qi buyi*." Many scholars have read "*wubei*" (lit., "to lack protection") and "*buyi*" (lit., "to be unaware") as a continuation of the previous twelve means, thus making this a total of fourteen.

Only Li Quan and Zhao Benxue identified their dissimilarities. Li referred to these two lines as "the key to military operations" and disconnected them from the preceding twelve means.[74] Zhao wrote, "Use the preceding twelve situations to make the enemy unsuspecting; make them unprepared for our attack, unconscious of our emergence, and have problems with gaps and inaccessibility. Then swiftly send forces to attack these points."[75] In his discussion Zhao perceptively determined that the preceding twelve means do not include offensive actions, and that offensive actions lie only in these two means. So, these two are actually the conclusion to the above twelve means and therefore must be listed separately.[76]

Overcoming the enemy lies in the opponents' weaknesses in either strength

---

[72]The *Shijia* (vol. 1, p. 2a) also quotes the *Taiping yulan* (vol. 270, "Bing bu" 1, p. 6b) as "*yin er lao zhi*."

[73]*Xunzi* has the line "as if *yi* it with a rope" (vol. 17, "Xing'e," p. 8a); Yang Jing's note. Because these two characters had the same pronunciation in ancient times, they were often interchangeable.

[74]This comment is located in the *Shiyijia* under the succeeding line of the text, "such victories of strategists never can be prematurely self-determined."

[75]*Sunzi shu jiaojie yinlei, shang*, p. 26b.

[76]*Sun Bin bingfa* was deeply influenced by Sun Wu's instruction. In "Weiwang wen" are two related entries: (i) The King of Wei asked, "Is there a method that can be used to attack ten with one?" Sun [Bin]-tzu said, "Yes. Attack their weaknesses; emerge to their surprise" (p. 41). (ii) Tian Ji said, "Is there a method if the enemy is massive and strong, and if a battle must be conducted?" Sun [Bin]-tzu said, "Yes. Strengthen fortifications and rouse their will. Strictly and systematically put troops under regulation. Avoid them and make them become arrogant. Draw their reactions and exhaust them. Attack their weaknesses; emerge to their surprise" (p. 42).

Of these two dialogues, the first one is simpler and the second is more detailed; their meanings totally agree with the writings of Sun Wu.

or mind. No other means for victory has existed other than "attack their weaknesses; emerge to their surprise."

26. "Such victories of strategists never can be prematurely self-determined" in the Chinese text reads "*ci bingjia zhi sheng, buke xianzhuan* [commonly read *xianchuan*] *ye.*"

The second to the last character in this line should be read *zhuan.*[77] (If read *chuan*, its proper interpretation will be unobtainable.[78]) In ancient times, "self-determined," or "privately [as opposed to officially] issued or created," was referred to as *zhuan.*[79] Before outland missions are discussed in *Sun-tzu's* preceding outline of military affairs, all surveys and deliberations stop at the point of whether or not victory can be assured. Operations for overcoming the enemy then must wait with complete preparedness for optimum opportunities to expose the enemy's shortcomings. Book 4, "Control," says that they "awaited the enemy's defeatability" (p. 53). Book 13, "Espionage," says, "stalk each other over several years to contend for victory in a single day" (p. 111). Both demonstrate the same basic principles.[80]

[77]E.g., the *Lunyu* has the line "has *chuan* not been practiced" ("Xueer"), about which Zheng Xuan noted, "In Lu, *chuan* is read as *zhuan*" (*Lunyu zhu* [*Han Wei yishu chao,* "Jing yi," vol. 4]). Sun Wu was a native of Qi. In ancient times, Qi pronunciation was similar to that of Lu, so the character *chuan* should be read *zhuan*. (Both Qi and Lu are in the present-day area of Shandong Province in eastern China.)
Also, the *Lüshi Chunqiu* has the line "*zhuan yu* peasants, do not belabor" ("Jidong ji"); Yu Xingwu wrote, "The ancient characters for *zhuan* and *chuan* were interchangeable" (*Zhuzi xinzheng,* p. 325).
Moreover, the Mawangdui silk text of the *Zhanguoce* reads "*chuan* [*zhuan*] depends on Chu's rescue, so Liang is certainly precarious" (sec. 26 [*Boshu zhujian,* p. 120]). The editor of the silk text identified *chuan* as the substitute character for *zhuan*.

[78]Cao Cao read the character *zhuan* as *chuan*, and interpreted this line, "*Chuan* is as if to say 'to reveal.'" However, no matter how this character is read, it has never had the definition of "to reveal," so this was Cao's own postulation. Du Mu also read *zhuan* as *chuan* and said, "*Chuan* means *yan* [to explain or comment]." "Victories of strategists" (p. 41) are not matters for "explanation" or "comment," so Du's commentary likewise is unacceptable.

[79]E.g., the *Zuozhuan* has the line "Zirong *zhuan,*" which Du Yu explained, "*Zhuan* means self-determined" (vol. 39, "Xianggong ershijiunian" [*Shisanjing,* p. 4353]; also, Takezoe Kokou's annotation [*Sashi kaishen,* vol. 19, p. 8] and Yang Bojun's note [*Chunqiu Zuozhuan zhu,* pp. 1158–59]). Moreover, *Xunzi* has the line "*jia* [the territory of *daifu*] do not dare *zhuanzao* carving and decoration" (vol. 5, "Wang zhi," pp. 9b–10a), which Yang Jing noted. "*Zhuanzao* means privately created."
The *Gongyangzhuan* has the line "when the Son of Heaven is on the throne, the feudal lords cannot *zhuan* the land ("Henggong yuannian" [*Shisanjing,* p. 4800]); what is meant by *zhuan* here is that the feudal lords self-determine their affairs (see the notes of He Xiu [Han, 129–82]), so the meaning here is the same as our own interpretation.

[80]The character *zhuan* also can be defined as *shan* (to dominate; to grasp) (see *Guangya,* "Shiyan," vol. 5 *shang,* p. 19b, as well as Book 6, "Superiority and Inferiority," comment 15). The meaning of *shan* uses

27. "Before armed conflict, the court's reckonings predict victory when more positive answers are gained" in the Chinese text reads *"fu weizhan er miaosuan sheng zhe, desuan duo ye."*

27a. The character *zhan* is today customarily used to mean "war," but in pre-Qin writings it generally indicates "battles."[81] By the end of that period, a distance still existed between *zhan* and today's concept of *zhanzheng*, or "war." The earliest instance where the term *zhanzheng* (war) can be found is from the Qin Dynasty,[82] but this was more than two hundred years after Sun Wu.

Therefore, *Sun-tzu's* use of the character *zhan* can be understood to mean such things as "armed conflict" or "battles."[83]

---

the vantage point of manipulating the enemy. However, *zhuan* here in Book 1 uses the perspective of attempting to seize a victorious opportunity.

[81] E.g., the *Gongyangzhuan* has the line "*zhan* cannot be called *fa*" (vol. 7, "Zhuanggong shinian chun," [*Shisanjing*, p. 4842]), which He Xiu noted, "Forces that withstand [each other] and bloodied blades are called *zhan*."
  Also, the *Zuozhuan* has the line "all have arrays called *zhan*" (vol. 9, "Zhuanggong shiyinian" *xia*, [*Shisanjing*, p. 3838]), which Du Yu noted, "Forceful and well prepared, each occupies its position, and success or failure is determined by will and strength." Kong Yingda annotated, "*Zhan* is a term for fighting together: both sides make arrays, no other flexible means will work, and each occupies its position; success or failure is determined by will and strength."

[82] According to the *Shiji*, Zhou Qingchen presented an ode to the emperor Qin Shihuang, saying, "Everyone is tranquil, [there are] no calamities from *zhanzheng*" (vol. 6, "Qin Shihuang benji," p. 89). What he was referring to as *zhanzheng* is roughly similar to today's "war."

[83] The term *zhengzhan* appeared during the pre-Qin period at a fairly late date. For example, the *Zhanguoce* has the line "*zhengzhan* with Qin" ("Zhaoce," 4, the passage "Wuguo fa Qin wugong," p. 419). The actual meaning of the term *zhengzhan* is to employ *zhan* in contending with someone, but this of course is different from *zhanzheng* (war). Also, *Wuzi* says, "Badger and exhaust them, but do not *zhengzhan* with them" (*shang*, "Liaodi," p. 4b); the term *zhengzhan* has the same meaning here as above.
  The pre-Qin period's references to war all employed euphemistic expressions. The "Yueling" section of the *Liji*, to cite one of many sources, has numerous examples: "weapons and chariots are not raised" ("Mengchun" [*Shisanjing*, p. 2935]), "weapons and armor are all raised" ("Jichun," [*Shisanjing*, p. 2951]), "chariots and weapons will come" ("Mengqiu," [*Shisanjing*, p. 2970]), "governmental concerns are raised" ("Zhongqiu" [*Shisanjing*, p. 2973], where "war" is one of its definitions), "troops are raised without stopping" ("Jiqiu," [*Shisanjing*, p. 2986]), "minor military operations are often raised" ("Mengdong" [*Shisanjing*, p. 2990]), and "a country has major military operations" ("Zhongdong" [*Shisanjing*, p. 2992]), are a few illustrations.
  Other ancient books have innumerable similar cases, but none of these euphemisms displays a unified form. Careful scrutiny of the characters themselves in these modes of expression do not literally spell out "war," as the above verbatim translations show, but the implication that these terms mean "war" can be seen from the context of the characters in the sentences.

27b. Insofar as the *miao* in *miaosuan* is concerned, most annotators generally recognize this character as meaning an ''ancestral shrine.'' This follows Zhang Yu's standpoint: ''The ancients who appointed commanders had to offer a ceremony in the ancestral shrine. They would give the commanders the finalized deliberations, and then they were sent out.''[84] Ceremonies such as he described did exist in ancient times, but such an explication is not appropriate in the interpretation of *Sun-tzu*. The reason is that since *Sun-tzu* in this paragraph says ''*miaosuan* predict victory'' and ''*miaosuan* predict no victory,'' this means that *miaosuan* are not yet finalized determinations, a fact that was overlooked by Zhang in his explanation here on *Sun-tzu*.

Miao in ancient times not only indicated ancestral shrines, but also the ''court.''[85] In this paragraph *Sun-tzu* has shown quite clearly that this is just a consideration of military affairs and has nothing to do with ceremonies. So, *miao* here ought to be the same as the ''court'' in ''the court departments'' (*langmiao*) mentioned in Book 11, ''The Nine Zones'' (p. 105). Both Li Quan and Du Mu defined *miao* as *miaotang*, which also meant ''court.''

With regard to ''*suan*,'' we have followed its basic meaning; see comment 27c.[86]

---

[84]Zhang's sources for this interpretation were the *Liji* (''Wangzhi'' [*Shisanjing*, p. 2882]) and *Baihutong* (*shang*, ''Sanjun'' [*Gujin yishi* edition, p. 41a]); this is also proved in the *Zuozhuan*, which has the line ''Chengzi accepted the sacrificial meat in the *she* shrine (vol. 27, ''Chenggong shisannian, sanyue'' [*Shisanjing*, p. 4146]).

[85]Jiao Xun, *Qunjing gongshitu*, ''Gongtu'' (*Huang Qing jingjie xubian*, ''Zhujing zongyi,'' pp. 14858–70).

[86]*Suan* 算 means ''to reckon'' or ''reckoning'' (*Shuowen*, 5 *shang*, ''Suan,'' p. 200). In *Sun-tzu*, this was often written as *suan* 筭 (tally). Duan Yucai noted in the *Shuowen* that no differentiation was made between these two characters in ancient books.

Miaosuan in the Eastern Han Dynasty was also called *miaomou*. (E.g., *Wenxuan*, the line ''the *mingming miaomou*'' [vol. 50, ''Hou Han Guangwudi zan'']; Li Shan's note. The *Hou Han shu* reads *mou* as *mo* [lit., ''to discuss a plan'']—they were interchangeable in ancient times [vol. 1, ''Guangwudi ji'' *xia*, p. 52].)

The *Shuowen* says that ''deliberation of a problem is called *mou*'' (3 *shang*, p. 92), so its definition is ''the court's deliberation,'' similar to the interpretation of *miaosuan* (the court's reckonings).

[87]*Shuowen*, 5 *shang*, ''Suan (tally),'' p. 200; Duan Yucai's note. Duan also noted, ''*Suan* is used to determine calendar days. The outcomes of deliberations are exactly like the outcomes of using tallies, so therefore whatever is referred to as *suan*, *chou*, or *ce* is the same thing'' (5 *shang*, ''Ce,'' p. 198).

27c. The character *suan* in *de suan* is the object of the verb *de* (to gain), so we know that this is the same as *suanchou*, or "tally."[87] In a game, a tally indicates the winning of points or scores; in a court's reckoning of military affairs, though, this indicates the gaining of a positive answer, so we interpret it accordingly.

28. For "completely," see comment 17.

"Clear" in the Chinese text, if its character form is followed, was originally read *"jian"* and means "to see" or "to be seen." It can also be read *xian* and means "to appear" or "clear."[88]

---

[88]The text here is merely borrowing the character *jian*, suggesting "vision" to express discernment. Thus, if we employ this character's meaning of "clear" at this point, a more apt interpretation is provided. Of course, if *jian* is read as "to be seen" here, that is not particularly erroneous.

MOBILIZING FOR ARMED CONFLICT

1. "Mobilizing for Armed Conflict" in the Chinese text reads "zuozhan." The character zuo in ancient times had three definitions: (i) shi (to create; to construct);[1] (ii) qi (to happen; to raise);[2] and (iii) wei (to do; to wage; to conduct).[3] Most people today are aware only of zuo's third definition, thereby overlooking its first and second definitions.

Sun Wu's discussion here in Book 2 has not yet reached the point of "waging war," but rather considers war's logistical burdens, just as Cao Cao explained: "If there is to be armed conflict, one must first reckon the expenses and take advantage of the enemy's provisions." Also, Zhao Benxue noted, "Zuo means 'to generate.' The court has already reached a finalized consideration, then distances are reckoned, expenses are discussed, and the affairs of armed conflict are raised."[4] So, we have adopted both their views and the preparations for armed conflict described in Book 2, which result in modifying the second definition as "mobilizing."

Regarding zhan, see Book 1, comment 27a.

2. "A thousand swift chariots, a thousand leather-armored chariots, a hundred thousand laced corselets, and drayage of provisions through a thousand miles, in addition to outland and domestic expenses, envoy and foreign advisory serv-

---

[1]E.g., Lunyu: "Shu [to conclude] but not zuo [to create]" (vol. 4, "Shuer," Jizhu edition, p. 1a; Zhu Xi's annotation).

[2]E.g., the Shuowen (8 shang, p. 378) and Shangjunshu ("Kenling," p. 7), the line "people who waste resources will not zuo"; Zhu Shiche's note.

[3]E.g., Erya, "Shiyan" (Shisanjing, p. 5610).

[4]Sunzi shu jiaojie yinlei, shang, p. 29b.

ices, and adhesive and varnishing materials, as well as vehicle and armor supplies" in the Chinese text reads *"chiju qiansi, geju qiancheng, daijia shiwan, qianli er kuiliang, ze wainei zhi fei, bin ke zhi yong, jiao qi zhi cai, ju jia zhi feng."*

2a. "Swift chariots" in the Chinese text reads *"chiju."* We are unable to know for sure exactly what type of chariots these were. But since *chiju* means "the chariots used to rapidly charge the enemy," we have interpreted *chi* as "swift."[5]

2b. "Leather-armored chariots" in the Chinese text reads *"geju."* This indicates the chariots and horses which were both protected by heavy leather armor.[6]

2c. "A hundred thousand laced corselets" in the Chinese text reads *"daijia shiwan."* Cao Cao wrote, "A hundred thousand *daijia* is the number of warriors and foot soldiers." All ensuing scholars have emulated his interpretation here. However, at the end of this paragraph in *Sun-tzu* it clearly states, "a hundred thousand troops are raised" (p. 43). We thus know that the number of raised troops is one hundred thousand. If we interpret *daijia shiwan* as Cao indicated, then isn't the number of raised soldiers increased to two hundred thousand?

In Book 13, "Espionage," Sun Wu said, "Generally, when raising a hundred thousand troops" (p. 111). This again shows that the accurate number of troops raised in *Sun-tzu* totals precisely a hundred thousand.

---

[5]Cao Cao noted, "*Chiju* was a light chariot." His explanation was based on Zheng Xuan's note in the *Zhouli* ("Chunguan zongbo xia: Jupu," the line "a concentration of light chariots" [*Shisanjing*, pp. 1781–82]), in which he obscurely explained that "light chariots" are *Sun-tzu*'s *chiju*. No one ever actually knew, though, why *chiju* meant "light chariots."

Book 9, "Troop Maneuvers," says, "When light chariots first emerge and situate on the flanks, this indicates deployed arrays" (p. 83), so we know that light chariots were used on the two flanks of battle arrays.

[6]Armor and shields in the pre-Qin era were all made out of hardened leather. The *Dadai Liji* has the line "weapons and *ge* are not touched" (vol. 1, "Zhuyan," p. 4b). (Qing) Wang Pinzhen annotated this, "*Ge* refers to the three hardened leathers, and Jia Kui's note on the *Guoyu zhu* states that the " 'three hardened leathers' are *jia* [armor], *zhou* [helmets], and *dun* [shields]." (This is identical to Wei Zhao's note in the *Guoyu* [vol. 6, p. 11b, "Ding sange"]. So, *ge* is interpreted here as "leather-armored.")

Therefore, Cao's interpretation here has to be erroneous.[7] Moreover, this paragraph from "Generally, fundamentals in using forces are" to "vehicle and armor supplies" (p. 43) includes eight items, and each refers to the costs involved; "expend thousands of pounds of gold per day" is actually the main part of this paragraph. In other words, what are listed in these eight items are no more than the objects for this outlay. So, *daijia* here is merely a name for a type of equipment.

Pre-Qin armor was generally constructed to protect mainly the torso.[8] Hardened leather rectangles were sewn together[9] and laced[10] for strength

[7]In the pre-Qin period, the term *daijia* (*dai* armor) was indeed widely used to indicate warriors and foot soldiers, and there are many examples of this in the *Zhanguoce* and other books. It was similar to the practice of using the character *bing* to mean "weapons," and later giving it the tacit meaning of "soldiers" or "forces." *Daijia* was a type of armor, and later it was also used to refer to those types of soldiers who were equipped with such armor. Once this extended meaning became customary, the original definition was often ignored; this is exactly where the mistake in Cao's explanation lies.

[8]Recent archaeological findings include such examples; see Yang Hong, *Zhongguo gubingqi luncong*, 1, "Chinese Ancient Armor and Helmets: Two, Leather Armor of the Yin and Zhou" (illustrations from this were also reprinted in *Gugong wenwu*, vol. 9, no. 12, p. 88). They can be further observed on the clay soldiers discovered in the tomb of the emperor Qin Shihuang (Yuan Zhongyi, *Qin Shihuang bingmatong yanjiu*, and Edmund Capon, *Qin Shihuang: Terracotta Warriors and Horses*).

[9]Cheng Dachang (Song, 1123–95) said, "Long ago, in the Three Dynasties [note: the Xia, Shang, and Zhou] before the Qin and Han, armies all employed leather armor, using that of rhinoceros and buffalo . . . all used leather rectangles, and when these rectangles were finished they were hardened with fire" (*Yanfanlu*, vol. 5, p. 133).

Zheng Xuan's note to the *Zhouli* reads, "*Zhu* . . . means the number of rectangles connected in torso and lower-body armor" (vol. 40, "Dongguan: Kaoguji: Hanren," the line "*xijia qizhu*" [the seven *zhu* of rhinoceros armor] [*Shisanjing*, p. 1982]). Jia Gongyan annotated, "One sheet meant one *zha* [rectangle]." So in pre-Qin times, armor basically was formed from separate pieces of hardened leather. That is why the *Guangya* explained that "*zha* are armor" (vol. 4 *xia*, "Shigu," p. 14a).

The *Zhanguoce* records, "[The lord of Yan] personally *xiao* [lit., 'cut'] armor" (vol. 29, "Yance" 1, p. 59); Wang Yinzhi explained, "*Xiao* meant 'sewed' " (*Dushu zazhi*, VIII-5, "Xunzi diwu: Chen shou [dao]," under "*buxiao*," p. 2a). We therefore know that this armor was created by sewing hardened leather rectangles together.

[10]The *Zuozhuan* has the line "silk-cord armor numbering three hundred" (vol. 29, "Xianggong san-nian" [*Shisanjing*, p. 4186]); Kong Yingda's annotation quotes Jia Kui: "Silk-cord armor is armor strung together with silk cords." *Dai* means "laces"; we can then infer that *daijia* was armor strung together with laces.

The "Yance" (see footnote 9) also records, "[The lord's wife] personally rolled armor *bing*" (see footnote 9); Takezoe Kokou (*Sashi kaishen*, vol. 14, "Zujia sanbai," p. 9) quoted Wu Shidao (Yuan, 1283–1344) in his annotations: "*Bing* are straightened cords; this refers to the cord used in tying together armor." Therefore, the laces used to tie armor rectangles together could also possibly have been made of thin leather cords.

in forming this armor. For this reason *daijia* is translated as "laced corse-lets." Although in the past *daijia* has often been translated into English as "mail-clad soldiers" or "mailed troops," this is erroneous.[11]

2d. "A thousand miles" in the Chinese text reads "*qianli*." Gu Yanwu (Ming, 1613–82) indicated that in the pre-Qin period, one *li* (lit., "Chinese mile") equaled 300 paces, and by the late Ming and early Qing this had increased to 360 paces. Therefore, a thousand *li* in pre-Qin terms was the equivalent of about 500 to 600 *li* in later times.[12] We can surmise, then, that what *Sun-tzu* refers to as "a thousand *li*" would actually be about several hundred miles today.

2e. "In addition to outland and domestic expenses, envoy and foreign advisory services" in the Chinese text reads "*ze wainei zhi fei, bin ke zhi yong*" and follows the Linyi text.[13] In the passage of *Sun-tzu* here, *ze* (translated here as "in addition to") acts as a break, with four entries underneath. In addition to this line, each of the preceding and succeeding entries lists two things, so we know that *bin ke* is not a single term, but indicates two separate items.

If we evaluate the characters *bin* and *ke* through their individual meanings in accordance with pre-Qin usage, *bin* meant an "envoy."[14] *Ke* indicates one who comes from a foreign country, normally serving in an advisory position.[15] We therefore interpret *ke* as "foreign adviser."

[11]Mail armor has never appeared in China. Such a misinterpretation not only allows Cao's error to persist (see above), but also adds another layer of misunderstanding.

[12]*Rizhilu*, vol. 32, "Li," pp. 755–76.

[13]The *Taiping yulan* (vol. 306, "Bingbu" 37, "Junxing," p. 1409) records this passage in the same way as the Linyi text. The later versions all read "domestic and outland." The outlays for armed conflict must consider the outland first, so we do not follow the later versions here.

[14]E.g., the *Liji* has the line, "when a *bin* enters the main gate, melodies are played" (vol. 25, "Jiaote-xing" [*Shisanjing*, p. 3130]); Zheng Xuan's note.

[15]E.g., the *Shuowen*, "*ke* means *ji* [alien dependent]" (7 *xia*); Duan Yucai noted, "[One] from this side who goes to another side is called a *ke*." Also see the *Zhanguoce* ("Qince" *shang*, the line "*Keqin Zhang Yi*," p. 53); Yokoda Yiko in *Senkokusaku seikai* follows the *Zizhi tongjian*'s annotation: "One who comes from the place of other lords to be a *qin* [minister] and is treated as a *ke*" (the passage "*Qin Huiwang wei Hanquanzi yue*," vol. 3 *shang*, p. 8).

3. The Chinese text reads *"rifei qianjin"* (lit., "daily expend thousand gold"). In the pre-Qin period, a *yi* was the standard unit of measurement for gold.[16] So, *qianjin* is shorthand for *qianyijin,* or "a thousand *yi* of gold."[17] A *yi* in ancient times had a weight of either 2.986 or 3.583 kilograms.[18] Therefore, *qianjin* (a thousand *yi* of gold) is approximately 2,986 or 3,583 kilograms. However, this term is used here merely to illustrate the large expense, rather than the actual amount, which is why we interpret it here as "thousands of pounds of gold."

4. "And, they will be capable of waging armed conflict" in the Chinese text reads *"qi yong zhan ye sheng."* The character *sheng* is generally thought to mean "victory"; however, a hundred thousand troops used in armed conflict may achieve victory, and also may not. Moreover, the following discussions are not about victory, so we know that this character is not used to express victory here, but follows its other definition of "having the sufficient ability to undertake a task,"[19] and we interpret it here accordingly.

5. "Even if there were an ingenious man" in the Chinese text reads *"sui you zhizhe."* This follows the later versions; the Linyi text lacks the character *you* (lit., "to have," so "there were") here.[20]

[16]E.g., *Shiji,* the annotation under the line *"yihuangjin yijin"* (lit., "one gold [weighs] one *jin"*) (vol. 30, "Pingjunshu," p. 446); see footnote 18.

[17]The *Zhanguoce* records "ten thousand *yi* of gold" (vol. 3, "Qince," p. 51); Gao You noted, "Ten thousand *yi* means *wanjin* [lit., 'ten thousand gold'], and twenty taels equals one *yi."*

[18]There are two explanations for *yi.* The first is that it equaled "twenty taels *[liang]"* (see footnote 16). The second is that it equaled "twenty-four taels" (*Wenxuan,* vol. 23, Ruan Ji's [Han, 210–63] "Yonghuai," the line *"huangjin baiyi"* [hundred *yi* of gold], p. 5b; Li Shan's note, which quotes Jia Kui's annotation). A tael is equivalent to about 14.929 grams today (Wu Luo, *Zhongguo duliangheng shi,* p. 47, table 12: "Table of Actual Amounts of Dynastic Weights Determined by Coins").

Certain scholars believe that *jin* means *tong* (variously interpreted as "copper," "brass," or "bronze"). However, *Guanzi* noted clearly that "gold indicates the outlay for expenses" ("Chengma," vol. 1, p. 14); we therefore understand that the *jin* referred to in *Sun-tzu* means "gold."

Also, some have interpreted *qianjin* as "a thousand ounces of silver" or "a thousand pieces of gold," which are mistaken as they have no historical basis.

[19]E.g., the *Shuowen* (vol. 13 *xia,* "Sheng," p. 706); also, the *Lunyu* records, "Holding the *gui*-tablet with a bowinglike manner, as if one does not *sheng"* (vol. 10, "Xiangdang" [*Shisanjing,* p. 5415]); Xing Bing's annotation.

[20]This line uses a supposition mood, so the addition of the character *you* makes the meaning more clear.

The Mawangdui silk text of the *Jingfa* notes, "If one sustains the sources of disorder, even if there were [*you*] a sage, he would be unable to exert solutions" ("Sidu" [*Boshu zhujian,* pp. 17–18]). The

6. "Thus, regarding forces we might hear of methodical swiftness, but we should never see cleverness cause protraction" in the Chinese text reads *"gu bing wen zhuosu, weidu qiao zhi jiu ye."*

The difficulty in this line lies in the two characters *zhuo* (lit., "stupid") and *qiao* (lit., "skillful"). This is because these two characters indicated a special manner of doing things in ancient times. If we fail to be aware of this, we lose any perception of their true meaning. Based on pre-Qin sources, *zhou* would today suggest "methodicalness," and *qiao* would suggest "cleverness."[21]

The *zhi* (lit., "of") in *qiao zhi jiu* is defined as *zhi* (to cause).[22]

7. "Would be without precedent" in the Chinese text reads *"wei zhi you ye"* and follows the later versions.[23]

8. "So, by not fully knowing the hazards of using forces, one cannot fully know the benefits of using forces" in the Chinese text reads *"gu bujinzhi yongbing zhi hai zhe, ze buneng jinzhi yongbing zhi li ye"* and follows the later versions.[24]

---

meaning and sentence pattern for this line are very similar to that of *Sun-tzu*, and *you* is used before the term "an ingenious man," so this can be used as a reference.

[21]With regard to *zhuo*, *Guanzi* notes, "A compass and T square are the rules for squares and circles; even with clever eyesight and skillful hands, they are not the equal of *zhuo* compasses and T squares to regulate squares and circles" (vol. 6, "Fafa," p. 92).

With regard to *qiao*, the *Liji* says, "a room by eye *qiao*" (vol. 50, "Zhongni yanju" [*Shisanjing*, p. 3502]); Zheng Xuan noted, "This means only clever eyesight is used, and one's best judgment is followed to build the room and not follow the rules."

From these we can understand that in pre-Qin times *zhuo* could be used to indicate "the manner of not following one's own inclinations, but absolutely obeying rules," and *qiao* could be used to indicate "the manner of following one's own inclinations and depending on one's innate ability."

[22]Pei Xuehai, *Gushu xuzi jishi*, vol. 9, "Zhi," nineteenth definition, p. 748.

[23]In the Linyi text this line reads *"wei you ye"* and does not have the character *zhi* (lit., "of"), which later generations interpreted as *neng* (to be able) (Wang Shumin, *Gushu xuzi xinyi*, 72, "Zhi," fifth definition, p. 111). As this line acts as a theatrical judgment, if the Linyi text is followed, then it becomes a discussion on the existence of an event, rather than of a truth, so this is not acceptable.

Zhi here was used in a similar fashion in the *Lunyu*, which also has the line *"wei zhi you ye"* (vol. 1, "Xueer," the passage *"Youzi yue"*), and the line *"wu wei zhi you de"* (vol. 7, "Shuer," the passage *"Zi yue, wen mo"* [*Shisanjing*, pp. 5333 and 5393]). Another example is in the Mawangdui silk text of the *Zhanguoce*, the line *"Chen wen zhi zhi"* (sec. 8 [*Boshu zhujian*, p. 98]).

[24]The Linyi text reads *"gu bujinyu zhi yongbing _____ ..."* (the rest missing). *Jinyu* in such later versions as the *Wujing* reads *jin* without the character *yu*. *Yu* here acts as a mood word and does not have a concrete meaning (see Pei Xuehai, *Gushu xuzi jishi*, vol. 1, "Yu," twenty-first definition, second explanation, p. 62).

9. "Thrice" in the Chinese text reads *"sanzai"* (lit., "three loads"), but *"san"* in other versions sometimes reads "additional" *(zai)*.[25]

10. "A country can be impoverished by its troops: when they are far away, there is distant drayage. When they are far away and there is distant drayage, then the citizenry will become impoverished. Places near markets will post high prices; high prices will then dry up the citizenry's finances. Once finances are dried up, there will be a dire need for heavier conscription and taxes" in the Chinese text reads *"Guo zhi pin yu*[26] *shi zhe: yuan zhe yuanshu; yuan zhe yuanshu ze baixing pin. Jinshi zhe guimai; guimai ze baixing caijie.*[27] *Caijie ze ji yu qiuyi.'*[28] From ancient times to the present, this paragraph has been recorded six different ways.[29] The points particularly worth discussing are listed below:

(a) "A country can be impoverished by its troops" should be observed from

[25]In the *Shijia,* Sun Xingyan and Wu Renji cite the *Taiping yulan* as their source (note: in vol. 332, "Caoyun," p. 1526). But in fact, the use of "additional" or "thrice" in this paragraph of *Sun-tzu* is not meant to be taken as a specific amount, but rather to indicate "numerous times."

[26]The *yu* in *"guo zhi pin yu shi zhe"* in ancient times was interchangeable with the character *yi* (with; by; through) ([Qing] Wu Changying, *Jingci yanshi,* vol. 1, "Yu," tenth definition, p. 12; also, Yang Shuda, *Ciquan,* vol. 9, "Yu," p. 15).

[27]In the Linyi text this portion is damaged, and there remains only *"gui_____."* Some scholars have hypothesized that the original text ought to have read *"gui__mai__ze cai__jie__,"* and therefore *"baixing"* was eliminated. (The small double lines acted as repeat marks.) But in fact, the preceding line could also quite possibly have been written *"gui__mai__, bai__xing__pin__"* and so have the term *baixing.* Until more factual proof is available, though, it remains uncertain.

From the grammar of this line we can see that *baixing* (citizenry) ought to have been the class which primarily supported the country's economy (see discussion [d] below). When this class became poor, then the country's finances naturally would face collapse.

[28]Zhang Yu's annotation on the term *qiuyi* says, "A country's supplies in a crisis force a *qiu* to pay the tax of a *dian."* This goes against the normal system. A *qiu* is 16 *jing* (the basic unit for tax), and a *dian* is 64 *jing,* so we know that the taxes became four times heavier. (According to scholars' general understanding, each *jing* was made up of eight farm units.)

[29](i) The *Shiyijia:* *"Guo zhi pin yu shi zhe yuanshu, yuanshu ze baixing pin; jin yu shi zhe guimai, guimai ze baixing caijie, caijie ze ji yu giuyi."*

(ii) The *Wujing* and the Sakurada versions are similar to the *Shiyijia,* except that *"jin yu shi zhe"* reads *"jin shi zhe."*

(iii) The Linyi text: *"Guo zhi pin yu shi zhe, yuan zhe yuanshu ze baixing pin; jinshi zhe gui_____ ze__ji qiuyi."*

(iv) The *Tongdian:* *"Guo zhi pin yu shi zhe, yuanshi yuanshu, yuanshi yuanshu ze ze baixing pin; jinshi zhe guimai ze baixing caijie"* (vol. 156, "Bing" 9, p. 821).

the perspectives of "the citizenry's property" and "the public's property," and is not solely caused by "distant drayage."

(b) "Distant drayage" is caused by distant military missions, so the term "when they are far away" *("yuan zhe"),* as written in the Linyi text, is necessary.[30] However, due to damage, we cannot ascertain what the intact Linyi text would have said;[31] most other versions reiterate this phrase, which indicates that a repeat of "when they are far away and there is distant drayage" *("yuan zhe yuanshu")* was part of the original text.

(c) Some of these texts record "near markets" *("jin shi")* as "near troops" *("jin shi").* When troops advance over a border, the people they are in the closest proximity to are the enemy's, not their own. Even if goods are sold at high prices, this is still the enemy's land, not ours.[32] Therefore, "near troops" is not acceptable, while the Linyi text's "near markets" is correct. Wang Xi once noted, "When near markets, goods surge in price"; this proved that some later versions retained "near markets." Because markets are used to generate a country's supplies and support war power, this system cannot deteriorate, or a country's strength will be weakened;[33] therefore, if goods are sold at high prices near mar-

---

(v) The *Taiping yulan:* "*Gu guo zhi pin yu shi zhe, yuanshi, shu* [note: *yuan* was omitted here] *ye, yuanshu ze baixing pin; jinshi ze guimai, guimai ze baixing xu, xu ze jie, jie ze ji yu qiuyi*" (vol. 332, "Caoyun," p. 1526).

(vi) Zheng Zhichun in *Zhuzi jinghualu:* "*Guo zhi pin yu shi zhe, yuanshu; yuanshu ze guopin. Jin yu shi zhe guimai, guimai ze baixing caijie*" (p. 1223).

[30]Both the *Tongdian* and the *Taiping yulan* have the term "remote troops" *("yuanshi"),* which is what "*yuan zhe*" indicates in *Sun-tzu.* The preceding line says, "a country can be impoverished by its troops," so we know that the subject of discussion here is "troops" *(shi). Yuanshi* would have been repetitive, thus we follow the Linyi text here.

[31]In the Linyi text, the right edges of the characters in this line were damaged, so it is possible that the repeat marks (=) on the edge were lost.

[32]Wang Xi wrote that "near troops" meant "about to go across the border," which is an attempt to twist the sentence around and so force it to make sense. However, in a preceding passage of *Sun-tzu* it says, "they equip themselves from the country and take advantage of the enemy's provisions" (pp. 44–45). We therefore know that markets did not act as direct furnishers of army supplies, so there would not necessarily have been anything in military operations directly to do with the line "areas near market districts posting high prices."

[33]*Guanzi* records, "A market is a regulator for goods. Therefore, when all goods are cheap, then no profits will be gained; when no profits are gained, then all affairs will be well managed; when all affairs are well managed, then all businesses will be under jurisdiction" ("Chengma: Wushiwu," p. 5a).

kets, then this system has been completely dismantled.[34] Because of this, the people's finances are exhausted, and then the country's resources definitely are deficient and it thereby faces economic collapse. From this we can see that this line certainly should read *"jinshi zhe guimai"* (places near markets will post high prices).

(d) "Citizenry" in the Chinese text reads *"baixing."* This Chinese term is usually recognized as meaning "the people." But throughout the entire book *Sun-tzu*, this term is used only the three times in this paragraph and the one time in the first paragraph of Book 13, "Espionage" (p. 111), in discussions on outlays for operations. Therefore, strictly speaking, *baixing* is not the term that can act interchangeably here with *min* (ordinary "people"), but rather indicates a specific class in ancient China of higher position and with greater economic power,[35] so we refer to *baixing* as "the citizenry."[36]

Weiliaozi says, "If those on the outside are inadequate for battle and those in the interior are inadequate for defense, then administrate through the market. The market is used to supply battles and defense." It also went on to say, "A market is the administrator of all goods. . . . [Those who] hold dominion over the world, yet do not possess the administration of all goods, cannot be said to possess the ability to conduct battles" (vol. 2, "Wuyi diba," p. 5a).

[34]The *Dadai Liji* says, "No merchants are near the markets" (vol. 5, "Zengzi zhiyan" *shang*, p. 2a). Markets were strictly regulated in ancient times, and merchants had to remain within the market areas. If areas near the markets had expensive merchandise, this of course would show that the country's financial situation was already extremely precarious.

[35]From the early Zhou Dynasty until at least the end of the Spring and Autumn Period, the term *baixing* (lit., "a hundred surnames") could be used to indicate a social class of definite position. The *Shijing* includes the phrase "the populace and the *baixing*" (vol. 9, "Xiaoya: Luming series: Tianbao" [*Shisanjing*, p. 881]), which contrasts the *baixing* with "the populace" *(qunli)*; Zheng Xuan noted, "The *baixing* are the surnames of all those with officially recognized positions *[baiguan]*."
Also, the *Guoyu* contrasts *baixing* with *zhaomin* (billions of people) (vol. 2, "Zhouyu," *zhong*, p. 3a); Wei Zhao explained, "The *baixing* are all those with officially recognized positions" and "those with officially recognized positions *[guan]* served the country and so were granted surnames." *Guan* indicated that this class was higher than that of ordinary people, while surnames *(xing)* indicated that they had been recognized by the lord or ruler. (*Guan* is today generally interpreted as "official," but in ancient times a genuine official had to have a certain position as well as a duty. The explanations by Zheng and Wei do not mention these duties or affairs, so we know they are referring only to the position itself.)

[36]The *Zhuzi jinghualu* reads "the citizenry will become impoverished" (*"baixing pin"*) as "the country will become impoverished" (*"guo pin"*). But if the country is already impoverished, how could there be further discussion? We therefore know this alteration is incorrect.

11. "Homes" in the Chinese text reads *"jia."* In ancient texts it was generally used to indicate a noble *daifu*'s feudal territory, but *Sun-tzu* here is discussing the citizenry's finances, so it refers to the citizenry's homes.[37]

12. In the Linyi text "seven" reads "six."

13. "Draft oxen and transport carts" in the Chinese text reads *"qiuniu daju."* Daju (lit., "large carts") were cargo carts for plains.[38] Land transport was mainly carried out with ox-pulled carts in ancient times, so we interpreted *qiuniu* (lit., *"qiu* oxen") as "draft oxen."[39]

14. "Actively" in the Chinese text reads *"wu."* The basic definition for this is "to move rapidly," so this was extended to mean "to actively perform a task,"[40] and we interpret it accordingly.

15. "Trounce the enemy" in the Chinese text reads *"shadi."* From individual character meaning this ought to be literally interpreted as "kill the enemy." However, the goal in conducting a battle is to overcome the enemy, and killing them is only one of the methods for achieving this goal. In pre-Qin times *sha* (to kill) was also used to mean "to trounce,"[41] so we interpret this term accordingly.

---

[37]E.g., *Guanzi* notes, *"Jia* and government storage centers compete for goods," as well as, "government storage centers will not accumulate goods but keep them among the people" ("Quanxiu," p. 7). Comparing these two examples with this passage from *Sun-tzu* shows that *jia* in pre-Qin times was also used to indicate the people's (or citizenry's) homes.

[38]The *Zhouli* records, *"Daju* have a height of three *ke* [units]" ("Kaogongji: Ju [today read Che] ren" [*Shisanjing*, p. 2018]); Zheng Xuan's note.

[39]Regarding the *qiu* of *qiuniu*, Li Quan noted, *"Qiu* means 'large,'" so *qiuniu* literally meant "large oxen." Cao Cao said, *"Qiuniu* means the oxen drafted from the *qiu* districts" (an explanation that was based on the ancient tax system; see footnote 28). The *Zhouli* says, "Now the prows of *daju* [large carts] are heavy and their steps are difficult" ("Kaogongji: Zhouren" [*Shisanjing*, p. 1974]); Zheng Xuan noted, *"Daju* indicates an ox cart," so we know that *qiuniu* were the oxen used to pull transport carts.

[40]*Shuowen*, 13 *xia*, "Wu," p. 706; Duan Yucai's note.

[41]E.g., the *Erya*, the line *"sha* [to kill] means *ke* [to overcome; to trounce]" ("Shigu" *shang* [*Shisanjing*, p. 5583]); Xing Bing annotated, *"Ke* also is *sha*," so we know that in ancient books these two characters were often interchangeable.

16. The Chinese text here can be read one of two ways: (i) "So, in chariot battles, when more than ten chariots are captured, reward the one who first captured them";[42] or (ii) the reading that we employed in the text, "So, in chariot battles when chariots are captured, the ten-chariot unit commander will reward the first to capture them"[43] (see p. 46).

Most follow the first reading, but why have a reward only when more than ten chariots are captured? We therefore follow the second reading. This is based on Cao Cao's interpretation and would then be the manner in which rewards were given on the battlefield.[44]

17. "Their soldiers are treated kindly when given care" in the Chinese text is read "shan er yang zhi" and follows the later versions.[45]

18. "Therefore, a commander who knows forces is the Guardian of the people's lives and the ruler of the entire country's security" in the Chinese text reads "gu, zhibing zhi jiang, shengmin zhi Siming, guojia anwei zhi zhu ye."

18a. "The Guardian" in the Chinese text reads "Siming," which in ancient times was a star regarded as a deity. From old records we know that this deity was in charge of the people's lives and fates.[46] Moreover, Book 10,

---

[42]"Gu juzhan, deju shicheng yishang, shang qi xiande zhe."

[43]"Gu juzhan, deju, shicheng yishang, shang qi xiande zhe."

[44]Regarding the phrase "shicheng yishang" (lit., "superior to ten chariots"), Cao said, "For shicheng is an officer, one in the rank of a zu [hundred soldiers] chief." (All army organization in pre-Qin times was based on five, so employing ten as a unit here is understandable; no detailed record exists of their chariot system, though.) So, the term shicheng indicated a "ten-chariot unit commander" on our side. Cao also pointed out, "[This] wishes to demonstrate the commander's generosity to those below." Chariot combat in the pre-Qin era constituted the main battle, so the immediate granting of rewards was necessary; such an interpretation is therefore more sensible.

[45]The Linyi text reads "gong [lit., be together] er yang zhi." This gong in ancient times was interchangeable with gong (lit., "to show respect")—e.g., the Yi Zhou shu says, "Being fond of the people, respecting the elders, and being kind to equals and the young is called gong" (vol. 6, "Xifa," Jiaoshi edition, p. 94)—so the intent of the Linyi text's character usage should be similar to that of the later versions.

"Terrain," describes the ideal commander as one "who advances not for glory, withdraws not to evade guilt, and cares only for the people's security along with the lord's interests" (p. 92). We therefore interpret this term as "the Guardian" (see Book 6, comment 9).

18b. "The people's lives" in the Chinese text reads *"shengmin."* This term can mean either "to take care of the people"[47] or "to protect the people's lives."[48] In military affairs, when commanders are able to conserve the country's resources and not deplete the people's livelihood, this closely appertains to "caring for the people's lives," so we interpret this term accordingly.[49]

18c. "Entire country" in the Chinese text is read *guojia.* In Zhou Dynasty feudal systems there was a lord's territory *(guo)*, and underneath it the territory

[46]Examples can be found in the *Liji* (vol. 46, "Jifa" [*Shisanjing*, p. 3447]; Zheng Xuan's note); the *Zhouli* (vol. 18, "Chunguan: Dazongbo" [*Shisanjing*, p. 1632]; Zheng Xuan's note); the *Chuci* ("Jiuge: Da Siming and Shao Siming" [vol. 2, pp. 51–55]; and even in records from the Han Dynasty, such as the *Shiji* (vol. 27, "Tianguan shu," p. 399; [Tang] Sima Zhen's annotation) and the *Fengsu tongyi* (vol. 8, pp. 5a–b).

[47]E.g., the *Zhouli*: "to *sheng* all of the people" (vol. 2, "Tianguan: Taizai" [*Shisanjing*, p. 1388]); Zheng Xuan's note. Also *Xunzi*: "*sheng* the people, who then obtain abundance" (vol. 7, "Wangba," p. 13a; Yang Jing's note).

[48]E.g., the *Lüshi Chunqiu*: "able to give *sheng* or death to one person" (vol. 7, "Mengqiuji: Huaichong," p. 9b); Gao You's note. Also, the *Zuozhuan*: "share reproach and *sheng* the people" (vol. 23, "Xuangong shiernian" [*Shisanjing*, p. 4082]).

[49]The true meaning of the term *shengmin* gradually became overlooked by scholars as early as the Han Dynasty. That is why the Eastern Han book *Qianfulun* quoted this phrase from *Sun-tzu* as *"min zhi Siming"* (the Guardian of the people) and omitted the character *sheng* (lives), while *guojia* (entire country) was rewritten as *er guo* (and the country) (vol. 5, "Quanjiang" [*Baizi quanshu*, p. 3b]). (Qing) Wang Jipei later criticized this error, but only revised *er guo* as *er guojia* (and the entire country) (*Qianfulun*, Wang edition, vol. 5, p. 14b).

Later scholars neglected further inquiry and believed that the altered texts were correct. (Both the *Tongdian* [vol. 148 "Bing" 1, p. 777] and the *Taiping yulan* [vol. 272, "Bingbu" 3: "Jiangshuai" *shang*, p. 1273] do not quote the term *shengmin*, and instead have *ren* [mankind; note: this was to avoid the Tang taboo character *min*], but otherwise follow the *Qianfulun*.)

By the Qing Dynasty, Sun Xingyan and Wu Renji completely accepted the Han and Tang versions and did not conduct research on pre-Qin usage, so they were unable to correct the errors in such works as the *Qianfulun*, but rather made further erroneous amendments (*Shijia*, vol. 2, p. 14b).

of *daifus (jia);* together these formed a feudal state.[50] We therefore interpret this term as "the entire country."[51]

---

[50]Confucius once said, "Those who administrate a *guo* or *jia* worry not about deficiencies, but about equitability" (*Lunyu,* "Qishi dishiliu" [*Shisanjing,* p. 5474]). Also, *Mengzi* noted, "Mencius [Warring States, 372–289 B.C.] said that in the people's normal discourse, all say '*tianxia* [lit., "beneath the sky"] *guojia.*' The fundament of *tianxia* lies in the *guo,* and the fundament of the *guo* lies in *jia*" ("Lilou" *shang* [*Shisanjing,* p. 5907]). So, *guojia* was an accepted term at that time. And, the concept of *guo* did not necessarily include *jia,* so the full term *guojia* was needed to describe the complete object (see footnote 51).

[51]From the Qin onward, *guojia* was used to indicate what was called *tianxia* (lit., "beneath the sky") in pre-Qin times, which meant China in its entirety and its surrounding "barbarian lands." Nowadays *tianxia* is used to indicate the whole world, while *guo* and *guojia* are used to signify individual countries (see footnote 50 and Book 1, comment 2b).

1. Another interpretation of this section is that the best policy is to keep our "country, army, battalions, companies, and squads" complete and undamaged. However, as (Tang) Jia Lin noted, "If their country is obtained in its entirety, our country will also be secure; this is optimum." His understanding here of strategy is undoubtedly superior to the other interpretation.

2. "So, the best military strategy is to crush their plans" in the Chinese text reads *"gu, shangbing fa mou."* *Fa* in ancient times had the definition of "to defeat," therefore "to crush."[1]

3. "Worst of all is to besiege their city fortifications" in the Chinese text reads *"qixia gong cheng."*[2]

4. "Besiege city fortifications only when no other option is left" in the Chinese text reads *"gong cheng zhi fa, wei budeyi ye"* and follows the later versions. The Linyi text does not have this line.

---

[1] *Shuowen*, 8 *shang*, "Fa," second definition, p. 385, and 3 *xia*, "Bai," p. 126; Duan Yucai's note. "To crush their plans" suggests that the enemy is made to surrender their plans and comply with us. Some opinions suggest that *fa mou* (lit., "to attack plans") indicates "attacking the enemy through schemes," which does not correlate with the text's purport because it does not say *"yi mou fa."*

[2] Sun Xingyan and Wu Renji followed both the *Tongdian* (vol. 160, "Bing" 13, p. 845) and the *Taiping yulan* (vol. 317, "Bingbu" 48, p. 1459) in changing *"qixia"* into *"xiazheng"* (the worst policy) (*Shijia*, vol. 3, p. 5b; note: The *Taiping yulan* misread *zheng* as *gong* [to attack]). *"Xiazheng"* grew out of Cao Cao's note here, "Besieging them is the worst policy," and scholars have debated this since early times. However, the Linyi text and later versions all read this as *"qixia."*

5. "A city blockade" in the Chinese text reads *"juyin."*[3] This was the procedure for besieging a city fortification. Cao Cao explained that this was "hilling up dirt nearby to their city fortifications," which was based on an ancient method.[4] We therefore say that *juyin* meant "a city blockade."

6. "Double, divide them; equal, be able to battle against them" in the Chinese text reads *"bei ze fen zhi, di ze neng zhan zhi"* and follows the later versions; this part is missing in the Linyi text. The *Shiji* has the line "ten to one, surround them; double, join them in battle."[5] A few scholars thereby felt that these two lines in *Sun-tzu* should be changed to read "double, join them in battle; equal, be able to divide them," but their sources for this are unreliable (see footnote 5), and so their deductions cannot be considered well grounded.[6]

---

[3]*Ju* in ancient times had the definition of "to blockade" (*kun;* e.g., *Guangya,* vol. 5 *shang,* "Shiyan," p. 5a).

[4]The procedure for creating a *juyin* is described in ancient books. The *Zuozhuan* says, "[On the date] *jiayin, yin* it, encircle the city fortifications, and approach the battlements" (vol. 30, "Xianggong liunian" [*Shisanjing,* pp. 4202–3]); Du Yu noted, "*Yin* means dirt mounds. Around the city fortifications make dirt mounds reach the battlements." Kong Yingda annotated, "*Yin . . .* have the same height as the city fortifications; thereby attack them."

[5]*"Shi ze wei zhi, bei ze zhan zhi"* (vol. 92, "Huaiyihou liezhuan," p. 922). This line is also quoted in the *Zizhi tongjian* (vol. 186, "Tangji" 2, p. 5810) as *"bei ze zhan"* without the character *zhi.* A few scholars have taken note of these, but what they might have ignored is that the *Shiji* quoted this in reference to the lord of Zhao, Cheng Anjun, while the *Zizhi tongjian* quoted it in reference to Shan Xiongxin and others.

On the same page of the *Shiji* it is noted, "Cheng Anjun was a literary scholar," while the *Zizhi tongjian* says that Shan Xiongxin was merely "adept at jousting" and "lightly changed loyalties" (p. 5812). So the ones to whom this quote was attributed were not strategists. It is also uncertain whether this line was taken directly from *Sun-tzu.* Nevertheless, when Cheng Anjun employed this method, he was captured by his opponent, Han Xin; and when Shan Xiongxin and the others requested that their lord follow this method, they lost as soon as they engaged in battle, and finally surrendered to their enemy, Wang Shichong. So its accuracy insofar as strategic principles are concerned is very doubtful.

The *Guliang zhuan* cites military strategic rules dating from the Spring and Autumn Period: "Double, attack; equal, battle [against them]; fewer, defend" (vol. 9, "Xigong ershiernian" [*Shisanjing,* p. 5208]). This is very similar to the line here in *Sun-tzu*'s text, so we believe that there are ancient sources for Sun Wu's doctrine.

[6]Book 3 here of *Sun-tzu* discusses offensive strategy. *Sun Bin bingfa* notes, "When the invader is double the defender, their power is balanced" (*xia,* "Ke zhuren fen," p. 96). So an invasion must be double that of our opponent in order for there to be balanced combat power, and they must be "divided" since our superiority is to be gained. If both sides are equal when we engage in battle, we must then rely on strategic capability. Such a perspective shows that this line of *Sun-tzu* must follow the later versions here in order to be accurate.

7. "Fewer, be able to evade them; weaker, be able to avoid them" in the Chinese text reads *"shao, ze neng tao zhi; buruo, ze neng bi zhi."*

7a. "Be able to" in the Chinese text of the above three lines reads *neng. Neng* also had the ancient reading of *nai* (then), so Wang Niansun suggested that *neng* here be read as *nai*,[7] and some contemporary scholars have followed his opinion. However, we cannot agree with Wang on this term of *Sun-tzu's*. Our reason is that in the text, from "ten to one, beset them" ("*shi, ze wei zhi*" on lists six conditions. They all have the same pattern, so if *ze* (then) is used once, then theoretically all should use *ze*, and if *ze neng* is used once, then all should use *ze neng*. But in fact, the first three conditions use *ze;* with "equal, be able to battle against them" ("*di, ze neng zhan zhe*") (p. 50), the next three suddenly change and use *ze neng* (lit., "then can") instead, so what was the reason for this?

By reviewing these three conditions where Sun Wu used *ze neng* with the previous three conditions where *ze* is used, we can clearly see that the latter three conditions using *ze neng* suppose that our military strength is not necessarily greater, and sometimes even worse, than the enemy. While conducting armed conflict in such situations, if one does not also have good strategic capabilities, we are afraid that even if one wanted to "battle" or "escape" or "avoid" the enemy, none of these could ever be achieved simply through the desire expressed in the character *nai* (then).

7b. "To evade them" in the Chinese text reads *"tao zhi."* (Qing) Yu Chang read *"tao"* as "to escape" and opined, "There certainly could not have been such a precept. Moreover, how could 'escape' be called '*neng*' [be able to; be capable of]?"[8] A few later scholars were also influenced by the annotations of Cao Cao and others, and so tried to adapt this term as meaning "to defend" *(shou).*[9]

[7]*Dushu zazhi*, IV-13, "Han shu dishisan" (pp. 13b–15a), under the line *"neng huo mie zhi."*

[8]*Xiangcao xujiaoshu*, p. 433.

[9]Cao Cao said, "[Have ourselves behind] high walls and steadfast fortresses, and do not engage them in battle." The *Sun-tzu* text he was working from could indeed have read "to evade them" *(tao zhi)* as "to defend" *(shou)*, as quoted in the *Guliang zhuan* (see footnote 5).

This line, though, discusses the condition in which the enemy's forces are great and ours are few, which is different from the line below where we are weaker than the enemy. When one is outnumbered, the first rule is to make certain that one is not entangled by the opponent. Therefore, although Cao's standpoint could be used at this time, after a while without succor, one would become easy prey, so the defense method espoused by Cao cannot quite fit *Sun-tzu's* teaching here.

A more appropriate explanation can be found in Du Mu's note: "Also, evade their strength, stalk their openings, and then issue a decisive attack for victory." We interpret *"tao"* accordingly.

8. "Thus, with a smaller force against them, conduct dynamic actions; with a larger force against them, conduct ensnaring actions" in the Chinese text reads *"gu, xiao di zhi, jian; da di zhi, qin ye."*

Cao Cao read this as *"gu, xiao di zhi jian; da di zhi qin ye"* and explained, "The small is unable to withstand the large." All scholars have used his interpretation as their archetype here. However, there are problems with this explication, because when "small" encounters "large," it cannot firmly withstand it; this has been common knowledge ever since ancient times. So, why would strategists particularly discuss this? If "small" has to firmly withstand "large," there would have to be extenuating circumstances; otherwise such an event would never occur. In such circumstances a mere warning has little effect.[10]

The function of this sentence is to act as a conclusion to the preceding discussion of using many or few troops, so strategic principles are presented. Thus, that the small cannot withstand the large is common knowledge, but the ability to make the small forceful and cause the large to seize the enemy concerns strategy. Later here in Book 3 it says, "By knowing how to apply many and few, there is victory" (p. 52), which can be used to prove our point, and we interpret this line accordingly.

---

[10]Cao Cao interpreted *xiao di* as "the small ones" and *da di* as "the large ones," which forces the interpretation of the two *di* (enemy; to withstand) here, showing he was not aware of their correct meaning. Moreover, Li Quan's annotation reads, "*Xiaodi* [a small enemy] which does not consider its strength and 'fights a rigid battle' will certainly be captured by *dadi* [a large enemy]." If both sides are the "enemy," then which would have been his own side in this conflict?

9. "So, a lord may harm the armies" in the Chinese text reads *"gu, jun zhi suoyi huan junzhe"* and follows the Linyi text. The Sakurada version reads this as "so, armies may be harmed by a lord" (*"gu, jun* [armies] *zhi suoyi huan yu jun* [a lord]"), while the *Wujing* and *Shiyijia* versions read this as "so, a lord may be harmed by armies" (*"gu, jun* [a lord] *zhi suoyi huan yu jun* [armies]"), which obviously is incorrect.[11]

10. "Interfering" in the Chinese text reads *"tong."*[12] When a lord personally intervenes in commanders' duties, this is improper, so we interpret it accordingly.

11. "This is called disrupting the armies and surrendering victory" in the Chinese text reads *"shiwei luanjun yinsheng."* In the preceding text *Sun-tzu* already has noted, "When the armies are both leery and suspicious" (p. 51), which is an example of "disrupting armies," and this causes the "calamities caused by other lords" to follow, an example of "surrendering victory."[13]

12. "Therefore, regarding forces" in the Chinese text reads *"gu, bing"* and follows the Linyi text. The later versions all read this as *"gu, yue"* (therefore, it is said).

13. "Perceiving," which is used six times in this passage, in the Chinese text reads *"zhi."* Zhi normally is understood to mean "to know," but here this character has a broader meaning, as it also involves anticipation and prediction. We therefore interpret it accordingly.[14]

---

[11]Book 6 has the line, "So, those sophisticated at battle dominate the adversary but are not dominated by the adversary" (*"gu, shanzhanzhe, zhi ren er buzhi yu ren,"* using *gu* to express the passive voice), which acts as proof.

[12]*Shuowen,* 7 *xia,* p. 357, where *"tong"* is defined as *"hehui"* (to intervene).

[13]*Yin* has the same meaning as "to guide" (*dao*) (*Guangya,* "Shigu" 3 *xia,* p. 21a), which is why Du Mu annotated this as "drawing the enemy and making them overcome us," so we interpret it accordingly. Cao Cao interpreted *yin* as "to snatch" (*duo*), but we do not know his source for this.

[14]When *zhi* was used by the ancient Chinese, it indicated all of the activities and knowledge received through the senses and the mind (*xin*) (see Zhu Junsheng, *Shuowen tongxun dingsheng,* "Zhi" ["Jie" section 11, p. 542]). "To know" therefore is incapable of completely relaying this connotation.

14. "There will be no unforeseen risk in any battle" in the Chinese text reads "*bai-zhan budai*." The *bai* (one hundred) in *baizhan* (lit., "one hundred battles") is merely a way of describing "all" or "without exception."[15]

   Dai means "danger" or "risk" *(wei)*.[16] However, there are no battles that do not contain danger, so we know that this *dai* should indicate "risk without proper preparation beforehand."

---

[15]E.g., the *Liji* has the line "those who administrate all of China make offerings to a hundred deities" (vol. 46, "Jifa" [*Shisanjing*, p. 3443]); Zheng Xuan noted, " 'A hundred' is borrowed as a round number." So the character *bai* is often a loose term, not an exact amount.

[16]E.g., the *Shujing* has the line "the inability to safeguard our descendants and the people is also *dai*" (vol. 20, "Qinshi" [*Shisanjing*, p. 545]); (Western Han) Kong Anguo's annotation defined *dai* as "peril" *(weidai)*.

CONTROL

1. "Control" in the Chinese text reads "*xing*" and follows the Linyi text.[1]

Cao Cao explained the content of this book as "It is about the armies' *xing* (shape; format). We move and they respond. Both sides withstand each other and mutually examine our conditions." However, at the conclusion of this Book 4, Sun Wu himself said, "Those who weigh victory engage their people in battle just as if they had released the floodgates on an extremely deep gorge—that is *xing*" (p. 56), so we doubt that "the armies' shape" or "examining the conditions" is sufficient.

The original meaning for *xing* in ancient times was "to mold" or "to control."[2] This character in *Sun-tzu* can therefore not be explained as a "shape" or "format." The *xing* for using forces should take as its definition "control," which

---

[1]All books from the pre-Qin era write *xing* as 刑 (to mold; to control; to confine; to contain). The title used in the later versions, 形 (shape; appearance; image; format; to see), exists because of changes by later scholars.

[2]The *Erya* notes in the line "*xing, fan*, and *lü* are *fa*" ("Shigu" *shang* [*Shisanjing*, p. 5581]) that the meaning of *fa* is "to control or regulate," and that it includes, along with *xing*, the meanings of "to mold" (*fan*), "to rule" (*lü*), and "a T square" (*ju*). Furthermore, (Han) Liu Xi's *Shiming* says that *fa* is "to force alignment [*bi*] and make confined" (vol. 6, "Shidianyi" [*Gujin yishi* edition, p. 4b]; however, Wang Xianqian's *Shuzheng bu* edition, p. 15a, quotes Bi Yuan's [Qing, 1730–97] opinion that "*bi* [forced] should be *bi* [banked up]").

Xunzi has the line "*xing* and *fan* are straight" (vol. 11, "Qiangguo," p. 1a); Yang Jing noted, "*Xing* is *fan* [a mold; to mold], and both mean *fa* [regulation; control]." The *Shuowen* records, "*Xing* means to punish a crime" (5 *xia*, p. 218), which refers to control of the criminal's behavior. Later, according to Duan Yucai, *xing* was borrowed to express the meaning of *dianxing* (criterion; model; archetype).

The modern scholar Ding Shanfu noted, "There is not one of the characters with the *jing* 井 component that does not have the meaning of 'to regulate by rule' or 'to confine with a mold' (cited from Chen Pan's *Han Jin yijian zhixiao*, p. 115b). The character *xing* (shape) was derived from *jing*, so that even if it is written in its ancient form, it appears as 形." Ding also noted, "Mr. Xu [Xu Shen (Han, 30–124), author of the *Shuowen*] believed that the *xing* of 'appearance' comes from the phonetic component 开. The

163

would then make the release of "floodgates on an extremely deep gorge" possible.

All uses of *xing* throughout the entire work *Sun-tzu*, with the exception of the *xing* in "terrain" (*dixing*) and a very few other instances, involve this point of view in their definition.

2. "Long ago, those sophisticated at strategy first created undefeatability and then awaited the enemy's defeatability" in the Chinese text reads "*xi shanzhe xian wei bukesheng, yidai di zhi kesheng.*"

2a. "Long ago, those sophisticated at strategy" (*xi shan [zhe]*"; "*zhe*" was a later amendment) follows the Linyi text, but the later versions read this as "those sophisticated at battles in ancient times" (*xi zhi shanzhanzhe*).

In pre-Qin times the character *zhan* indicated a situation in which both sides were already engaged in combat.[3] Also, the last part of Book 4 here says, among other things, "victorious forces first achieve victory and then conduct battle" (p. 55). So, at this point the discussion concerns an enemy that has not yet been engaged in combat and should therefore not read "those sophisticated at battles" (*shanzhanzhe*), but follow the Linyi text.[4]

The literal interpretation of *shanzhe* is "the sophisticated one," but from the context of *Sun-tzu* we can see that *shanzhe* actually indicates those who are sophisticated at strategy or tactics, so we interpret it accordingly.

characters on the Han 'Gao Biao stele' write the 形 as based on *jing*." (Zhang Shunhui's *Shuowen jiezi yuezhu* also quotes (Qing) Gui Fu, saying, "The character *xing* should follow the phonetic component *jing*" [vol. 17, p. 22a]. Ding went on to note that *jing* "was a vessel used in molding clay, so characters that have developed from *jing* . . . all have the meaning of 'to regulate by rule' or 'to confine with a mold'" [*Han Jin yijian zhixiao*, p. 116a].)

To regulate by rule and to confine with a mold are forms of control. The definitions of *xing* here must be based on the above explanations.

[3]See Book 1, comment 27a.

[4]The difference between *shanzhanzhe* and *shanzhe* can be clearly seen in the book *Sun Bin bingfa*: in "Ke zhuren fen" (*xia*, pp. 96–98), where tactics are discussed for engaging the enemy and attempting to surpass them, the term *shanzhanzhe* (those sophisticated at battles) is employed; but in "Shanzhe" (*xia*, pp. 100–101), where it discusses employing an active manner other than battle against the enemy, the term *shanzhe* (lit., "the sophisticated one") is used instead. This, then, proves to have been a specific pre-Qin Chinese military term that was lost over the ensuing years.

2b. "Created" in the Chinese text reads "*wei.*" In ancient times, *wei* and *zuo* (to create) were mutually definable (see Book 2, comment 1).[5]

3. "For undefeatability, defend; with defeatability, attack" in the Chinese text reads "*bukesheng, shou; kesheng, gong ye*" and follows the Linyi text. The later versions read "for undefeatability, then defend; with defeatability, then attack" ("*bukesheng zhe shou ye, kesheng zhe gong ye*"), so they have similar meanings. The two *zhe* characters in the later versions are defined as *ze* (then).[6]

4. "Defense is for sufficiency; attack is for deficiency" in the Chinese text reads "*shou ze youyu, gong ze buzu*" and follows the Linyi text. The later versions read "defense is for deficiency; offense is for sufficiency" ("*shou ze buzu, gong ze youyu*"), so the conditions have been flipped. Let us view some ancient records of this line:

(i) Zhao Chongkuo (Western Han, 137–52 B.C.) in his report said, "I learned from strategy that when an attack is deficient, then defense will be sufficient."[7]

(ii) Feng Yi (Eastern Han, d. 34) once wrote, "Oh, when an attack is deficient, the defense will be sufficient."[8]

(iii) Wang Fu (Eastern Han) quoted this line from *Sun-tzu* as, "An attack often is deficient and a defense usually is sufficient."[9]

(iv) But Huangpu Song (Eastern Han) is recorded as saying, "Undefeatability lies in ourselves; defeatability lies in the enemy. Their defenses are insufficient; our offenses are sufficient. The sufficient one moves in the highest

---

[5]E.g., the *Liji* has the line "raising pigs and *wei* wine" (vol. 38, "Yueji" [*Shisanjing*, p. 3324]); Zheng Xuan's note.

[6]Pei Xuehai, *Gushu xuzi jishi*, vol. 9, "Zhe," twelfth definition, p. 760.

[7]"*Chen wen bingfa gong buzu ye, shou youyu*" (*Han shu*, vol. 69, "Zhao Chongkuo zhuan," p. 861).

[8]"*Fu, gong ze buzu, shou ze youyu*" (*Hou Han shu*, vol. 17, "Feng Yi zhuan," p. 284).

[9]"*Gong chang buzu, er shou heng youyu ye*" (*Qianfulun*, vol. 5, "Jiubian" 22, p. 18a). Wang Fu was born between 105 and 125 and died between 148 and 189; he was slightly older than Huangpu Song.

reaches of the heavens; the insufficient one falls into the deepest bowels of the earth.''[10]

(v) And Cao Cao (Eastern Han, 155–220) had as his interpretation, ''The reason for us to take the defensive is because strength is insufficient; the reason for us to take the offensive is because strength is sufficient.''

The above materials clearly show that the Linyi text reliably recorded the lines from *Sun-tzu* here, while the later versions all used a common text that probably had been altered by late Han scholars sometime before both Huangpu Song and Cao Cao.

The two *ze* characters in this sentence are defined as *yi* (for).[11]

5. ''Long ago, those sophisticated at a defense were as if concealed in the deepest bowels of the earth, and those sophisticated at attack were as if moving in the highest reaches of the heavens. They were thus able to secure themselves and achieve complete victory'' in the Chinese text reads ''*xi shanshouzhe, cang yu jiudi zhi xia, shangongzhe dong yu jiutian zhi shang; gu neng zibao er quansheng ye.*'' This follows the later versions, whereas the Linyi text does not have the two ''*yu*'' (in) characters or the phrase ''those sophisticated at attack'' (*shangongzhe*). ''*Yu*'' shows where the action is taking place.[12] As for ''*shangongzhe,*'' the end of this line says, ''they were thus able to secure themselves and achieve complete victory'' (p. 54). ''Secure themselves'' (*zibao*) here refers to defense, and ''achieve complete victory'' (*quansheng*) to offense. The Linyi text therefore must have overlooked the phrase ''those sophisticated at attack.''

China in ancient times had the expression *tiandong dijing*, or ''moving heavens and still earth''; *Sun-tzu* in this section describes the movement and stillness of those adept at using forces.[13]

---

[10]''*Bukesheng zai wo, kesheng zai bi; di shou buzu, wo gong youyu; youyu zhe, dong yu jiutian zhi shang; buzu zhe, xian yu jiudi zhi xia*'' (*Hou Han shu*, vol. 71, ''Huangpu Song zhuan,'' p. 1048). It is uncertain in what years Huangpu Song was born and died, but from his career we can calculate that he was about ten years older than Cao Cao.

[11]Pei Xuehai, *Gushu xuzi jishi*, vol. 8, ''Ze,'' nineteenth definition, p. 600.

[12]Yang Shuda, *Ciquan*, vol. 9, ''Yu,'' fifth definition, p. 2.

[13]In the Chinese, ''the deepest'' and ''the highest'' literally read ''nine'' *(jiu)*.

Wang Zhong (Qing, 1744–94) in his *Shuxue* (''Neipian: Shi san jiu'' *shang*, pp. 2a–b) noted, ''If something cannot be confined by the number three, then it is referred to as 'nine' in order to express its large

6. The phrase "is not absolute perfection" both here and in the preceding line of the Chinese text reads "*fei shanzhishan zhe ye*" and follows the later versions. The Linyi text has two copies of Book 4, referred to as copies "A" and "B." In copy A, these two lines read, respectively, "*fei shan* ____[the rest missing]" and "*fei* ____ *ye*"; in copy B, the first line is missing, while this line reads "*fei shanzhe ye*" (which ought to be interpreted as "not the one who is sophisticated at strategy").

7. "For" in the Chinese text reads "*gu*" and follows the later versions. The Linyi text does not have this character, but from the text's intimation, the character "*gu*" here seems more appropriate. "*Gu*" is often interpreted as "so." However, since the succeeding text is not a result of the preceding description, but rather is an explanation of the cause, we interpret it accordingly.[14]

8. "So, the battles of those sophisticated at strategy do not have unorthodox victories" in the Chinese text reads "*gu shanzhe zhi zhan, wu jisheng*"; this reading follows the Linyi text. The later versions all read "so the victory of those sophisticated at battles" ("*gu shanzhanzhe zhi sheng ye*"), with "*shanzhe*" given as "*shanzhanzhe*" (see comment 2a), and they omit the phrase *wu jisheng* (do not have unorthodox victories).

9. "Because their victories contain no miscalculations" in the Chinese text reads "*gu qi sheng bute*."

9a. "Because" in the Chinese text reads "*gu*"; see comment 7.

9b. "Victory" in the Chinese text reads "*sheng*" and follows the Linyi text. The later versions read "*zhansheng*" (victory in battle). Because the en-

---

amount. This was an abstract number in the language. . . . *Sun-tzu* says, '*shan shou zhe cang yu jiudi zhi xia, shan gong zhe dong yu jiutian zhi shang*' [Wang is quoting from later versions, and its interpretation is the same as that of our text; see p. 54]; this cannot be explained as 'it is nine,' so we know that 'nine' is an abstract number."

Moreover, the *Shuowen* records, "Nine is a change in *yang*. Its form is to wend back and forth before reaching its maximum condition" (14 *xia*, p. 745). So, *jiu* does not necessarily mean "the number nine," but rather its utmost amount, the absolute extent of something.

[14]Yang Shuda noted, "This character's meaning is extended from *jiu* [old; original]" (*Ciquan*, vol. 3, "Gu," fifth definition, p. 15).

suing text says "victorious forces first achieve victory and then conduct battle," we can see that what *Sun-tzu* meant by "victory" here was not necessarily that which is gained through battle, so the later versions' text is obviously unacceptable here.

10. "Those sophisticated at strategy" in the Chinese text reads "*gu shanzhe*"; this part of the Linyi text is missing, so it is inferred from the preceding line. The later versions all read this as "those sophisticated at battle" ("*shanzhanzhe*") (see comment 2a).

11. "Therefore, victorious forces first achieve victory and then conduct battle" in the Chinese text reads "*shigu, shengbing xian sheng er hou zhan*" and follows the Linyi text. The later versions read "therefore, victorious forces first achieve victory and then seek battles" ("*shigu, shengbing xian sheng er hou qiu zhan*"). Because it says to "first achieve victory," a situation thereby completely comes under our domination. In such a case, once we desire to fight, the enemy would have no alternative but to fight; using "seek" (*qiu*), therefore, is incorrect. This error perhaps was the result of the phrase "seek victory" in the succeeding line.

12. "The controllers of victory and of defeat" in the Chinese text reads "*shengbai zheng*" (*zheng*, lit., "straight" or "controller") and follows the Linyi text. The later versions read "*shengbai zhi zheng*" (with *zheng* here literally meaning "policy"). From the foregoing text we know that "*sheng*" (victory) lies with ourselves and "*bai*" (defeat) lies with the enemy. The ones who can make this happen are the "controllers" of the situation, so we choose the Linyi text here. "*Zheng*" (controller) and "*zheng*" (policy) actually were interchangeable in ancient times.[15]

13. "There is a rule" in the Chinese text reads "*fa*" and follows the Linyi text. The later versions all read "forces' rules" (*bingfa*).

   Some previous scholars have felt that the principles discussed in this paragraph are formulas for the reckoning of a country's strength, using land (*di*) to indicate

---

[15]E.g., the *Shuowen*, 3 *xia*, "Zheng," p. 124. Also, the *Liji*, the line "to straighten its *zheng* [lit., 'policy']" (vol. 58, "Shenyi" [*Shisanjing*, p. 3610]); Zheng Xuan's note.

the country's territory and measurement (*liang* [their translation]) to indicate its resources, thereby producing the weight (*cheng*), which compares both sides' manpower and material strengths. If so, this begs a question: with further deduction, is "weighing determines victory" ("*cheng sheng sheng*") an assured result? If yes, this formula means that a large country will always be victorious over a small country, and small countries will always be defeated. In fact, Sun Bin clearly addressed this during the pre-Qin period: "Do masses of people mean victory? Then tallies can determine battles. Does wealth mean victory? Then the measurement of grain can determine battles. Do sharp weapons and strong armor mean victory? Then victory is easily perceived."[16] Cao Kuai (Spring and Autumn Period) once said, "A large country is difficult to anticipate,"[17] which is indeed true, but if the mere reckoning of a country's size, manpower, or material can determine victory or failure, then this argument, we are afraid, is unsound.

14. "Those who weigh victory engage their people in battle just as if they had released the floodgates on an extremely deep gorge" in the Chinese text reads "*chengshengzhe zhanmin ye, ru jue jishui yu qianren zhi xizhe.*"

14a. "Those who weigh victory" in the Linyi text reads "*chengshengzhe.*" The later versions all read "the victorious ones" (*shengzhe*). The preceding passage uses "weighing" (*cheng*) to express how victorious strength overwhelms the losing side, therefore the phrase "those who weigh victory" is more apt here.

14b. "Engage their people in battle" in both the Linyi text and the *Shiyijia* version read this as "*zhanmin ye*"; the *Wujing* and Sakurada versions read it as "battle" (*zhan*). This discusses the creation of power on the battlefield and so cannot be fully expressed with the single character *zhan*. We therefore follow the Linyi text and the *Shiyijia* version here.

"*Zhan min*" is as if saying "to make their people fight." This is written

---

[16]*Sun Bin bingfa, xia,* "Ke zhuren fen," p. 97.

[17]"Zhuanggong shinian," *Zuozhuan* (vol. 8, *Shisanjing,* p. 3833).

with the mood of "making [or causing] someone to do something," which we interpret as "engage their people in battle."[18]

14c. "An extremely deep gorge" in the Chinese text reads "*qianren zhi xi*."[19] "*Ren*" was an ancient measurement for height that had various interpretations, e.g., eight feet or seven feet, and sometimes even four feet or five feet six inches.[20] Nevertheless, "*qianren*" (a thousand *ren*) here serves only to describe the gorge's great depth, so we do not directly translate it.

[18]See Book 1, comment 21, footnote 70.

[19]"*Xi*" (gorge) follows the later versions. This part is missing from copy A of the Linyi text (see comment 6), while in copy B it reads "*xia*" (lit., "crevice"), so it has a similar meaning.

[20]Hu Yuanyi, "Shi ren" (*Shisong jingshi wenlu*, pp. 1b–2b [*Dingchou congbian*]).

COMBAT POWER

1. See Book 1, comment 19a.

2. "Through organization and squad training" in the Chinese text reads *"fen shu shi ye."*

    Cao Cao's interpretation of *fen shu* is, "The *buqu* system is called *fen*, and *zu* [a hundred-soldier unit] *wu* [a five-soldier unit] are called *shu*."[1] His explanation of *fen*, in fact, is borrowed from Zheng Xuan's standpoint,[2] which employs a Han system to describe a pre-Qin structure.[3]

    From the positions of Cao and Zheng we can say that *"fen"* indicates "organization."[4]

    As for *shu* (lit., "number") when used in a military sense, this precisely indicates the methods for "squad training."[5] It was from this that soldiers were able to develop their synchronized power in combat.[6] All pre-Qin armies used five-

---

[1] In pre-Qin times, this was generally read as the term *zuwu*, meaning "the fundamental army unit," rather than two separate subjects, *zu* and *wu*.
   Buqu was a type of troop system during the Han Dynasty (see Book 1, comment 12a).

[2] *Liji*, the line *"fen* face to face and move forward"; Zheng Xuan noted, *"Fen* is as if saying *buqu*" (vol. 39, "Yueji" [*Shisanjing*, p. 3342]).

[3] Also see Book 1, comment 12a. Zheng Xuan's use of "as if saying" is a circumspect manner of expression, but Cao Cao's explanation lacks this caution of Zheng's, which could cause misunderstanding.

[4] *Xunzi* says, "Rites and music are then well managed, *fen* and proper position are then clear" (vol. 11, "Qiangguo," p. 1b); Yang Jing noted, "*Fen* means a differentiation between upper and lower." Therefore, *fen* here is also used from the perspective of "organization."

[5] *Guanzi* records, "Physically train them with the *shu* of signals and orders" (vol. 6, "Bingfa," p. 95); Yin Zhizhang noted, "This describes the *shu* of kneeling and rising."

[6] E.g., the *Shujing* says: "Today's affairs do not go beyond six paces or seven paces, stopping, and arraying the rows," and "do not go beyond four strikes, five strikes, six strikes, seven strikes, stopping,

man squads as their basis.[7] So, Cao Cao had a reason for saying *"zu wu* are called *shu"*; however, the vagueness of his description caused later readers to misinterpret *zu wu* as part of army organization.

3. "Signals and designations" in the Chinese text reads *"xing ming."* Because *xing* and *ming* are a complementary pair, *xing* indicates what can be seen.[8] Cao Cao explained, "Battle standards and flags are called *xing,* gongs and drums are called *ming."* But Book 7, "Armed Contention," notes, "When voice cannot be clearly heard, drums and gongs are used; when eyesight cannot clearly observe, battle standards and flags are used" (p. 72). Therefore, both "drums and gongs" and "battle standards and flags" had the same basic function, so how could they be given separate classifications?

As a matter of fact, *ming* (lit., "a name" or "a title") in ancient Chinese military affairs indicated the various troops' designations.[9] Troops were combined under a particular crest designation and banner, and then they were directed through the signals of "battle standards" and "drums and gongs." Either many or few could thereby be dispatched into battle without loss of coordination.

4. "Fully" in the Chinese text reads *"bi"* and follows the Linyi text. The later versions read this as *"bi"* (must; certain; ensure). Wang Xi noted that *"bi"* (must) is an incorrect character that actually should read *"bi"* (fully). In fact,

---

and arraying the rows" (vol. 11, "Mushi" [*Shisanjing,* p. 389]). This is what Li Jing (Tang, 571–649) meant by "use six paces and seven paces, six strikes and seven strikes, in combat training methods" (*Li Weigong wendui, shang,* p. 6a).

[7]E.g., *Li Weigong wendui;* Li Jing noted, "Of all the soldier-training techniques, only five-squad methods are fundamental" (*zhong,* p. 3a).

[8]E.g., *Shuowen,* 9 *shang,* "Xing," p. 429; Duan Yucai's note.

[9]The *Zhouli* says, "[In] midsummer . . . discriminate between the uses of signals and *ming.* Leaders use their gates as *ming.* Countries and districts all use their own *ming. Daifu* territories use their titles as *ming. Xiang* [probably 'county'] territories use provinces as *ming.* Rural areas use towns as *ming."* It also says, "Countrysides display *zhao* banners, officials display *yu* banners; all write on them their offices and their titles" (vol. 29, "Xiaguan: Dasima" [*Shisanjing,* pp. 1805–6]).

Zheng Xuan noted, "*Ming* means the crest used for differentiation. Those of *xiang* and *sui* territories are called *ming,* those of *daifu* territories are called *hao,* and those of officials are called *shi.* In the country these demonstrate their posts; in the army these also demonstrate their systems." We therefore may say that *ming* are "designations."

these characters were often interchangeable in ancient times.[10] However, if it is read as meaning "certain" or "ensure," the line makes no sense.

5. "Contrasts in strength" in the Chinese text reads *"xu shi."*[11] The literal translation is "deficiency and sufficiency." It should indicate, though, a concentration of our forces used in assaulting the enemy's weaknesses, so we interpret this term accordingly.

6. "Regular actions" and "irregular actions" in the Chinese text read *"zheng"* and *"ji."* Cao Cao interpreted them as two different forces, which have been translated by others as "the normal force" and "the extraordinary force"; if these are correct, how could they "perpetually engender each other" and be "like a ring without a breach," as the succeeding text describes them? We therefore know that such an interpretation is incorrect.

7. "Those sophisticated at creating irregular actions" in the Chinese text reads *"shanchujizhe."* (Song) Zheng Youxian opined, "How could a single irregular action be able to cause change?" and so he suggested that this line should actually read *"shanchujizhengzhe"* (those sophisticated at creating irregular and regular actions).[12] What Zheng did not take into account was that "creating irregular actions" *(chuji)* is the same as "change." The text of *Sun-tzu* therefore does not contain any errors here.

    Moreover, Sun Xingyan and Wu Renji suggested that "creating irregular actions" *(chuji)* should read "to dispatch forces" *(chubing);* this was due to incorrect sources they employed.[13]

---

[10]See Wang Niansun, *Dushu zazhi,* IX-18, under the line *"zhan wushi bi qi si,"* the last sentence of the note, p. 26b.

[11]It is also possible that this could be read *"shi xu"* (lit., "sufficiency and deficiency"); see Book 6, comment 1.

[12]*Sunzi yishuo,* p. 5b.

[13]*Shijia,* vol. 5, p. 5a. Sun and Wu stated that their proofs could be found in the text of *Beitang shuchao.* However, a printing of this book from the (Qing) Guangxu period that we used for verification (Kong edition, vol. 116, "Mouce" 5, p. 511) gives this term as *"chuqi,"* which is identical to the *Sun-tzu* text. We know, then, that the edition of the *Beitang shuchao* that Sun and Wu worked from was erroneous at this point.

8. "Rivers and seas" in the Chinese text reads *"hehai"* and follows the Linyi text. The *Wujing* and the Sakurada versions read *"jianghai"* (rivers and seas), while the *Shiyijia* reads *"jianghe"* (rivers).

9. The "five tones" in the Chinese text reads *"wusheng."* The names for the five tones are *zhi, yu, gong, shang,* and *jiao.*[14] The "five colors" in the Chinese text reads *"wuse";* the five colors are blue-green, red, yellow, white, and black, and correspond with the five directions.[15] The "five tastes" in the Chinese text reads *"wuwei";* the five tastes are sour, bitter, spicy, salty, and sweet.[16] The ancient arrangement of these matters all complement the seasons, directions, and five natural elements.[17]

10. "Irregular and regular perpetually engender each other like a ring without a breach" in the Chinese text reads *"jizheng huan xiangsheng, ru huan zhi wuduan"*[18] and follows the Linyi text. The later versions read "irregular and regular engender each other like following a ring's rim without a breach" (*"jizheng xiangsheng, ru xunhuan zhi wuduan"*).

[14]*Guanzi* says, "The sound of *zhi* is like a toted pig which becomes alert and startled. The sound of *yu* is like a horse whinnying in the wilderness. The sound of *gong* is like a cow lowing in its stall. The sound of *shang* is like a sheep separated from its flock. The sound of *jiao* is like a pheasant perched on wood and crying: its sound is strong yet clear" (vol. 19, "Diyuan," p. 311). The *Liji* has the phrase *"wusheng"* (vol. 22, "Liyun" [*Shisanjing*, p. 3078]); Zheng Xuan noted, "The five tones are *gong, shang, jiao, zhi,* and *yu,"* which is an order different from that in *Guanzi.*

[15]*Liji,* "Wuse" (vol. 22, "Liyun" [*Shisanjing*, p. 3078]); Kong Yingda's annotation. Note: the five directions are east, south, center, west, and north.

[16]*Liji,* "Wuwei" (vol. 22, "Liyun" [*Shisanjing*, p. 3078]); Zheng Xuan's note.

[17]See the *Liji,* vol. 22, "Liyun," under *"wuxing zhi dong"* (Shisanjing, pp. 3078–80); Kong Yingda's annotation.

[18]Notes in the *Yinqueshan Hanmu zhujian* *"Sunzi bingfa"* ("Shi," p. 49) provide three examples of lines similar to that in the Linyi text: as quoted in an annotation to the *Wenxuan* (vol. 6, "Weidufu" [note: under the line *"zhi jizheng yi sifa,"* meaning "to operate irregular and regular actions in trouncing all enemies," p. 128]), as quoted in the *Shiji* ("Tian Dan liezhuan" [note: vol. 82, p. 857]), and as quoted by Wang Xi in an annotation under a line earlier in the text, *"sanjun zhi zhong . . . jizheng shi ye"* (the armies' legions . . . through regular and irregular actions).

10a.   "Huan" (lit., "ring") in the phrase *"huan xiangsheng"* in ancient times
was interchangeable with *"huan"* (lit., "to return"; "to go around"; "to
repeatedly go back and forth"; hence, "perpetually").[19] This character is
used here to clarify the meaning of the succeeding text: "like a ring without a breach—who can limit them?" (p. 58). For this reason, when the
later versions lost this character, this line's meaning was impaired. Moreover, all of the ancient sources for this line from *Sun-tzu* have this character (see footnote 18), so we know that the Linyi text should be followed
here.

10b.   "Without a breach" *(wuduan)* describes the actual condition as like a ring,
so the later versions' addition of "to follow a rim" *(xun)* is an extraneous
character.[20]

11.   "The strength of a cataclysmic flood" in the Chinese text reads *"jishui zhi ji"*
and follows the later versions. The Linyi text reads "the strength of water" (*"shi
zhi ji"*). Since no explanation is given as to how water can have strength, this
line in the later versions is more sensible. The omission of the character *"ji"* (lit.,
"to urge") could also have occurred as a copying error.[21] The second *"ji"* (lit.,
"swift") in this line in ancient times was often defined as *zhuang* (strong;
strength).[22]

[19]For *"huan"* (to return; to repeatedly go back and forth) see *Shuowen,* 1 *xia,* p. 72; Duan Yucai's note.
Also, the *Yili* has the line *"bujin huan* [lit., 'ring'] *fu"* (vol. 35, "Shisang li" [*Shisanjing,* p. 2445]); Zheng
Xuan noted, "In ancient writings, *huan* could be read *huan* [lit., 'to return,' but here meaning 'to follow
a rim']."

[20]In addition to the quotes from ancient sources of *Sun-tzu* as noted in footnote 18, *Xunzi* recorded,
"From beginning to end, from end to beginning, like a ring without a breach" (vol. 5, "Wangzhi,"
p. 7a). This shows that "a ring" *(huan)* was referred to in pre-Qin times, rather than "following around
a ring's rim" *(xunhuan,* which means "circulation" today).

[21]*Sun Bin bingfa* says "when there is a correct method for handling water," its strength can be gained
(see comment 12b). Also, *Heguanzi* recorded, "Water when discharged becomes violent" (*xia,* p. 3b),
which proves our own standpoint.

[22]*Erya,* "Shiyan" (*Shisanjing,* p. 5610). Also, Hao Yixing's (Qing, 1757–1825) annotation to the *Erya
yishu* (p. 382) quotes the *Guangya* in defining this as *jian* (strong; dynamic).

12. "The strike of raptors which would even be able to produce destruction shows a restrained release of force" in the Chinese text reads *"zhiniao zhi ji, zhiyu huizhe, jie ye."*

12a. "Strike" in the Chinese text reads *"ji"* and follows Sun Xingyan and Wu Renji's critical notes.[23]

12b. "Produce destruction" in the Chinese text reads *"huizhe."* This is a complementary passage to the preceding "float rocks." We therefore know that the character in *zhe*'s position should be the object of *hui*. However, the character *zhe* is mainly defined as "to break" or "to damage."[24] Neither of these is appropriate as an object. The character *zhe* can also be defined as "a riding crop";[25] although a riding crop can act as an object, what would be the meaning of "destroy a riding crop"? We then find that *Sun Bin bingfa* has the line "when there is a correct method for handling water, it can float rocks and break boats";[26] this is probably similar in meaning to this passage from *Sun-tzu*. So, we suspect that the term *huizhe* might possibly be similar to *"zhezhou"* (to break boats), but one edition used *hui* (__) (to destroy [something]) and another used *zhe* (__) (to break [something]). Someone probably later carelessly combined the two editions and formed the term *huizhe* while losing the objects. In recent years a number of scholars have created their own forced explanation of this, such as "breaks the body of its prey," and so forth, which is unacceptable.

Cao Cao interprets this line as "start to attack the enemy"; he does not explain the characters, but rather focuses on the sentence's meaning.

12c. "A restrained release of force" in the Chinese text reads *"jie."* The basic meaning of *jie* is "restrained." From such illustrations in *Sun-tzu* as this

---

[23]*Shijia*, vol. 5, p. 7a. *Ji* (strike) had the ancient reading *ji* (lit., "swift").

[24]*Shuowen*, 1 *xia*, p. 45. Also, the *Shijing*: "Do not *zhe* my medlar tree" (vol. 4, "Zhengfeng: Qiangzhongzi" [*Shisanjing*; p. 712]); Mao Heng's note.

[25]The *Guangya* says, "*Zhe* means *duo*," which is "a riding crop" (vol. 8 *shang*, "Shiqi," p. 21a). Also see the *Shuowen*, 5 *shang*, "Duo," p. 198; Duan Yucai's note.

[26]*Xia*, "Jizheng," p. 123.

line's "strike of raptors" and the succeeding text's "pulling the trigger," etc., we can surmise that *jie* was used to indicate force with a restrained release. If other than this, massive destructive power could not be created (see comment 13).

13. "Instantaneous" in the Chinese text reads *"duan."* Cao Cao defined *duan* (lit., "short") as "close" *(jin),* and succeeding scholars have followed this. However, the preceding line in *Sun-tzu* uses "the strike of raptors" as its example; for a raptor to strike, it must gain great height in order to produce the power of its swoop, so this action cannot be described as "close." Also, the next line in *Sun-tzu* says, *"jie* [a restrained release of force] is as if pulling the trigger," which uses a crossbow as its illustration. In ancient times the crossbow had the greatest range of any weapon, so how could it be said to be "close"? We therefore know that Cao's view is improper.

Since ancient times *duan* has been used not only with regard to short distances, but also with regard to short durations of time.[27] Whenever power is gradually released over a period, it will lose its ability both to achieve a distant discharge and to create destruction. Restrained power must be released with instantaneous synchronization, like "a raptor's strike" or "the pulling of the trigger," which *Sun-tzu* used in attempts to illustrate his meaning, but were still misunderstood by Cao Cao.

14. "Stillness" in the Chinese text reads *"ci"* and follows the Linyi text. The later versions read "advantages" *(li).* The preceding text says "leave opportunities" *(yu zhi,* lit., "to give them"), which already includes "advantages," so this does not need to be repeated.

For "contain," see Book 6, Comment 11.

[27]The *Shujing* has the line "the sun is *duan* [short] and the star Ang is used to align [the span of] midwinter" (vol. 2, "Yaodian" [*Shisanjing,* p. 251]; the star Ang is located in the White Tiger constellation). Zhu Junsheng noted that the sun's movements "pass by swiftly, so it was described as *duan* [short]" (*Shuowen tongxun dingsheng,* "Duan," p. 757). Also, *Sun-tzu* in Book 6, "Superiority and Inferiority," says, "the sun has short and long spans" (p. 68); this uses "short" and "long" in relation to speed and so proves our position here. Since the "strike of raptors" and "pulling the trigger" have speeds that are faster than the blink of an eye, we interpret *duan* accordingly.

Huilin's *Yiqiejing yinyi* says that *duan* can be defined as *cu* (compelling, swift, instantaneous) (vol. 16, the term *"shouduan,"* which quotes from the *Cangjiebian,* p. 5b).

Ci (usually translated as "this") has as its basic definition "stillness" *(zhi)*,[28] and we have followed this in our interpretation.

15. "Soldiers" in the Chinese text reads *"zu"* and follows both the Linyi text and the *Shiyijia*. The *Wujing* reads this as *"ben"* (lit., "fundamental"; "main") while the Sakurada version reads this as *"shuai"* (lit., "to lead").[29]

---

[28]*Shuowen, 2 shang*, p. 69.

[29]*Shuai* is a mistaken reading for *zu*, for their forms are similar. As for *ben*, Zhang Yu explained that this meant "imposing and well-ordered troops," so if we follow his interpretation, this would have indicated the main forces, which makes sense, too. (*Li Weigong wendui, xia*, p. 7b, in quoting this line of *Sun-tzu*, also reads *zu* as *ben*.) The characters *zu* and *ben* were often mixed up in ancient times (e.g., the term *benyang* in *Zhuangzi* [vol. 9, "Daotuo," p. 21a]; Lu Deming indicated that *"ben* can also be read *zu"* [*Jingdian shiwen*, p. 403]). "Emerging to their surprise" (p. 41) often takes advantage of difficult terrain, so we follow the Linyi text and the *Shiyijia* here (see Book 1, comment 16, footnote 52).

SUPERIORITY AND INFERIORITY

1. The Chinese text reads *"shixu"* and follows the Linyi text. Later versions read *"xushi."*[1] The literal translations for *shi* and *xu* are "sufficiency" and "deficiency"; the discussion of these in *Sun-tzu*, though, shows that *shi* actually indicates "superiority" and *xu* indicates "inferiority," so we do not follow the literal translations.

2. "Sun-tzu said, Generally" in the Chinese text reads *"Sunzi yue, fan"* and follows the later versions. These characters are missing from the Linyi text, possibly because they were inadvertently dropped.

3. "Await battle" in the Chinese text reads *"dai zhan"* and follows the Linyi text. Later versions read "await the enemy" *(dai di)*, and so there is very little difference in the meaning. However, the succeeding text says "rush into battle," so the Linyi text is clearly preferable here.

4. "Enemies" in the Chinese text reads *"di"* and follows the Linyi text. The later versions read *"diren."*[2]

---

[1]With the exception of the Linyi text, ancient books have often given this term as *shixu*; e.g., *Guanzi* notes, *"Shixu . . .* is called *jishu* [the analysis of numbers]" (vol. 2, "Qifa," p. 28). *Shixu* was expressly an ancient term. Moreover, in this book's discussion *shi* is addressed first, and then *xu*, which also corresponds to the Linyi text. *Xushi* later was a common term, so the title was possibly changed to accommodate this mode of expression.

[2]*Diren* in later times, and up until today, has meant "enemies," but in the pre-Qin period it was used to mean "the adversary in conflict"; see Book 11, comment 8b.

5. "When steady, be able to move them" in the Chinese text reads "*an neng dong zhi.*" We doubt that this was part of the original *Sun-tzu*, but rather was a later addition; the previous sentence reads "when enemies are at ease, be able to exhaust them," so it already includes the crux of this line. Although this sentence is included in later versions, it is not a part of the Linyi text.

6. "Emerge where they have to rush over, and rush over to their surprise" in the Chinese text reads "*chu qi suo bi qu, qu qi suo bu yi,*" which follows Sun Xingyan and Wu Renji's critical note in the *Shijia.*[3] Some later versions such as the Sakurada are similar to Sun and Wu's readings, while the *Wujing* and *Shiyijia* read "have to rush over" *(bi qu)* as "not rush over" *(bu qu)*, which is incorrect. The Linyi text has only "emerge where they have to rush over" ("*chu qi suo bi qu*") and does not have "rush over to their surprise" ("*qu qi suo bu yi*"). But, if the enemy is aware of our actions, then not only will our actions to "emerge where they have to rush over" be in vain, but we will also run the risk of being destroyed. For this reason we surmise that the Linyi text must have dropped the phrase "rush over to their surprise."

7. "Without threat" in the Chinese text reads "*buwei*" and follows the Linyi text. Later versions all read instead "*bulao*" (not fatigued). Armies cannot be said to march a thousand miles and still not be fatigued, so we follow the Linyi text here.

8. "Cannot attack" in the Chinese text reads *bugong* and follows the later versions. The Linyi text reads this as "*bi* [lit., 'must']—" (second character missing, but the phrase probably originally meant "must attack"). Subsequently the text says

---

[3]Sun and Wu said, "The original text [i.e., the *Shiyijia*] reads 'not to rush over' [*bu qu*]. Note: All annotations to the preceding text that read *bu qu* are incorrect. This has been corrected in accordance with the *Yulan* [i.e., the *Taiping yulan*, vol. 270, 'Bingbu' 1, 'Xubing' *shang*]."

Their mention of "all annotations" includes Cao Cao's explanation of the preceding line—"be able to make enemies approach of their own accord by laying advantages; be able to make enemies not approach by laying hazards"—which says, "emerge where they have to go rapidly, attack where they have to rescue." Cao also explained the line ":when steady, be able to move them" (p. 63) as "attack what they certainly cherish, emerge where they have to come rapidly, and then force the enemy to rescue it."

"against those sophisticated at defense, enemies will be unsure of how to attack" (p. 63) and "once we do not want to conduct battle, even if defense is a line drawn on the ground, the enemy will be unable to engage us, by positioning where they are deceived into not going" (p. 64). We therefore know that the phrase "must attack" strays from *Sun-tzu*'s doctrine of actively controlling the enemy, so it cannot be used.

9. "The Fates" in the Chinese text reads *"Siming."* The meaning of this is examined in Book 2, comment 18a. As the situation here is still deliberated with regard to the enemy, we interpret *Siming* accordingly.

10. "Achieve an advance that cannot be withstood by rushing their weak sectors; achieve a withdrawal that cannot be entrapped by departing with unsurpassable rapidity" in the Chinese text reads *"jin bukeying zhe, chong qi xu ye; tui bukezhi zhe, yuan bukeji ye"* and follows the Linyi text.[4] The later versions all read "achieve an advance that cannot be defended by rushing their inadequate sectors; achieve a withdrawal that cannot be pursued with a swiftness that cannot be surpassed" (*"jin er bukeyu zhe, chong qi xu ye; tui er bukezhui zhe, su bukeji ye"*). *Ying* indicates "to withstand."[5]

   This section discusses a situation in which one is engaged with the enemy. *Tui* (lit., "to retreat") describes withdrawing when the enemy may still have the likelihood of protracting us into combat, so referring to this as "achieve a withdrawal that cannot be entrapped" (*"tui bukezhi"*) makes sense.[6] But using the character *zhui* (to chase) here instead of *zhi* (to trap; to be entrapped) indicates that there is already a distance between the two armies and that *tui* (to retreat) has already been completed; this does not complement the text of *Sun-tzu* here.

   The action of withdrawing from combat is called *yuan* (to depart; commonly

---

[4]The original remnants of the Linyi text read *"jin bukeying zhe, chong* _____ *kezhi zhe, yuan* ____"; later versions have supplied the missing characters.

[5]*Shuowen*, "*ying* means *feng* [to meet]" (2 *xia*, p. 72). This indicates meeting up against the enemy, so it is interpreted accordingly.

[6]*Zhi* is defined as *jin* (to be bound): e.g., the *Zhanguoce* has the line "a net could not *zhi* it" (vol. 8, "Qice" 1, the passage "Lord Jingguo will build a city fortification at Xue," p. 164); Gao You's note that *zhi* meant "to trap."

known as meaning "far").[7] The phrase *bukeji* (cannot be surpassed) describes a very rapid withdrawal from action, thus making our opponent incapable of overtaking us. So, reading this line as "*su* [swiftness] *bukeji*" in accordance with the later versions would be repetitive.[8]

From the above we may conclude that the Linyi text is preferable here to the later versions.

11. "So, those who are sophisticated at command contain the adversary but are free of containment" in the Chinese text reads "*gu, shanjiangzhe xing ren er wuxing*" and follows the Linyi text.

11a. *Xing* should basically be defined as "control,"[9] but the situation discussed in this section is where the enemy is already engaged, so we use "contain" and "containment" here as our interpretation.

11b. The reading "*shanjiangzhe*" (those who are sophisticated at command) was not included in the later versions. This phrase, though, more clearly indicates that the succeeding discussion concerns a situation on the battlefield. *Jiang's* ancient definition also was "to lead" or "to command" (*shuailing*).[10] Since this is a situation where the enemy is already engaged, we know that *jiang* actually should indicate "commanding battles" rather than just commanding our troops.

11c. "*Wuxing*" (are free of containment) is read "*wo wuxing*" in the later versions, and so has an extra *wo* (I; we) character.

12. "We are the few and the enemies are the many: be able to use few in striking the many when those who battle against us are confined" in the Chinese text

---

[7]E.g., the *Lunyu* has the line "the ones without benevolence will *yuan yi*" (vol. 6, "Yanyuan," under "Fanchi asked about benevolence," p. 128); (Liang) Huang Kan's annotation.

[8]*Su* 速 probably originally was written as *yuan* 遠, but since this form was later not understood, this character was changed to one with a similar shape: *su*.

[9]See Book 4, comment 1.

[10]*Shuowen*, 3 *xia*, p. 122; also, Xuanying's *Yiqiejing yinyi*, vol. 22, "Yuqie shidi lun," 23, under the term "*junshuai*," p. 9b.

reads *"wo gua er di zhong, neng yi gua ji zhong zhe, ze wu zhi suo yu zhan zhe yue yi."*

12a. "We are the few and the enemies are the many" in the Chinese text reads *"wo gua er di zhong"* and follows the Linyi text. The later versions read "then we are the many and the enemy are the few" (*"ze wo zhong er di gua"*).[11] When the reading follows the later versions, it makes some sense. However, using the few to attack the many and using the weak to fight against the strong are both extremely important topics in the conduct of armed conflict. These are also the considerations that commanders have studied ever since ancient times. The conclusion to the passage following this line contains the following: "In my judgment, though Yue's troops are many, how can this promote their victory? So it is said, victory can be grasped," and "Though the enemies are numerous, they can be made unable to engage in combat" (p. 66). What this section discusses is expressly the theory of using the few to attack the many, so we follow the Linyi text here.

12b. "When those who battle against us are confined" in the Chinese text reads *"ze wu zhi suo yu zhan zhe yue yi."* Du You noted, "It says few and easy to overcome," and Du Mu wrote, "*Yue* is as if saying 'few.'" If these are true, what is the difference between this and the later line, "those who battle against us will be few" (p. 65)? The original definition for *yue* was "to bind."[12] We thereby use the context of this passage to interpret *yue* as "to be confined."

Perusal of the relationship between this line and the preceding text shows that regardless of other factors, this line is the reason for the foregoing line, not its result. We know, then, that the character *ze* is defined as *yi* (for; because; when).[13]

[11]The Linyi text does not include this first character *ze* (then), in addition to the other discrepancies.

[12]*Shuowen*, 13 *shang*, p. 653.

[13]Wu Changying, *Jingci yanshi*, vol. 8, "Ze," eleventh definition, p. 92.

13. "By perceiving where battlefields will lie and by perceiving when battles will happen" in the Chinese text reads *"zhi zhan zhi di, zhi zhan zhi ri"* and follows the later versions. The Linyi text first mentions "when" and then "where." When discussing war strategy, the possible location of the battlefield is commonly known first, while the date of the battle is anticipated by studying the developing trends, so we do not follow the Linyi text here.

14. "By not knowing where battlefields will lie and by not knowing when battles will happen, the front cannot support the rear, the rear cannot support the front, the left cannot support the right, and the right cannot support the left" in the Chinese text reads *"buzhi zhan zhi di, buzhi zhan zhi ri, qian buneng jiu hou, hou buneng jiu qian, zuo buneng jiu you, you buneng jiu zuo"* and follows the Linyi text. The later versions first discuss "left" and "right," then "front" and "rear." In battle arrays, the front and rear of the arrays are generally the main sectors, and then left and right are used as supports. We therefore do not follow the later versions here.

15. "Victory can be grasped" in the Chinese text reads *"sheng keshan ye"* and follows the Linyi text. The later versions read "victory can be created" (*"sheng kewei ye"*), which is incorrect. The next line reads "though the enemies are numerous, they can be made unable to engage in combat" (p. 66), which precisely matches the meaning of "grasped." Moreover, Book 4, "Control," clearly notes that "victory can be perceived, but it cannot be created" (p. 53). Sun Wu's logic is so infallible that we know this line should be according to the Linyi text.

16. "Plan, but know the calculation of gains and losses" in the Chinese text reads *"ce zhi, er zhi deshi zhi ji."*

> **16a.** The interpretation of this line requires that the character *er* (but; then) be defined first, as this concerns the manner in which something is known beforehand and afterward.
>
> A few lines before this, *Sun-tzu* notes, "By perceiving where battlefields will lie and by perceiving when battles will happen, battles can be launched over a thousand miles" (pp. 65–66). This means "visualizing

beforehand." Book 13, "Espionage," notes this even more clearly: "So, as for enlightened lords or distinguished commanders, the reason they can overcome the adversary when action is taken and achieve unparalleled success is prescience" (p. 112). Therefore, knowing an action beforehand is an unchangeable precept of Sun Wu. These show that *er* here suggests "but" rather than "then."

16b. The order of the four situations following this line—*ce zhi* (to plan),[14] *zuo zhi* (to mobilize),[15] *xing zhi* (to control),[16] and *jiao zhi* (to fight)[17]—are very similar to the book titles in *Sun-tzu:* "Surveying," "Mobilizing for Armed Conflict," "Planning an Offense," "Control," and "Armed Contention," etc.

17. "Victory is determined" in the Chinese text reads *"zhisheng."* The basic definition of *zhi* is "to sever" *(duan).*[18] Once something is severed, it is determined or demarcated, so *zhi* is interpreted here accordingly.[19]

[14]*Shuowen* (5 *shang,* "Ce," p. 198); Duan Yucai's note: "Planning is called *chouce.*" Also, *zhi* has no explicit meaning; see Wang Yinzhi's *Jingzhuan shice* (vol. 9, "Zhi," tenth definition, p. 201) as well as Yang Shuda's *Ciquan* (vol. 5, "Zhi," third definition, p. 3). We therefore interpret these characters according to the suggested meaning of the preceding verb.

[15]See Book 2, comment 1. The Chinese text reads *"zuo zhi"* and follows the later versions. The Linyi text reads *"ji zhi"* (*ji* may be defined as "to achieve" [*Shuowen,* 13 *shang,* p. 666; Duan Yucai's note]).

The ancient pronunciation of today's *zuo* was *tsak,* while today's *ji* was pronounced *tsiek,* so they were similar (Zhou Fagao, *Hanzi gujin yinhui,* pp. 1 and 253) and ought to have been interchangeable. Moreover, textual criticism notes in the *Shijia* (vol. 6, p. 21a) say that the *Tongdian* (vol. 150, "Bing" 3, p. 785), *Taiping yulan* (vol. 290, "Bingbu" 21, p. 1339), the Li Quan annotated version, and Zheng Youxian's *Sunzi yishuo* (vol. 6, p. 21a) all read this as *"hou zhi";* the *Changduanjing* (vol. 9, "Liaodi," [*Hanhai congshu,* p. 1197]) also reads this as *"hou zhi."*

Hou means "to reconnoiter" *(siwang)* (*Shuowen,* 8 *shang,* p. 378), so the rendition by the above versions would mean that one should reconnoiter the enemies and then "perceive the causes for action and inaction"; this would make sense, but it does not fit in with the descriptions in the other three situations here.

[16]See Book 4, comment 1.

[17]E.g., Dai Tong wrote, "Horned animals use their *jiao* [horns] to butt each other, so it is used to mean the *jiao* in *jiaodou* [to conduct conflict or to fight] and *jiaoshengfu* [to fight for victory]" (*Liushu gu,* vol. 18, p. 13b).

[18]*Shuowen,* 4 *xia,* p. 184.

[19]The *Liji* notes, "Generally, *zhi* of the five *xing* [laws or penalties] must be according to the rationale of heaven" (vol. 13, "Wangzhi" [*Shisanjing,* p. 2905]); Zheng Xuan noted, *"Zhi* means 'to decide.'"

18. "Water's movement avoids the high and runs downward" in the Chinese text reads *"shuixing* [lit., 'to move'; 'movement'], *bi gao er zou xia"* and follows the Linyi text. Later versions read "water's shape [or format] avoids the high and tends downward" (*"shui zhi xing* [lit., 'shape'], *bi gao er qu xia"*). Pre-Qin books often used *xing* (movement) and *xing* (shape) interchangeably.[20]

"Avoids the high and runs downward" describes water's flow, so we know that the Linyi text is better here.[21]

19. "A force's victory avoids superiority and strikes inferiority" in the Chinese text reads *"bingsheng bi shi ji xu"* and follows the Linyi text. Later versions read *"bing zhi xing* [lit., 'the format or appearance'], *bi shi er ji xu."* "Avoids superiority and strikes inferiority" is a technique for achieving victory, so we know that the Linyi text is more pertinent than the later versions here.

20. "So, water conforms to terrain in determining movement" in the Chinese text reads *"gu, shui yin di er zhi xing"* and follows the Linyi text. Later versions read *"shui yin di er zhi liu"* (lit., "water determines its flow by following terrain"). The meaning of *xing* (movement) and *liu* (flow) are similar, but because a preceding passage used the Linyi text's *shuixing,* we do not follow the later versions here.[22]

21. "Forces do not have immutable combat power, nor do they have unchangeable control" in the Chinese text reads *"bing wucheng shi, wuheng xing"* and follows the Linyi text. Later versions read *"gu, bing wu changshi, shui wu changxing"* (lit., "so, forces cannot adhere to a constant combat power, water cannot adhere to

---

[20]E.g., *Liezi,* "the two mountains Taixing [lit., 'shape'] and Wangwu" (vol. 5, "Tangwen," p. 32a); (Jin) Zhang Zhan noted, "*Xing* [shape] is to be read as *xing* [to move]."

[21]This line is quoted exactly the same as the Linyi text in the Tang book *Chengui* ("Liangjiang" [*Luo Xuetang xiansheng quanji,* VI, pp. 2476–77]).

[22]This is quoted exactly the same way in the Linyi text as in the *Wenxuan* (vol. 58, "Zhu Yuan bei wen," the line *"zhisheng jiyuan,"* p. 1078; Li Shan's note). Also see *Luo Xuetang xiansheng quanji* (VI, p. 7352), in which a fragment of a Tang edition of the *Wenxuan* quotes this line as *"shui kun, yin di er zhi xing"* (when water is blocked, it conforms to terrain in determining movement), and the *Zhuzi zhiyao* (vol. 3, p. 56 [*Qunshu zhiyao*]). The *Beitang shuchao* reads *"zhi xing"* as *"panxing"* (*pan* movement) (vol. 113, the annotation under the line *"yin di liao sheng,"* p. 3b); the meaning of *pan* here is the same as *zhi* (to determine).

a constant form''). A textual criticism note to the Linyi text observes, ''The passage which succeeds this says *'neng yu di hua zhi wei shen'* [lit., 'being able to accommodate the enemy's changes can be considered supreme']. This is a specific reference to military affairs, so it appears that 'water' is inappropriate here.''[23]

The passages preceding this line—from ''thus, the control of forces is like water'' to ''are considered supreme'' (pp. 67–68)—discuss force employment, and water is used here as an illustration. The function of this illustration is concluded by the line ''forces conform to the enemy in determining victory'' (p. 68). From this point on, the text should be seen as a discussion focusing solely on forces. If, though, this is perceived as one more argument concerning water, it becomes superfluous. This shows that using water as the subject here is erroneous.

22. ''Those who are able to adapt to changes in the enemy and achieve victory are considered supreme'' in the Chinese text reads *''neng yin di bianhua er qusheng zhe, wei zhi shen''* and follows the later versions. The Linyi text reads ''to be able to adapt to the enemy's changes is considered supreme'' *(''neng yu di hua zhi wei shen'')*. Because the preceding discussion already concerns the moment of the forces' victory, it appears that the Linyi text overlooked the part that says *''qusheng''* (to achieve victory).

23. After this line the Linyi text has the two characters *''shen yao''*; the purpose for these characters is unknown, but perhaps acted as a subtitle.

[23] *Yinqueshan Hanmu shujian ''Sunzi bingfa,''* pp. 58–59, note 38.

ARMED CONTENTION

1. "Sets up bases in coordination with the order of battle" in the Chinese text reads *"jiaohe er she."* This was a special pre-Qin military term. Cao Cao interpreted it as, "The army gate is a *he* gate . . . and two armies facing each other are *jiaohe.*"[1] Most scholars have emulated this position, but it contains unacceptable points.

In this book *Sun-tzu* says, "The difficulties in armed contention are: turning the circuitous into the direct . . . set forth after the adversary but arrive before the adversary" (p. 69) and "conducting a forced march over a hundred miles while contending for advantages" (p. 70). These clearly describe two armies that are widely separated. If we follow Cao's interpretation, though, that these two armies are not far apart, this obviously was not Sun Wu's meaning here.

Cao's explanation that "the army gate is a *he* gate" probably came from Zheng Xuan, but his interpretation is suspect.[2] Ancient records show, insofar as we can understand, that *he* were the flanks of battle arrays.[3] *Jiao* here means "sequentially connected."[4] So, *jiaohe* was another way of saying "to sequentialize *he*,"

---

[1]From the context we surmise that Cao intended *jiao* to mean "in contact."

[2]The *Zhouli* says, "Use battle standards as the gate for the left and right *he*" ("Xiaguan: Dasima" [*Shisanjing*, p. 1809]), about which Zheng Xuan commented, "Army gates were called *he.*" Since the *Zhouli* refers to the gate for the left and right *he*, then *he* clearly was not the gate itself. Unless additional proofs can be found to document Zheng's standpoint, it must be considered unacceptable.

[3]*Hanfeizi* records, "Li Li fought against the men of Qin. He told the left *he*, 'Rapidly advance, the right *he* has already advanced.' He then galloped to the right *he*, saying, 'The left *he* has already advanced'" (vol. 11, "Waichusuo" *zuo shang*, p. 215). From this record we can see that *he* indicates "flank."
Yang Shuda explained, "The left and right *he* refer to the left and right armies. This is because army gates were called *he*. This meaning was extended so that their army also came to be called *he*" (*Jiweiju jiawenshuo, shang,* "Shi he"). From this, Yang attempted to make an academic compromise.

[4]The *jiao* of *jiaohe* is interchangeable with the character *jie* (to contact, to join) (*Shuowen,* 12 *shang,* "*jie* means *jiao,*" p. 606; Duan Yucai noted, "*Jiao* are crossed legs, extended to express 'crossed' or 'contacted'").

meaning that each of the armies' flanks had its confirmed troop order for battle. The *she* in the phrase *"er she"* is as if saying "to situate."[5] *"Jiaohe er she"* is therefore interpreted as "sets up bases in coordination with the order of battle."

2. "Armed contention has advantages; armed contention has risks" in the Chinese text reads *"junzheng wei li, junzheng wei wei."* The verb *wei* (lit., "to do") in both lines is defined as *you* (to have).[6]

3. "By bringing the camp" in the Chinese text reads *"jujun."* *Ju* literally means "to raise," and *jun* here indicates the army camp.[7] So, *"jujun"* is "to move the camp." The *jun* of *"weijun"* (by laying the camp aside) in the next passage has the same meaning.

4. "All of the armies' commanders could be ensnared" in the Chinese text reads *"qin sanjun jiang."* The later versions read *"qin sanjiangjun"* (three generals could be ensnared). Book 1, comment 13a, has shown that *jiangjun* is no more than a title. The one who leads armies in battles is the commander, in which case this should read *junjiang* or, as *Sun-tzu* records, *"jiang."* Du You noted, "If care is not used with the above two matters, the commanders of the three armies

---

Wang Yinzhi said, "*Jie* means the *jie* of 'sequence.' The *Guangya* records, '*Xu, jie, cha,* and *di* all are sequences' "; the annotation remarks, "The *Shuowen* said *jie* means *ci*. *Ci* means *di* [sequential]. *Ci* is interchangeable with *ci* [the order of], [meaning] 'sequentially connected,' as well as 'arranged in order' " (see *Jingyi shuwen,* vol. 21, "Guoyu" *xia,* the line *"qian jun jiehe,"* p. 521).

[5]E.g., the *Zhouli,* under the line *"zhang wang ci zhi fa"* (vol. 6, "Tianguan: Zhang ci" [*Shisanjing,* p. 1455]); Jia Gongyan's annotation.

[6]E.g., Wang Yinzhi, *Jingchuan shice,* "Wei," tenth definition (vol. 2, p. 59).

[7]The *Shuowen* says, "*Jun* means encirclement" (14 *shang,* p. 734); this definition uses the likeness of the ancient character form of *jun,* which depicts surrounding chariots. Wang Yun (Qing, 1784–1854) wrote, "Deduction of the *Zuozhuan*'s use of 'brush fence' as the meaning of *jun* shows that *jun* is what is today called 'a camp' " (*Shuowen shili,* vol. 9, pp. 33a–b).

Also, the *Zuozhuan* records, "The rest of the Jin troops were unable to *jun*" (vol. 23, "Xuangong shiernian" [*Shisanjing,* p. 4083]); Du Yu noted, "Could not create a camp." This proves that Wang Yun's interpretation was correct. Wang's use of a brush fence as the meaning of *jun* came from the *Zuozhuan,* where Kong Yingda annotated, "When the ancients applied forces, a fortress wall and moat were built where they stopped to protect against the unexpected. A brush fence was used as the camp wall when they intended to pare their forces as a way of showing that they did not distrust each other" (vol. 38, "Xianggong ershiqinian" [*Shisanjing,* p. 4331]).

(sanjun zhi jiang) will be ensnared by the enemy." His annotation shows that the version he followed read *"sanjun jiang."*[8]

In pre-Qin times, large countries that sent troops into battle always used three armies, which were divided into the middle army, upper army, and lower army.[9] *San* is therefore interpreted here as "all." When all the armies' commanders have been ensnared, the armies' destruction is inevitable.

5. "The spearhead force's commander" in the Chinese text reads *"shangjiang"* and follows the Linyi text. The later versions read *"shangjiangjun,"* but *jiangjun* is incorrect (see comment 4). As noted in the previous discussion, the three armies were divided into the upper, middle, and lower armies.[10] *Shangjiang* indicated the commander of the upper army.[11] Du You said that the *shangjiang* was "the spearhead force's commander" *(qianjun zhi jiang);* Zhang Yu's annotation reads, " 'The spearhead force's commander may be thwarted' *[jue shangjiang]* indicates the advance army which marches first." We interpret this line accordingly.

6. "Secure allies" in the Chinese text reads *"yujiao."* Cao Cao explained, "If the enemy's condition and deliberations are unknown, we cannot establish allies *[jiejiao]*"; his source is unknown.

Yu means "to settle" *(an),*[12] hence "secure."

---

[8]Zhang Zhichun recorded regarding the phrase *"sanjun jiang"* here in *Sun-tzu* that "a previously [seen one] was written *'sanjiangjun,'* which was a mistake made in later writings" (*Zhuzi jinghualu,* vol. 18, textual criticism note, p. 1238).

[9]See Sun Yirang, *Zhouli zhengyi,* vol. 54, "Xiaguan: Sima," the annotation after the passage *"fan zhijun"* (generally, regulating the army), p. 2237.

[10]Proof can also be found in the *Zuozhuan,* which records, "In the Jin troops' rescue of Zheng, Xunlinfu commanded the middle army, Shihui commanded the upper army, and Zhao Suo commanded the lower army" (vol. 23, "Xuangong shiernian" *xia* [*Shisanjing,* p. 4075]). The most important of the three armies was the middle, the next was the upper, and the least was the lower. The *Guoyu* also says, "[Wengong] established the three armies and appointed Xihu to command the middle armies as its *dazheng* [chief commander]" (vol. 10, "Jinyu" 4, p. 20a; for *dazheng,* refer to Wang Yinzhi, *Jingyi shuwen,* vol. 21, pp. 18b–19a).

[11]Some believe that *shangjiang* indicated the "field marshal," but this is incorrect; see Du You and Zhang Yu's annotations below.

[12]*Erya,* "Shigu" *xia* (*Shisanjing,* p. 5596). *"Yujiao"* is therefore interpreted as "to secure allies." Zhang Yu annotated this line, "Their deliberations are unknown, so anxiety that they will be erratic is likely."

7. "Forces achieve missions with unexpectation" in the Chinese text reads *"bing yi culi."*[13] The character *cu* (today only read *zha*) here means "unexpectation."[14] And *li* indicates the fulfillment of a task.[15] *Culi* is interpreted accordingly. Book 1 says, "attack their weaknesses; emerge to their surprise" (p. 41) and Book 11 says, "follows unexpected routes to attack where they are unaware" (p. 97); both of these lines can be used to confirm our above discussion.

8. "Thus, they act as swiftly as the wind; they march as steadily as forests; invading like fire, standing firm like mountains, as unpredictable as rain clouds, striking like thunder and lightning" in the Chinese text reads *"gu, qi ji ru feng, qi xu ru lin, qinlue ru huo, budong ru shan, nanzhi ru yin, dong ru leiting."* The descriptions in this section were greatly influenced by the classical writings from before that time, and were especially inspired by the *Shijing*.[16] This is the typical form of a pre-Qin book.

---

[13]Some read the character *cu* as *zha* and thereby interpret it as "deception," which is incorrect here; see footnote 14.

[14]The *Gongyangzhuan* records the phrase *"cu zhan buri"* (vol. 12, "Xigong sanshisannian" [*Shisanjing*, p. 4913]); He Xiu noted, "*Cu* 詐 [commonly read *zha*] was read *cu* 卒 [unexpectedly; suddenly]; this is of the Qi dialect." Yu Yue said, "Sun-tzu originally was from Qi; he read *zha* as *cu*" (*Zhuzi pingyi bulu*, vol. 3, under the line *"yi li dong zhi, yi cu dai zhi,"* p. 8). Moreover, Chen Li (Qing, 1809–69) wrote in the *Gongyang yishu* (vol. 37, under the line *"cu zhan* [lit., *'cu* battle'] *buri"* [*Huang Qing jingjie xubian*, p. 12630]): " '*Cu* battles' indicates 'unexpected [battles]'; 'unexpected' means 'suddenly.' The *Guangya*, 'Shiyan,' notes that 乍 means *zhan* [temporarily] [note: vol. 5 *xia*, p. 10b; Wang Niansun's notes]. In 'Dinggong banian,' *Zuozhuan*, it says, 'Huanzi *cu* told Lin Chu' [note: vol. 55 (*Shisanjing*, p. 4652)], and the annotation reads, '*Cu* means *zhan*; *zhan* means "suddenly." ' Not to fight on the appointed date [suggests] an imminent moment for subterfuge, so both meanings can be included."

[15]*Guangya*, "Shigu," 3 *xia*, the line *"li* means 'to accomplish,' " p. 12b.

[16]"They act as swiftly as the wind": see the line *"wanglü dandan, ru fei ru han"* (the omnipotent troops of the king are as flight, are as raptors) (vol. 18, "Daya: Dang series: Changwu" [*Shisanjing*, p. 1243]).
"They march as steadily as forests": see the line *"Yin Shang zhi lü, qi hui ru lin"* (the troops of the Yin Shang concentrate like a forest) (vol. 16, "Daya: Wen Wang series: Daming" [*Shisanjing*, p. 1093]). Also, the *Shujing* says, '*jiazi, meishuang, Zhou shuai qilü ruo lin, hui yu Muye*' (on the date *jiazi* by dawn, King Zhou [of the Shang] led his troops like a forest to concentrate on the outskirts of Mu) (vol. 11, "Zhoushu: Wucheng" [*Shisanjing*, p. 392]). *Lin* (forest) indicates that the warriors are numerous and their battle arrays are orderly. (This explanation refers to Ma Ruichen's [Qing, 1782–1853] standpoint in *Maoshi zhuanjian tongshi*, vol. 24 [*Huang Qing jingjie xubian*, p. 2625].)
"Invading like fire": see the line *"ru huo lielie, ze mo wo gan'e"* (blazing like a fire, then none dare stand against us) (vol. 20, "Shangsong: Zhangfa" [*Shisanjing*, p. 1353]).
"Standing firm like mountains": see the line *"ru shan zhi bao"* (like the root of a mountain) (vol. 16,

9. "Invade a countryside and rule the people; expand one's land and rule the advantageous points" in the Chinese text reads *"luexiang fenzhong, kuodi fenli."*

9a. In the line *"luexiang fenzhong,"*[17] *lue* means "to snatch" or "to invade" *(duoqu)*.[18] The object of *lue* is *xiang* (countryside).[19] *Fen* is defined as *zhi* (to rule).[20] *Zhong* indicates "their people." So, *"luexiang"* denotes "to invade a countryside," and *"fenzhong"* is "to rule the people."[21]

"Daya: Wen Wang series: Daming" [*Shisanjing*, p. 1093]); this means defending firmly, being like a mountain, neither frightened nor moved, and follows Kong Yingda's annotation.

"Striking": see the line *"ru lei ru ting, Xu fang zhen jing"* (like thunder, like lightning, the Xu kingdom was terrified) (vol. 16, "Daya: Wen Wang series: Daming" [*Shisanjing*, p. 1242]). Also, the *Yijing*, the line *"zhen jing baili"* (terrified over a hundred miles) (vol. 5, "Zhen diagram: Guaci" [*Shisanjing*, p. 126]); this means "the distant are frightened and the near are petrified" and follows the "Zhuanci."

(Qing) Jiang Nan in the *Xuepu yuli* indicated, "Among the five classics' [*Shijing, Shujing, Yijing, Liji,* and *Chunqiu*] descriptions of combat power, the *Shijing*'s is the most detailed, and military strategists often emulate its lines" (the section "Jingyan bingshi," p. 3b [collected in Wu Xinglan's *Yihai zhuchen* compendium]).

[17]The *Shiyijia* notes that *"luexiang"* in another version reads *"zhixiang"* (lit., "to point at directions"), and the annotations of Jia Lin and Wang Xi refer to that version. Also, both the *Tongdian* (vol. 162, "Bing" 15, p. 857) and the *Taiping yulan* (vol. 313, "Bing bu" 44, p. 1441) quote this term from *Sun-tzu* as *"zhixiang."* Because this reading obviously does not have any strategic meaning, it could not have been the correct text of *Sun-tzu*.

[18]*Shuowen*, 12 *shang*, Chen Changzhi wood-block edition, p. 258.

[19]In pre-Qin times, *"xiang"* originally was a local administrative unit (see the *Zhouli*, vol. 11, "Xiang-shi," and vol. 12, "Xiang daifu" [*Shisanjing*, pp. 1536 and 1542]; also see *Guanzi*, vol. 1, "Mumin: Liuqin wufa" and "Lizheng: Shouxian and Shengguan," pp. 3 and 11–12).

A *"xiang"* at that time was the main source of production and labor conscription, and it cannot be directly translated. But since it was made up of the areas outside of the walled cities *(guo)*, it would have been similar to the "countryside," so we interpret it accordingly.

[20]*Xunzi,* the line "needless to say that the *fen* concerning the way of the early kings and the conventions of benevolence and righteousness, as well as the *Shijing, Shujing,* the rites, and music" (vol. 2, "Rongru," p. 13a); Yang Jing noted, "*Fen* means *zhi.*"

Also, the *Dadai Liji* says, "*Fen* through the way is called Fate" (vol. 13, "Benming," p. 3a); Wang Pinzhen noted, "*Fen* means *zhi.*" This *"zhi"* does not follow its pre-Qin usage, so we interpret it as "to rule."

[21]Scholars have interpreted this line much as Du Mu did: "In separate turns send all of our men in to proceed." Zhang Yu also annotated, "The savings of the people in the countryside are not much. We must separately send forces in to seize them from different areas, then there will be enough to use."

If their explanations are followed, then *Sun-tzu* would have to read *"fenzhong luexiang."* So, Du and Zhang's readings twist *Sun-tzu*'s text. However, *Sun-tzu*'s meaning here is completely intelligible, and it suggests exactly what it states.

9b. In the line *"kuodi fenli,"* *kuo* is defined as *da* (to enlarge), which indicates developing something, so we interpret it as "expand."[22] *Li* means "advantages," and since this is a discussion of land, we know that *li* here actually indicates "advantageous points." Wang Xi's annotation says, "Occupy where it is advantageous to us; do not let the enemy grasp it."

10. "The means of circuitous as direct" in the Chinese text reads *"yuzhi zhi dao"* and follows the Linyi text. In the later versions the character *ji* (calculations)[23] is substituted for *dao* (means).[24] The discussion at this point in *Sun-tzu* concerns a confrontation with the enemy that could occur at any time, so measures for actions are to be firmly grasped. Therefore, "means" is more appropriate here than "calculations" *(ji)*.

11. The long paragraph of quoted material in this section, from *"Junzheng* reads . . ." until "these are fundamentals in employing legions," has been different in every edition from ancient times to the present. After reviewing the various versions of *Sun-tzu*, we find that the Linyi text is more logical, so we generally follow it. The remnants of the Linyi text's lines here are as follows:

Therefore, *Jun* _____["]drums and gongs[a] _____when eyesight cannot clearly observe, battle standards and flags are used.["] Therefore, in day battles emphasize battle standards and flags; in night battles emphasize drums and gongs.[b] These drums, gongs, battle standards, and flags are used to unify the ears and eyes of the people. The people are then united _____.

The discussion is as follows:

(a) This is not a conclusion to the previous text, so we should follow the later versions and eliminate "therefore" *(gu)*. Because the characters between *"Jun"* and "drums" *(gu)* are missing in the Linyi text, the later versions

[22]*Erya*, vol. 1, "Shigu" *shang* (*Shisanjing*, p. 5579); Xing Bing's annotation.

[23]Some translations interpret *yu* as "indirect," but the context of the succeeding text of *Sun-tzu* shows that this is not acceptable. For *ji*, see Book 1, comment 1, footnote 6.

[24]See Book 1, comment 20, the last paragraph.

are relied on to fill in the gaps. Pre-Qin texts often employed rhymes; "gongs" (*jin*) and the previous line's "flags" (*qi*) in ancient Chinese were rhymes, so the Linyi text is more acceptable here than the later versions' "gongs and drums."[25]

(b) The section from "therefore" until "gongs" was moved in the later versions to the end of the paragraph after "these are fundamentals for employing legions," writing instead "so, in night battles emphasize gongs and drums;[26] in day battles emphasize battle standards and flags. These are used to modify men's ears and eyes." (Night battles relied on gongs and drums, while day battles relied on battle standards and flags, so they were said to "modify" the ears and eyes of men.) The reason drums and gongs were emphasized at night, and battle standards and flags were emphasized in the day, was "to unify the ears and eyes" of the troops as well as their actions in battle. So, the later versions' explanation that these would "modify" their ears and eyes is meaningless.

12. "The morale of the armies can be dampened, and the sense for commanding battle arrays can be dampened" in the Chinese text reads "*gu, sanjun keduoqi, jiangjun keduoxin.*"

12a. Since this section is not the conclusion to the preceding text, we know that the first character here, "*gu*" (lit., "so"), acts as a mood word and has no tangible meaning.[27]

---

[25]E.g., the *Beitang shuchao*, vol. 120, "Qi," the line "*shi zhi ermu,*" p. 528; *Tongdian*, vol. 149, "Bing" 2, p. 779; and *Taiping yulan*, vol. 338, "Bing bu" 69, p. 1552, and vol. 340, "Bing bu" 71, p. 1561, "Qi." In all of these sources, "*jingu*" is given as "*guduo.*" *Duo* was a type of gong, so we know that the version they followed was the same as the Linyi text.

[26]This follows the *Wujing* version. The *Shiyijia, Shijia,* and Sakurada versions all read "fire and drums." However, pre-Qin signals for battle only used drums, gongs, and various types of flags (see *Guanzi*, vol. 6, "Bingfa: Sanguan," p. 95). *Sun Bin bingfa* notes, "In the day emphasize flags; at night emphasize drums," not fire. We therefore know that fire was not mainly used as a battle signal in pre-Qin times.

The Western Han book *Huainanzi* has the line "when in the day, emphasize flags; when at night, emphasize fire" (vol. 15, "Binglue," p. 16a), so the *Shiyijia* and other later writers probably followed *Huainanzi* in altering *Sun-tzu.*

[27]See Pei Xuehai, *Gushu xuzi jishi,* vol. 5, "Gu," eighth definition, p. 315.

12b. "Morale" in the Chinese text reads "*qi.*" Insofar as battles are concerned, "morale" has been referred to as *qi* since ancient times.[28]

12c. "Sense" in the Chinese text reads "*xin*" (lit., "heart"). Due to the practical circumstances surrounding battle, we interpret it accordingly.[29]

12d. "Commanding battle arrays" in the Chinese text reads "*jiangjun.*" These two characters are written this way in the Linyi text as well as in the later versions, so we know without a doubt that this follows the original text of *Sun-tzu.* In *Sun-tzu,* a general or commander is referred to as a *jiang.*[30] We therefore know that the character *jiang* here is a verb and interpret it as "to command," while *jun* is its object.

Jun (lit., "army") indicates "battle arrays."[31]

13. "Therefore, in the beginning morale is high, then slackens, and at last dissipates" in the Chinese text reads "*shigu, zhaoqi rui, zhouqi duo, muqi gui*" (lit., "therefore, in the morning, morale is high; during the day, morale slackens; by evening, morale dissipates"). In the Tang Dynasty, Li Jing noted, "What *zhaoqi rui* indicates is not limited by a time span, for a day's beginning and end are used as

---

[28]E.g., in the *Zuozhuan,* Cao Kuai noted about battle, "With the first drumroll, *qi* is raised" (vol. 8, "Zhuanggong shinian" [*Shisanjing,* p. 1833]). Today, "morale" is referred to in Chinese as *shiqi* (warrior's *qi*). "Morale" in ancient times was also referred to as "*nu*"; see Book 1, comment 22.

[29]*Guanzi* notes, "The *xin* is where *zhi* [mind; intellect] is situated" (vol. 13, "Xinshu" *shang,* p. 221). Also, Wang Yinzhi said, "*Xin* means *si* [the ability to think]" (*Jingyi shuwen,* vol. 27, under the line "*mou, xin ye,*" pp. 634–35).

[30]See Book 1, comment 13a.

[31]The *Lunyu* notes, "Weilinggong asked Confucius about arrays. Confucius replied, 'The matters of *zudou* [the implements used in the rites] I have heard of before. The matters of *junlü* I have never studied'" (vol. 15, "Weilinggong" [*Shisanjing,* p. 5465]). Confucius used *junlü* in replying to Weilinggong about arrays, so *jun* indicates "battle arrays." Therefore, Xing Bing's annotation on *junlü* concerns the use of forces.

In the ensuing passage of *Sun-tzu* it states, "Await disorder with discipline; await clamor with calmness—this is how to handle sense" (p. 73). This says that we and the enemy are facing each other in arrays and waiting for an opportunity to attack. These all point to the character *jun* here as meaning "battle arrays."

illustrations. If after three drumrolls the enemy's neither slackens nor dissipates, how can it be forced into slackening or dissipating?"[32] We therefore interpret "morning," "day," and "evening" as "beginning," "then," and "at last."

"*Gui*" is basically defined as *wang* (to go away).[33] Morale is described in *Sun-tzu* as "going away," so it is interpreted here accordingly.

14. "A frontal attack" in the Linyi text reads "*ying*" (lit., "to go toward"; "to face").[34] *Ying* indicates the enemy's approach, and therefore we advance to face them, so we know that this describes "a frontal attack."

15. "With elite soldiers, do not attack them; with baited forces, do not devour them" in the Chinese text reads "*ruizu wugong; erbing wushi*" and follows the *Wujing* and the *Shiyijia* versions. The Linyi text does not have these two lines, while the Sakurada version moved these to Book 8, "The Nine Adaptations"; see comment 18.

16. "With surrounded organized troops, leave a gap; with orderly retreating troops, do not block them" in the Chinese text reads "*weishi yique*;[35] *guishi wu'e.*" *Shi* (troops) indicates an organized body of soldiers, so its actions must include plans.[36] If the enemy's organization is still intact while they act to execute their plans, yet we rigidly attempt to either beset them or block their retreat, our losses would be great.

---

[32]*Li Weigong wendui, xia*, p. 4a.

[33]*Guangya*, "Shigu" 1 *shang*, p. 5b.

[34]Later versions all read "*ni*" (to confront). In ancient times these two characters were interchangeable (*Shuowen*, 2 *xia*, "Ni," p. 72; Xu Shen's explanation).

[35]"Leave a gap" ("*yique*") follows the Linyi text; the *Wujing* and *Shiyijia* versions read "must have a gap" ("*bique*"); the Sakurada version reads "do not seal up" ("*wuzhou*").

[36]I.e., Book 2, "Mobilizing for Armed Conflict," says, "only then are a hundred thousand troops raised" (p. 43), and Book 13, "Espionage," notes, "generally, when the raising of a hundred thousand troops" (p. 111); since "raise" was used in both lines, this allows us to visualize the meaning of *shi* (troops) as an organized body.

17.   "With desperate foes, do not exceedingly push them" in the Chinese text reads "*qiongkou wupo*" and follows the later versions.[37] The Linyi text does not have this line.

18.   The passage from "fundamentals in using forces are" to "these are fundamentals in using forces" has been recorded in various ways:

(i)   Both the *Wujing* and the *Shiyijia* have 43 characters in this passage.

(ii)   Extant portions of the Linyi text, from "with the enemy backed by a mound, do not issue a frontal attack" to "these are the fundamentals in using forces," total 22 characters.

(iii)   The Sakurada version relocated this passage of 43 characters to the first paragraph of Book 8, "The Nine Adaptations," but it first completely eliminated the 11 characters that translate "fundamentals in using forces are" and "these are fundamentals in using forces," leaving only the 8 remaining items (totaling 32 characters), from "with high buttes, do not fight toward them" to "with orderly retreating troops, do not block them." This presentation in the Sakurada version has the same perspective as Liu Ying (in his *Wujing qishu zhijie*).

We now may consider the various versions' total number of characters in Book 7:[38]

(i)   The *Wujing* totals 476 characters.[39]

(ii)   The *Shiyijia* totals 477 characters.[40]

[37]"Exceedingly push" in the *Wujing* and *Shiyijia* versions reads "*po*," while the Sakurada reads "*bi*"; they both mean "to push" or "to compel."

[38]In the *Sunzi jiaoshi*, which Wu Jiulong edited, he had observations on this passage that are similar to ours.

[39]In the paragraph beginning with "*Junzheng* reads," the two lines "*wei zhi gujin*" (drums and gongs are used) and "*wei zhi jinqi*" (battle standards and flags are used) have two more *zhi* characters than the *Shiyijia*.

[40]It has three more *gu* characters than the *Wujing* in the lines "*gu junzheng wei li*" (so, armed contention has advantages), "*gu sanjun keduoqi*" (so, the morale of the armies can be dampened), and "*gu shanyongbingzhe, bi qi ruiqi*" (so, those sophisticated at using forces avoid their high morale).

(iii) The Sakurada version totals 434 characters.[41]

(iv) The Linyi text has a record at the end of Book 7 that there are 465 characters in this book.

In the paragraph beginning with *"Junzheng* reads . . ." some differences exist between the way in which the *Wujing,* the *Shiyijia,* and the Linyi text record this, but their substance is generally the same, the main disparity being that the Linyi text does not have the 8 characters *"suoyi bianren zhi ermu ye."*[42] If these 8 characters are eliminated from the *Wujing* and *Shiyijia,* then the *Wujing* has 468 characters and the *Shiyijia* has 469 characters. If the *Wujing* and *Shiyijia* are then compared with both the Linyi text's record of having 465 characters and the extant text itself, this shows that the content of the two later versions complement that of the Linyi text. And we know that the last paragraph in Book 7 was actually written with 43 characters in ancient times.

We can therefore state that the Sakurada version's transfer of the last paragraph of 43 characters was not Sun Wu's intent. No reason was given for such a relocation. However, Liu Ying made an announcement after this last paragraph: "This originally was taken from *'Jiubian'* [Book 8, 'The Nine Adaptations'] and misplaced here";[43] he was following the Zhang Pen version, which transferred this paragraph to the beginning of "The Nine Adaptations."[44]

Liu Ying lived during the early Ming, so the latest date for the Zhang Pen edition had to have been the Yuan Dynasty (probably before 1368). The Saku-

---

[41]When compared with the *Wujing* and *Shiyijia,* we see that the Sakurada version has one more *yang* character than the *Wujing* in the line *"nanzhi ru yinyang"* (lit., "as unpredictable as yin and yang"). In addition to this extra *yang,* the Sakurada version also has two more *zhi* characters than the *Shiyijia* in the paragraph beginning with *"Junzheng* reads," but has three less *gu* characters than the *Shiyijia,* as shown above. So, its total content is basically similar to that of the *Wujing* and *Shiyijia.* If the final eliminated paragraph is returned to the Sakurada version, its total reaches 477 characters, and it has only one extra *yang* character, like the *Shiyijia.*

[42]"These are used to modify men's ears and eyes." This was given as the last line in the quote from the *Junzheng,* but we do not agree with its inclusion in *Sun-tzu* here; see comment 11, discussion (b).

[43]*Wujing qishu zhijie, zhong,* p. 24a.

[44]See Book 8, comment 1. The Zhang Pen edition is no longer extant; the only record of it is in Liu Ying's discussion.

rada version was found in Japan during 1851;[45] this was at least 483 years later than the Zhang Pen version. The elimination of this last paragraph and its transfer to Book 8 is a characteristic unique to these two versions, so it suggests the possibility that the Sakurada version could have been influenced by the Zhang Pen version.

[45]Hattori Chiharu, *Sonshi hyohō kōkai,* "Introduction," "Three: The Editions and Development of *Sunzi bingfa,*" p. 12.

COMMENTS ON BOOK 8

―――――

THE NINE ADAPTATIONS

1. "The Nine Adaptations" in the Chinese text reads *"jiubian."* Cao Cao annotated this as "adapt to its regularity." *Jiu* (lit., "nine") is not a concrete number, but rather indicates "the maximum amount."[1] Liu Ying wrote under this title,

> Note: The contents of this book are jumbled. Because of this, many have blindly followed it before; only Zhang Pen could have been able to correct them. His edition was once published. When I was eighteen or nineteen I encountered the upheaval of the [end of the] Yuan, so I was taught to read it by my father. This book has been lost for more than forty years, but I can still generally remember it. I will rectify the interpretation as follows according to its order to help novices easily understand it.[2]

Zhao Benxue agreed with Liu's opinion,[3] but we have proved that this viewpoint contains some unacceptable points.[4]

2. "Compartmentalized zones" in the Chinese text reads *"pidi"* and follows the *Wujing* and *Shiyijia* versions, while in the Linyi text this part is missing. In the ancient classics, *pi* was customarily defined as *hui* (broken);[5] however, we modified the definition given in *Sun-tzu* for this type of zone (see p. 95 and comment 4) to acquire this interpretation.

---

[1]See Book 4, comment 5, footnote 13.

[2]*Wujing qishu zhijie, zhong,* p. 24b.

[3]*Sunzi shu jiaojie yinlei, zhong,* pp. 53b–54a.

[4]See Book 7, comment 18.

[5]*Erya,* vol. 1, "Shigu" *shang* (*Shisanjing,* p. 5582).

3. "Unite allies" in the Chinese text reads "*hejiao*" and follows the *Wujing*. The *Shiyijia* reads this as "*jiaohe*" (allies are united),[6] while in the Linyi text this part is missing.

4. Throughout this paragraph no definition has been given for *di* (zone; terrain). As this is contrary to Sun Wu's style of writing, his explanatory passage must have been mislaid somewhere other than in Book 8. In Book 11, "The Nine Zones," is one section that defines six kinds of areas—severable zones, key traffic zones, dominant zones, susceptible zones, surrounded zones, and lethal zones (pp. 101–2)—and it has no relationship to the rest of Book 11, so this probably is the missing passage and should be included as follows:

Where away from the country, at a distance from the border, and troops are set is a severable zone. Where many places converge is a key traffic zone. Where deeply penetrated is a dominant zone. Where shallowly penetrated is a susceptible zone. Where the rear is blocked and the front is narrow is a surrounded zone. Where inextricable positions lie is a lethal zone.

If the six definitions listed here are compared with the paragraph under discussion, the definitions lack compartmentalized zones *(pidi)*, while this paragraph is missing both dominant zones *(zhongdi)* and susceptible zones *(qingdi)*.

How many areas are there, then, in *Sun-tzu* and how should they be listed? No sources exist that delineate this, but the above discussion actually gives us a total of seven zones. Compartmentalized zones are undefined, yet Book 11 says, "Where there is a maneuverable mountain forest, obstacle, or swamp and the passes are difficult to forge is compartmentalized" (p. 95). As for methods of adaptation in dominant and susceptible zones, Book 11 says, "with susceptible zones, do not halt" and "with dominant zones, conduct appropriations" (p. 95), as well as "with susceptible zones we will urge then to advance swiftly" and "with dominant zones we will maintain our food supply" (p. 95).

---

[6]The criticism of Sun Xingyan and Wu Renji points out that this reading is incorrect (*Shijia*, vol. 8, p. 1b). In the Sakurada version, the first part of Book 8 was erroneously altered at a later time and so was eliminated (see Book 7, comment 18).

We refer, therefore, to *Sun-tzu*'s own definitions for these zones in determining their interpretations.

5. "Some lords' orders need not necessarily be accepted" in the Chinese text reads *"junming you suo bushou"* and follows the later versions of *Sun-tzu*. Appendix 2, "The Four Adaptations," in the Linyi text has the line "some lords' orders should not be carried out" *("junling you suo buxing")*, where *"bushou"* is read *"buxing."*

If a lord's order is to be rejected, it should not be an act of defiance with regard to the planned strategic goals. This is what Book 10, "Terrain," meant by "so, when the ways for battle are definitely victorious, even if the lord orders no battle, the battle may still be waged; when the ways for battle are not victorious, even if the lord orders a battle, the battle may still not be waged" (p. 92). Also, Book 1, "Surveying," notes, "When commanders do not heed our surveys and are appointed, defeat is assured; dismiss them" (p. 40), and Book 12, "Attacks Using Fire," says, "So we say, an enlightened lord considers these and distinguished commanders follow them" (p. 109). These all confirm our understanding here.

Xunzi[7] records, "There are three orders which are not accepted from a lord: when one would rather be killed than be forced into a flawed situation, when one would rather be killed than forced into a thwarted attack, and when one would rather be killed than forced into oppressing the people. These are the three loftiest principles." However, these were the views of Xunzi, not Sun Wu.

6. "The advantages in the nine adaptations" in the Chinese text reads *"jiubian zhi li"* and follows the *Wujing* and Sakurada versions. The *Shiyijia* reads this as *"jiubian zhi dili"* (the terrain's advantages in the nine adaptations), which is incorrect.[8]

7. "Fulfilled" in the Chinese text reads *"shen"* (now read only as *"xin"*). In ancient times the character with the form of *xin* (lit., "credibility"; "to believe") was

---

[7]Vol. 10, "Yibing," p. 7a.

[8]Sun Xingyan and Wu Renji's criticisms have already noted that the *Shiyijia*'s reading mistakenly added an extra *"di"* (terrain) character (*Shijia*, vol. 8, p. 7a).

actually read as meaning *shen* (lit., "unfolded"),[9] which therefore came to be interpreted as "fulfilled."[10]

8. "Make other lords work on our behalf through successes" in the Chinese text reads *"yi zhuhou zhe yi ye."* *Ye* indicates "an achievement."[11]

The first character, *"yi,"* means *shi* (to make a person work on one's behalf).[12] The success of an affair is used to make other lords work on our behalf, so we know that *"yi* [lit., 'with'; 'for'; 'through'] *ye"* indicates "sharing successes."

Cao Cao noted, *"Ye* means *shi* [lit., 'affairs']. Make them fatigued, much like emerging when they return or returning when they emerge." He defined *ye* here as *shi*, which is unacceptable (see footnote 11). He also defined the first character, *yi*, as "make them fatigued," but the source for his definition is unknown. The rest of his interpretation has a certain tactical value, but it does not follow Sun Wu's meaning here.[13] Moreover, he heedlessly took *Sun-tzu's* use of the term *zhuhou* (lit., "feudal lords") to mean "the enemy" (see below). In addition to Cao's interpretation, the others—such as Du Mu, who wrote, "This says to fatigue the enemy and make them unable to rest"—irrationally emulated Cao's words without evincing the slightest doubt.

In *Sun-tzu*, whenever *zhuhou* are mentioned, this always indicates feudal lords other than the enemy;[14] sometimes they are even allies.[15] So, the explanations

[9]*Shuowen*, 8 *shang*, "Shen," p. 381; Duan Yucai noted, *"Shen* in all ancient books is written the same as *xin."*

[10]*Guangya*, the line *"shen* means *li* [lit., 'to manage'; 'to be managed']" (vol. 2 *shang*, p. 18b); our interpretation evolved from this.

[11]The *Yijing* has the line "reveal through *shiye"* ("Kun diagram: Wenyan" [*Shisanjing*, p. 33]); Kong Yingda's annotation says, "Whatever is being performed is called *shi*, and *shi* that succeeds is called *ye."* Also, the *Zhanguoce* notes, "Listen more and utilize it to fit the situation; in this way the *shi* will not spoil the *ye"* (vol. 19, "Zhaoce" 2, the section "Qing gong Zhao," p. 361). These prove that *shi* and *ye* are, as Kong pointed out, two different matters.

[12]*Guangya*, "Shigu" 1 *xia*, p. 19a. Also, *Shuowen*, 3 *xia*, "Yi," p. 121; Duan Yucai's note.

[13]Actually, Cao Cao's example comes from "Zhaogong sanshinian," *Zuozhuan* (vol. 53, Shisanjing, pp. 4614–15).

[14]E.g., Book 2, "Mobilizing for Armed Conflict," says "then other lords will take advantage of these complications and rise up" (p. 44).

[15]E.g., Book 7, "Armed Contention," says, "by not knowing other lords' minds, one cannot secure allies" (p. 71). This is identical to another line in Book 11, "The Nine Zones" (p. 103). Book 11 also

of Cao Cao and such scholars as Du Mu appear to have ignored the rules of term usage in *Sun-tzu;* they therefore can definitely not be accepted.

9. "Rapidly take action" in the Chinese text reads *"qu." Qu* should have the basic definition of "to move rapidly";[16] however, when it is used in referring to feudal lords, this is not simply a question of their coming or going, so we interpret it accordingly.

notes, "where a lord conducts battles in his individual sector is separated" (p. 94). That *zhuhou* (feudal lords) here indicates our allies is very clear.

[16]*Shuowen, 2 shang,* "Zou," p. 64; Duan Yucai's note.

COMMENTS ON BOOK 9

TROOP MANEUVERS

1. "Studying" in the Chinese text reads "*xiang*." This was originally defined as "to thoroughly examine,"[1] so it is interpreted here accordingly.

2. "Observe the safe and position on heights" in the Chinese text reads "*shisheng chugao*." *Sheng* (safe) and *gao* (heights) are the two fundamental requirements in *Sun-tzu*'s discussion on terrain superiority. Cao Cao noted, "*Sheng* [lit., 'life'; 'alive'] means *yang*." Since ancient times the southern sides of lands, especially highlands, have been referred to as "*yang*,"[2] so many succeeding annotations have interpreted "*shisheng*" as "facing south."

   Later in this book the text reads, "generally armies . . . prize southerly sites [*yang*] over northerly sites [*yin*]" (p. 80), so if *sheng* here means *yang*, why didn't Sun Wu write *yang* instead of *sheng*? Also, even if *sheng* is interpreted as "the south," its meaning is no more than a direction.

   Direction with regard to terrain is decided by how it assists in achieving superiority over the enemy. So, the choice of a particular direction is merely conditional. "Position on heights," though, is an inherent strategic requisite,[3] but this still is inadequate.

---

[1] *Shuowen, 4 shang,* p. 134; Duan Yucai's note.

[2] The northern sides of lands, particularly lowlands, were referred to as "*yin*," and the belief also existed that "the south governs life and the north governs death," so this was a product of cultural tradition. Even so, relying on such an explanation for this line of *Sun-tzu* is unreliable.

[3] Du Mu once pointed out that "with regard to 'the heights' and 'the south,' one can relinquish the south for the heights, but one cannot relinquish the heights for the south" (Book 10, "Terrain," the paragraph beginning "with obstacled terrain" [p. 89 in our text], Du Mu's annotation [*Shiyijia, xia,* p. 3b, and *Shijia,* vol. 10, p. 5a], where he discusses the battle of Xiao between the Qin and Jin states during the Spring and Autumn Period).

In *Sun-tzu*, the achievement of terrain superiority demands a thorough perception of "the lethal" *(si)* and "the safe" *(sheng)*. And, as a matter of fact, "*sheng*" here expressly means "safe." Lethal and safe terrains coexist as a pair of opposites. Therefore, the domination of safe terrain is none other than the domination of an enemy trapped in lethal terrain. The two major necessary conditions for victory in battle terrains are "the observation of the safe" and "positioning in the heights."

3. "A high position" in the Linyi text reads "*hong*" (today commonly read "*jiang*," meaning "to descend" or "descendant"), while the later versions read "*long*" (lit., "high").[4] While these two characters are distinct today, they had the same reading in ancient times; even after the Han Dynasty these two characters remained interchangeable.[5]

4. "Cling" in the Chinese text reads "*yi*" and follows the Linyi text. The later versions read "*biyi*" (must cling). *Sun-tzu* at this point is merely discussing general principles; individual criteria have to be taken into account when encountering the enemy, so "must" is not needed here.

5. "Position in the peripheral sites" in the Chinese text reads "*chuyi*." Previous annotations by Cao Cao, Du Mu, etc., of this line hold that *yi* means "a level area" on a plain that is advantageous to our chariot and cavalry charges. But where on a plain is it not level? And how can one then explain the next line— "with the right flank backed by height" (p. 80)—for where on a plain is it high?

---

[4]Both the *Tongdian* (vol. 156, "Bing" 9, p. 824) and the *Taiping yulan* (vol. 306, "Bing bu" 37, p. 1409) use the same character as the Linyi text in quoting *Sun-tzu* here.

Zhang Yu (who cited the "*long*" of the later versions) indicated that this character in another version reads "*jiang*"; we therefore know that during his time, the Song Dynasty, this character still retained two readings.

[5]While today this character is read *long* 隆, in ancient times its reading came from *hong* 降 (today read *jiang*; see *Shuowen*, 6 *xia*, "Long," p. 276, and 14 *xia*, "Jiang [lit., 'to descend'],'' p. 739), so these two characters had the same pronunciation and were interchangeable.

An example of this can be found in a line from the *Jin shu:* "shenshi jiang [also, hong] jia" (vol. 22, "Yuezhi" *shang*, "Yingsong shen ge," p. 168); (Liu Song) Guo Maoqian quoted this line in the *Yuefu shiji* as "*shenshi longjia*" (vol. 1, "Jin, Jiaosige: Yingsong shen ge," p. 8a).

Only the peripheral areas of a plain are high, so we know that the character *yi* does not indicate "level ground," but was borrowed to mean "peripheral sites" (also read *yi*).[6]

6. "The advantages in all these four army positionings were used by the Yellow Emperor to achieve victory over all his enemies" in the Chinese text reads *"fan sijun zhi li, Huangdi zhi suoyi sheng sidi ye."* "Four army positionings" (*sijun;* lit., "four armies") indicates the previous passage's four army positionings in mountains, rivers, swamps, and plains.

As for *"sheng sidi"* (lit., "to achieve victory over four emperors"), who are the four emperors? *Sun-tzu* does not provide further explanation. They could have been enemies from the four regions described in the foregoing text, or even enemies from the four directions of north, south, east, and west.[7] We therefore use a more general stance to interpret it as "all of his enemies."

7. "Prize southerly sites over northerly sites" in the Chinese text reads *"guiyang er jianyin."* For *"yang"* and *"yin,"* see comment 2.

8. "Occupy the safe" in the Chinese text reads *"yangsheng"* (lit., "to cultivate or feed the living"). Cao Cao noted, " 'Yangsheng' means to head for water and grass, to let out to graze, to care for oxen and horses." Scholars often have followed his interpretation. The problem with this standpoint is that *Sun-tzu* is currently in the middle of a discussion on terrain, so why would he make a sudden unrelated digression about livestock?

We believe that this was not carelessness on the part of Sun Wu, but rather a misunderstanding by the annotators. Their misinterpretation lies with the char-

---

[6]E.g., the *Yijing* has the line "lost sheep in the *yi*" (vol. 4, "Dazhuang diagram: Liuwu" [*Shisanjing*, p. 98]); Wang Yinzhi noted, "[In Lu Deming's *Jingdian*] *shiwen* [note: p. 24], the character *yi* [lit., 'a level area'] is read as the *yi* in *jiangyi*, or the edge of an area." Wang also noted, "In ancient times the character *yi* in *jiangyi* was usually written as *yi* [of 'a level area']" (*Jingyi shuwen*, vol. 1, under the line *"sangyang yu yi,"* p. 24).

[7]In Appendix 3 there is a story about the Yellow Emperor conquering his enemies in the east, south, west, and north. However, that record was written during the Warring States Period, so it has no direct relationship with this passage of *Sun-tzu* (see the introduction to Appendix 3).

acter *yang* (lit., ''to feed''), which had the ancient, obsolete definition of *qu* (''to take,'' so ''to occupy'').[8] If we overlook the pre-Qin meaning of *yang*, we would read it using the common definition of ''to feed'' or ''to raise''; in this way *sheng* (safe) would have the forced reading of ''livestock'' *(sheng)*.[9]

9. ''These ensure victories, and the armies may avoid disease'' in the Chinese text reads *''shiwei bisheng, jun wu baiji''* and follows the Linyi text.[10] The later versions read *''jun wu baiji, shiwei bisheng''* (the armies may avoid disease, and these ensure victories), which is exactly the opposite arrangement of the Linyi text.

    If we pay special attention to this passage from ''generally, armies prefer'' to ''may avoid disease,'' we will find that this seems incongruous with the preceding and succeeding text; it is possible that omissions or misplacements are involved.

10. ''Be positioned'' in the Chinese text reads *''chu''* and follows the Linyi text. The later versions read *''bichu''* (must be positioned). At this point *Sun-tzu* is discussing general principles, so ''must'' *(bi)* would not have been used; we therefore do not follow the later versions.

11. ''When rainwater rises and currents approach, halt crossing until it has subsided'' in the Chinese text reads *''shang yushui, shuiliu zhi, zhishe, dai qi ding ye''* and follows the Linyi text. The later versions read ''when rainwater rises and spray from the broken waves comes [see footnote 12], those wishing to cross, wait until it has subsided'' *(''shang yushui, mo zhi,''[11] yushezhe, dai qi ding ye'').*

---

[8]Wang Niangsun, *Dushu zazhi*, VIII-7, under the line *''zhi suo yang,''* p. 23b. Also, *Shijing*, vol. 19, ''Zhousong: Qingmiao series: Zhuo,'' the line *''zunyang shihui''* (*Shisanjing*, p. 1302); Mao Heng's note.

[9]E.g., the *Lunyu* has the line ''the lord granted *sheng*'' (vol. 10, ''Xiangdang'' [*Shisanjing*, p. 5418]); Zheng Xuan's note.

[10]Sun Xingyan and Wu Renji's textual criticism says, ''The *Tongdian* [note: vol. 156, 'Bing' 9, p. 824] records, 'These ensure victories and the armies may avoid disease.' The *Taiping yulan* [note: vol. 306, 'Bing bu' 37, p. 1409] is identical. Note: Mei [Yaochen] and Zhang [Yu's] annotations are both the same as that of the *Tongdian*'' (*Shijia*, vol. 9, pp. 8b–9a). The lines they cite correspond to this line in the Linyi text.

''Disease'' is not a main consideration in strategy (except, of course, for modern biological warfare), so it is preferable to note this after the conclusion of ''these ensure victories.''

[11]Du You and Zhao Benxue read this as *''shangyu, shuimo zhi...''* (lit., ''rain rises, the water's spray [or foam] approaches...''); all other ancient readings have been *''shang yushui, mozhi.''*

The supposition in this line is that a large amount of rainwater has rushed down, so that currents naturally appear in the flow and it is no longer safe to ford, which is why the next line says "halt crossing until the water is still." The Linyi text is therefore easier to understand here than the later versions' renditions.[12]

Cao Cao followed the later versions and annotated, "One fears that when halfway across, the water will suddenly rise." While this certainly is worth keeping in mind, this line of *Sun-tzu* describes water that has already risen, so one should ascertain when the flow has subsided before crossing.

12. "Generally, if terrain consists of severed ravines, gigantic pits, gigantic prisons, gigantic coops, gigantic traps, and gigantic rifts" in the Chinese text reads *"fan di you juejian,*[13] *tianjing, tianlao, tianluo, tianxian, tianxi.'"*[14] The explanations for these various terrains change with each annotator, so we have listed them below:

(i) Severed ravines *(juejian)*: "Have deep mountains and vast waters" (Cao Cao). "Two banks which are deep, widely separated, and impassable" (Jia

[12]*Yinqueshan Hanmu zhujian "Sunzi bingfa"* says, "The *Taiping yulan,* vol. 306 [note: 'Bingbu 37'], quotes this as *'shan yushui, shuimo zhi,'* repeating the character *shui,* as does the Linyi text," and "we suspect that *mo* 沫 is an incorrect form of the character *liu* 流" (p. 69).

However, based on our observations in ancient writings, we conclude that *mo* (lit., "foam") should indicate the spray stirred up by the currents. A very clear illustration of this can be seen in the *Liezi,* which has the line "Confucius went sightseeing at the Lü cliffs; the waterfall was tens of meters [high] and there was flowing *mo* for tens of miles" (vol. 2, "Huangdi" 2, p. 5a). *Mo* here indicates what the currents had created by colliding with each other; as it was carried along by the currents, this was referred to as *liumo* (flowing spray).

Furthermore, the second definition of the character *pu* (commonly, "waterfall") in the *Shuowen* is *mo* (11 *shang,* p. 562); Duan Yucai's note quotes Ma Rong's "Changdifu" (*Wenxuan,* vol. 18, p. 322) that it meant "sprayed *mo*" and explained that this was "*mo* leaping on the waters." In the *Wenxuan,* (Tang) Lü Xiang annotated this line, "the ferocity of water spews forth *mo*." These descriptions show that *mo* is the spray produced by breaking waves.

Today *mo* means "foam"; but if it is read as meaning "foam" here, this not only disagrees with its ancient definition, it also makes the line difficult to understand. From the above discussion we can further comprehend that *mo* was merely a different edition's version, rather than a misreading of *liu.*

[13]Wang Xi postulated that *"juejian"* should actually read *"jue tianjian"* (lit., "cross over gigantic valleys"), since, he announced, the character *tian* had been lost; however, we cannot agree with him. The rest of this sentence reads "one must strive to skirt them and never go near" (p. 81), so why discuss "crossing over" here?

[14]This reading follows the later versions; the extant part of Linyi text has slight variations in the characters, but its meaning is the same.

Lin). "Deep and precipitous to the front and rear, with waters crossing between them" (Mei Yaochen). "Deep, precipitous valleys that are uncrossable" (Zhang Yu).

(ii) Gigantic pits *(tianjing):* "High in every direction but depressed in the center" (Cao Cao). "The terrain cups down and vast waters collect there" (Du Mu). "The center is sunken" (Jia Lin). "Steep slopes in every direction with a valley in the center" (Mei Yaochen). "High on the outside and low in the center, where all the water accumulates" (Zhang Yu).

(iii) Gigantic prisons *(tianlao):* "Where deep mountains may be transversed; like a cage" (Cao Cao). "Compressed mountain valleys which can cut off passage" (Du Mu). "Valleys in every direction that are difficult, interspersed with water and grasses, with a sloping center, and with both entry and exit arduous" (Jia Lin). "Surrounded in three directions; easy to enter but difficult to exit" (Mei Yaochen). "Like a jail" (Wang Xi). "Exacting surrounding mountain terrain with a narrow entrance" (Zhang Yu).

(iv) Gigantic coops *(tianluo):* "Capable of cooping someone up" (Cao Cao). "Densely covered with forests; deep and far-reaching reeds" (Du Mu). "Rough and twisting roads, partly wide, partly narrow; must inch along and be inconvenienced; hard to walk in" (Jia Lin). "Densely covered with grasses and woods; hard to use blades and arrows" (Mei Yaochen). "Like a net or coop" (Wang Xi). "Tangled trees and with dense reeds" (Zhang Yu).

(v) Gigantic traps *(tianxian):* "Caved-in terrain" (Cao Cao). "Valley's water clear and wide with an unfathomable depth; paths are muddy, impassable to men and horses" (Du Mu). "Marsh-filled land" (Jia Lin). "Low and muddy, impassable to chariots and horses" (Mei Yaochen). "This means those places full of ditches, sinks, and mud" (Wang Xi). "Moors and mudflats in which chariots will founder and horses cannot find their footing" (Zhang Yu).

(vi) Gigantic rifts *(tianxi):* "Paths in the valley are compressed, terrain is several meters deep, and the length is several tens of meters long" (Cao Cao). "Terrain filled with ditches and sinks; the depressions have wood and rocks" (Du Mu). "Difficult and widely separated on both sides; narrow and long slopes for several miles; passage difficult in the middle; both entrance and exit blockable'' (Jia Lin). ''Two mountains facing each other; a tunnel-like path that is compressed and treacherous'' (Wang Xi). ''The path is compressed and the land is full of caves and sinks'' (Zhang Yu).

In conclusion, we can see that these all are extremely disadvantageous types of terrain for conducting combat. We have followed the literal character definitions for our interpretations here.

Tian (heavenly) and *da* (large; gigantic) had analogous meanings and were interchangeable in pre-Qin times, so *tian* can be read as meaning ''gigantic'' here.[15]

13. ''In army maneuvers, where obstacles, flooded lowlands, tall reeds, mountain forests, or thick vegetation lie and could be used for hiding, carefully reconnoiter and search them—hidden enemies might be positioned there'' in the Chinese text reads ''*junxing you xianzu, huangjing, jiawei, shanlin, yihui, kefunizhe, jin fu suo zhi—jian zhi suochu ye.*''

13a. ''*Junxing*'' (in army maneuvers) follows the *Shiyijia*. The Linyi text is damaged at this point, while the *Wujing* and Sakurada versions read ''*junpang*'' (by the armies). Sun Xingyan and Wu Renji's criticism says that this should read ''*junpang,*''[16] but their view is erroneous: reconnoitering and searching should be completed before the armies arrive; waiting for this to be done ''by the armies'' would be too late.

13b. ''*Shanlin*'' (mountain forests) follows the later versions; the Linyi text reads ''thickets'' *(xiaolin)*. The next phrase, ''thick vegetation'' *(yihui)*, encompasses thickets, so we do not follow the Linyi text here.

[15]The *Guangya* says that ''*tian* means large'' (1 *shang*, ''Shigu,'' p. 1b); Wang Niangsun's annotation. Also, *Zhuangzi* has the line ''solely fulfill his *tian*'' (vol. 2, ''Dechongfu,'' p. 23a); Lu Deming explained, ''In Cui's version, the character *tian* is read *da*'' (*Jingdian shiwen*, vol. 26, ''Zhuangzi yinyi'' *shang*, p. 372). Furthermore, Yu Shengwu said, ''*Tian* and *da* were interchangeable in ancient times'' (*Xunzi xinzheng*, vol. 1, under the line ''*qi de tian sha*'' [*Zhuzi xinzheng*, p. 252]).

[16]*Shijia*, vol. 9, p. 11b.

13c. *"Kefunizhe"* (could be used for hiding) follows the Linyi text; the other versions do not have this line.

13d. *"Jian zhi suochu ye"* (hidden enemies might be positioned there) follows the Linyi text; the other versions differ slightly.[17] *"Jian"* (originally, "evil-doer")[18] here means "hidden enemies."

14. "Where they situate is on level ground: this indicates possible advantages" in the Chinese text reads *"qi suojuzhe yi, li ye"* and follows the Linyi text.[19] Du Mu noted, "This says that the enemy is not situated in barriers but on a level area, which must expedite their actions." Zhao Benxue explained, "When setting a camp or deploying arrays, a reliance on barriers makes sense. On the other hand, when leaving barriers and situating on level ground, there could very possibly be unexpected forces to the rear."[20]

15. "Pincer movement" in the Chinese text reads *"fu."* In basic military terminology, this character indicates "ambush troops."[21] But since the preceding line already discusses ambush, this *fu* must indicate something else. *Fu* in pre-Qin times could also describe how a round net was cast over something, as in capturing an entire army.[22] We therefore interpret it as a "pincer movement."

[17]The *Wujing* and Sakurada versions read *"ci fujian zhi suo ye"* (these are where the hidden enemies are), the *Shiyijia* reads *"suo"* as *"suochu"* (are positioned), and the *Shijia* reads *"suocangchu"* (the hiding place).

[18]*Shuowen,* 12 *xia,* "Jian," p. 632; Duan Yucai's note. The later versions all read this as *"fujian"* and follow Zhang Yu's interpretation: "[the enemy's] ambush troops or spies."

[19]The *Wujing, Shiyijia,* and Sakurada versions all read *"juzhe yi"* as *"juyi zhe."* Sun Xingyan and Wu Renji pointed out this error, saying it should read *"juzhe yi"* (*Shijia,* vol. 9, p. 13a). Their correction matches this line in the Linyi text.

[20]*Sunzi shu jiaojie yinlei, zhong,* p. 78a.

[21]E.g., the *Zuozhuan* records, "wait for them with three *fu*" (vol. 4, "Yingong jiunian" [*Shisanjing,* p. 3762]; Du Yu noted, "*Fu* means 'ambush troops' ").

[22]The *Zuozhuan* records, "*Fu* and defeat them is to seize someone's troops" (vol. 9, "Zhuanggong shiyinian" [*Shisanjing,* p. 3838]); Kong Yingda's annotation.
Cao Cao noted, "The enemy expands their arrays and swells their flanks in order to *fu* us." Zhang Yu wrote, "They must have come through the obstacles, grasses, and woods, so the animals are startled and fearfully run away." Li Quan disagreed, writing, "To come unexpectedly is called *fu,*" but the source for his assumption cannot be found in either character definitions or pre-Qin records.

16. "Firewood is being cut and collected" in the Chinese text reads *"qiaocai."* Li Quan altered this to read "firewood is coming" *(xinlai),* but this is problematic.[23]

17. "Camp is being set" in the Chinese text reads *"yingjun." Jun* indicates "camp."[24] *Ying* means *zhi* (to manage; to set up).[25]

18. "When running about and arraying forces, this indicates a joint operation" in the Chinese text reads *"benzou zhenbing zhe, qi ye"* and follows the Linyi text; the Sakurada version is the same. The *Wujing* has an extra *er* (and; then) character between *zou* and *zhen;* the *Shiyijia* reads *"zhenbingju"* (to deploy forces and chariots) instead of *"zhenbing."* Zhao Benxue has already pointed out that the character *ju* should not be used here.[26]

Qi means "an engagement." When all troops are engaged, this indicates a large action is being conducted, so we interpret it as "a joint operation."[27] Even today, when the enemy constantly moves its troops, we know that there will soon be a large-scale attack.

19. "When partially advancing, this indicates a lure" in the Chinese text reads *"banjin zhe, you ye"* and follows the Linyi text. The later versions read "when partially

[23]Li Quan made this change because of an event that happened during the Spring and Autumn Period: "Regarding the phenomena of smoke and dust," Li said, "when Jin's troops invaded Qi, they dragged firewood behind them. The Qi people ascended a mountain to observe them and were fearful of the numbers of their legions, so [they] escaped by night."
There are two difficulties with his story. First, in the example he gave the dust should have been high, strong, and broad, rather than what *Sun-tzu* refers to here as "streaked and scattered." Second, when something that can be used "is coming," such as tea, rice, or firewood, the inherent Chinese meaning is that it will be served. So, the example he gave not only is totally unrelated to what is being discussed here, it is simply absurd. This in turn greatly misled some careless readers, who twisted it into "deceptive warfare."

[24]See Book 7, comment 3, footnote 7.

[25]The *Shijing* recorded, "The Count of Cao *ying* it" (vol. 15, "Xiaoya: Yuzao series: Shumiao" [*Shisanjing*, p. 1064]); Mao Heng's note.

[26]*Sunzi shu jiaojie yinlei, zhong*, p. 82a.

[27]*Shuowen*, 7 *shang*, "Qi," p. 317; Duan Yucai's note. Li Quan wrote, "Battles are scheduled and are about to be exercised, so they run about." Jia Lin also noted, "Running about will not occur during regular schedules, so this must be because remote forces are about to enter; the schedule has a countdown; they will certainly unite in attacking us, and we should quickly make preparations."

advancing and partially withdrawing, this indicates a lure" ("banjin bantui zhe; you ye"). A partial advance is an attempt to make the enemy approach, and it always includes an easy withdrawal. This easy withdrawal cannot be perceived by the enemy, or how could they be "lured"? We therefore know that the phrase "partially withdrawing" in the later versions was an addition. If one talks about advancing and also retreating, this only adds to the reader's confusion; no wonder previous annotators all mistook this as an example of a "chaotic appearance." If it were not for the Linyi text, this line probably would never have been correctly understood.

20. "Water details" in the Chinese text reads "jiyi" and follows the Linyi text. The later versions read "ji er" (draw water and), so while this is close to the Linyi text, it is not as clear.[28]

21. "Exhaustion" in the Chinese text reads "lao" and follows the later versions. The Linyi text reads "laojuan." Lao and juan commonly are understood to have the same meaning, but, strictly speaking, they connote different types of fatigue.[29] Lao describes physical exhaustion, while juan means mental weariness, so juan is unnecessary in this line of Sun-tzu. Moreover, a few lines later Sun-tzu says, "When officers are enraged, this indicates mental weariness" ("li nu zhe, juan ye").

22. "When horses are fed grain, meat is eaten, and the army no longer has water jars or returns to its encampment, this indicates desperate foes" in the Chinese text reads "shuma roushi, jun wu xuanchui, bufan qishe zhe, qiongkou ye" and fol-

[28]Sun Xingyan and Wu Renji pointed out that both the Tongdian (note: vol. 150, "Bing" 3, p. 788) and the Taiping yulan (note: vol. 291, "Bing bu" 22, p. 1347) quoted this as "jiyi" (water details); yi in the Taiping yulan was mistakenly in the form of she (lit., "to establish"). However, the Changduanjing quoted this as "ji er" (vol. 9, "Liaodi" [Hanhai congshu, p. 1198]), which is identical to the later versions.

[29]The Lunyu has the line "[Yan Yuan said,] 'will not apply lao' "; Huang Kan's annotation indicates that lao means laoyi (physical labor) (Jijie edition, vol. 3, "Gongzhichang," p. 50).
The Lunyu also says, "Zigong asked about governing. Confucius said, 'Be the first one to start, then lao zhi [put them to work].' When asked for clarification, Confucius said, 'Wujuan' [have no weariness]' "; Huang Kan's annotation says that juan means xiejuan (mental weariness) (Jijie edition, vol. 7, "Zilu," p. 129). From these two descriptions we can plainly see the differences between these two characters.

lows the *Shiyijia*. The first half of this line is missing from the Linyi text. Both the *Wujing* and the Sakurada versions read "when horses are killed and meat is eaten, this indicates the army no longer has provisions; when water jars are not returned to their encampments, this indicates desperate foes" (*"shama roushi zhe, jun wuliang ye; xuanchui bufan qishe zhe, qiongkou ye"*).[30]

With the exception of Li Quan, all of the ancient annotators refer to the *Shiyijia*'s rendering of the text, so such versions as the *Wujing* are not followed here.

23. "When disorderly and shirking, but words are spoken guardedly" in the Chinese text reads *"junjun xixi, xuyan ruru zhe, shizhong ye."* *"Junjun"* indicates the soldiers' "disorder,"[31] while *"xixi"* indicates that they "shirk their duties."[32] *"Xuyan ruru"* means that the officers "speak carefully" to avoid their men's displeasure.[33]

24. "Be certain to regard this cautiously" in the Chinese text reads *"bijincha ci"* and follows the Linyi text. The later versions read *"ci"* (this) as *"zhi"* (it), which has a similar meaning, but *"zhi"* does not connote as powerful a mood as the Linyi text's version.

[30]The *Tongdian* (vol. 150, "Bing" 3, p. 788), *Taiping yulan* (vol. 291, "Bing bu" 22, p. 1346), and the *Changduanjing* (vol. 9, "Liaodi" [*Hanhai congshu*, p. 1198]), though, all record this line in the same way as the *Shiyijia*.

[31]*Erya*, vol. 4, "Shixun" (*Shisanjing*, p. 5628).

[32]See the *Erya*, the line *"xixi, bugongzhi ye"* (vol. 4, "Shixun disan" [*Shisanjing*, p. 5630]). The Linyi text reads this as *"jianjian"* (jian, lit., "a gap"), but it is uncertain what this phase actually means here. *Zhuangzi* describes it as "minor knowledge focusing on individual matters" (vol. 1, "Qi-wulun," p. 11b; Guo Xiang's note). Yu Yue said that *jianjian* probably meant "to spy on others" (Wang Xianqian's Jijie edition, p. 7, quoting from the *Zhuzi pingyi*).

[33]This reading follows Sun Xingyan and Wu Renji's criticisms (*Shijia*, vol. 9, p. 22a). The later versions all read this line as *"xu yu ren yan zhe"* (when gently speaking to others). However, Sun and Wu corrected this to *"xuyan ruru"* by following the *Tongdian* (note: vol. 150, "Bing" 3, p. 788; the current edition reads this as *"xuyan renru"*) and the *Taiping yulan* (note: vol. 291, "Bing bu" 22, p. 1347). The *Changduanjing* quotes this line of *Sun-tzu* as *"xuyan ruru"* (vol. 9, "Liaodi" [*Hanhai congshu*, p. 1198]), which serves to bolster Sun and Wu's viewpoint.

In the Linyi text, the remnant of this line reads "___ yan ren zhe" (lit., "___ say about someone"), so the meaning is unclear.

As for *"ruru,"* Sun and Wu noted that it meant a careful or cautious manner. Zhang Binlin pointed out that in ancient times *"ru"* meant *"na"* (tongue-tied) ("Wenshi" 2 [*Zhangzhi congshu*, p. 77]). We modified the description in this paragraph of *Sun-tzu* to interpret *"ruru"* accordingly.

25. "They still will be useless" in the Chinese text reads *"ze bukeyong ye"* and follows the later versions. The Linyi text reads *"ze buyong"* (lit., "then not use"), which omits the character *"ke"* (will be).

26. "So, unite them through benevolence and regulate them through strictness— these ensure internalized discipline" in the Chinese text reads *"gu, he zhi yi wen, qi zhi yi wu—shiwei biqu."*

26a. *"Gu, he zhi yi wen, qi zhi yi wu"* follows the Linyi text.[34] Cao Cao noted, *"Wen* [lit., 'literary'] means benevolence, while *wu* [lit., 'martial'] means rules." The *Shangjunshu*[35] records, "All those with rewards are *wen,* and all those with punishments are *wu."* We know, then, that in the pre-Qin period the character *wen* was used to indicate "a kind method,"[36] and *wu* was used to indicate "a strict method."

26b. As for *"shiwei biqu,"* the preceding line shows that *"qu"* (lit., "to take") concerns soldiers. A description of *qu* can be found in *Guanzi*[37]: "If rewards and punishments are not effectively meted out, then the people will not have *qu."* His ensuing text describes what he meant by *qu:* "When rewards and punishments are meted out where they can be seen, then even when they cannot be seen, will they be challenged?" and "when rewards and punishments are not meted out where they can be seen, to expect improvement to occur when they cannot be seen is impossible." This shows

---

[34]The later versions read *he* (to unite) as *ling* (to order). The preceding text discusses the importance of bonds with soldiers, so *he* is correct, while *ling* was a misreading of this character.

This line is quoted identically to the Linyi text in *Huainanzi* (vol. 15, "Binglue," p. 265), *Beitang shuchao* (vol. 113, "Lun bing" 1, p. 499), and *Taiping yulan* (vol. 296, "Bing bu" 27, p. 1364).

Wen in the Linyi text has the form of *jiao* (lit., "to cross"). Actually, *wen*'s basic definition is "crossed strokes" (*Shuowen*, 9 *shang*, p. 429). This could therefore have been either the miswriting of a similar character or an ancient, unconventional character form.

[35]Vol. 3, "Xiuquan," p. 49.

[36]The *Guoyu* has the lines "chariots have a puissant *wu"* (Wei Zhao defined *wu* as *wei* [omnipotence]) and "[when] the masses are subordinate, it is *wen"* (vol. 10, "Jinyu" 8, p. 10b); this indicates having the morality of *wen,* which causes the populace to follow.

[37]Vol. 1, "Quanxiu," p. 6.

that *qu* is the automatic observance of rules,[38] so we interpret it as "internalized discipline."

Internalized discipline can only assure efficiency; but the achievement of victory requires far more than just this. Some annotators did not ascertain the correct interpretation for *qu* and instead explained this as meaning that "victory is certain." This definition is problematic. Not only has *qu* never had the meaning of "victory is certain," but victory cannot be ascertained only through rewards and punishments.

27. "The ingrained execution of orders" in these three lines reads *"ling suxing"*[39] in the Chinese text. It is conceivable that in ancient times other versions read this as *"ling sushen"* (the ingrained effectiveness of orders).[40]

[38]The previous line from *Guanzi* says, "when the people are many but soldiers are weak, it is because the people do not have *qu*" ("Quanxiu," p. 6); Yin Zhizhang noted that *qu* meant *quze* (lit., "to choose rules"), which indicates when the people automatically heed the rules. His definition agrees with our discussion.

[39]Sun Xingyan and Wu Renji's criticism here (*Shijia,* vol. 9, p. 26b) notes that the second of these three lines, *"ling busuxing"* (fail to establish the ingrained execution of orders) (p. 87), is quoted in both the *Tongdian* (note: vol.. 149, "Bing" 2, p. 779) and the *Taiping yulan* (note: vol. 296, "Bing bu" 27, "Faling," p. 1364) as *"ling su buxing"* (orders fail to establish ingrained execution).

Only the character *"su"* of this line is extant in the Linyi text, and it is located at the beginning of the line, so it probably was written *"su buxing,"* thereby omitting the character *"ling"* (order).

[40]*Sun Bin bingfa* records, "The King of Wei asked, 'How can the people be made to have ingrained obedience?' Sun [Bin]-tzu replied, '*Sushen*' [ingrained effectiveness; *shen* today is read *xin*]" ("Weiwang wen," p. 41). His answer uses the same viewpoint as the text of *Sun-tzu* under discussion here, and the employment of the character *shen* (effectiveness) is worth noting.

Also, Sun Xingyan and Wu Renji's criticism notes that the third of these lines, *"ling suxing zhe"* (the ingrained execution of orders) (p. 87), should be changed to read *"ling su xinzhu zhe"* (the conduct of orders is known to always be reliable); they cite as proof the *Tongdian* (note: vol. 149, "Bing" 2, p. 779), the *Taiping yulan* (note: vol. 296, "Bing bu" 27, "Faling," p. 1364), and the annotations of Du Mu, Chen Hao, Zhang Yu, and others. However, we suspect that *zhu* was a later addition.

COMMENTS ON BOOK 10

TERRAIN[1]

1. "Barbed" in the Chinese text reads *"guazhe"* (lit., "the barbed one"). This is self-interpreted by *Sun-tzu* here as "where advance is possible but return is inexpedient" (p. 88). *Sun-tzu*'s intent was originally quite clear, but Mei Yaochen wrote in his annotation, "Terrain like a net: will be entangled when entered." This distorted the meaning into "advance is possible, but return is impossible," which was not what *Sun-tzu* intended.[2]

2. "Be ready at the gorge mouth to await the enemy" in the Chinese text reads *"biying zhi yi dai di."* Cao Cao noted, "Must be in front, flush with the gorge mouth; deploy arrays and defend it." This follows the definition of *ying* (full).[3]

3. "Hunt for them" in the Chinese text reads *"cong zhi."*[4] *Cong* (lit., "to go after") indicates "to go and attack an enemy in an inferior situation."[5]

4. "Heavens or the terrains" in the Chinese text reads *"tian di"* and follows the *Wujing* and Sakurada versions; the *Shiyijia* reads this as simply *"tian"* (the heavens). The purpose of this line is to act as a bridge between the preceding and

[1]All of Book 10 is missing from the Linyi text.

[2]As a result, a few scholars have interpreted this term of *Sun-tzu* as "entangling" or "entrapping," both of which are obviously incorrect.

[3]When a vessel is full, it is filled to the rim or mouth; see *Shuowen*, 5 *shang*, "Ying," p. 214.

[4]Earlier in this line, the Chinese text reads *"wucong"* (do not hunt [for them]), with the object *"zhi"* (them) omitted; *"cong zhi"* (hunt for them) is the regular pattern here.

[5]E.g., the *Shujing* records, "The Xia troops lost the battle; Tang then *cong* them" (vol. 8, "Shangshu: Tangshi" [*Shisanjing*, p. 340]); Kong Anguo noted, "*Cong* means 'to chase and fight with them.'"

succeeding text. The preceding text discusses "the terrain" but not "the heavens," so the *Wujing*'s reading is preferable.[6]

5. "What they might do" in the Chinese text reads "*qi neng.*" *Neng* is basically defined as "ability," so it is "what can be achieved." This is interpreted accordingly to fit both the context and *Sun-tzu*'s description here.

6. "The duties of the spearhead force's commander" in the Chinese text reads "*shangjiang zhi shou ye.*"[7]

7. "A commander" was originally omitted in the Chinese text as it was understood from the context, but is included in the English interpretation for clarity.

8. "Soldiers who are treated kindly but cannot be ordered, cared for but cannot be employed" in the Chinese text reads "*ai er buneng ling, hou er buneng shi*" and follows the *Wujing* and Sakurada versions. In the *Shiyijia* the order of the two parts in this line is reversed.

9. "By perceiving the geographical factors and perceiving the cyclic natural occurrences, victory thereby is complete" in the Chinese text reads "*zhi di, zhi tian, sheng naikequan.*"

    9a. "By perceiving the geographical factors and perceiving the cyclic natural occurrences" ("*zhi di, zhi tian*") follows the *Taiping yulan*'s records.[8] The *Wujing*, *Shiyijia*, and Sakurada versions all read "*zhi tian, zhi di.*"

[6]The first discussion on this can be found in Zhao Benxue's *Sunzi shu jiaojie yinlei* (*xia*, p. 6a); under this line the annotation reads, "One version does not have '*di*' [terrains], which is incorrect." Next to this line the discussion in large type says, " '*Tian*' [the heavens] possibly is extraneous." *Tian* indeed is very possibly a later addition.

[7]For *shangjiang* (lit., "commander of the upper army") see Book 7, comment 5. For *shou*, see Book 1, comment 12b. *Shou* is commonly read *dao* (lit., "the way").

[8]This discussion follows Sun Xingyan and Wu Renji's criticism (*Shijia*, vol. 10, p. 16a) that the line here can be seen in the *Taiping yulan* (vol. 322, "Bing bu" 53, p. 1480). They also mentioned Du You's annotation in which he says, "know the terrain's advantages; know the heavens' timing," which has "*di*" first and "*tian*" second.

9b. "Victory is thereby complete" *("sheng naikequan")* follows the *Wujing* and Sakurada versions. The *Shiyijia* reads this as "victory will be unlimited" *("sheng naibuqiong"),* which is incorrect.[9]

Sun and Wu pointed out that the *Tongdian* (note: vol. 150, "Bing" 3, p. 785) and Du You's annotation both concluded this line with *"sheng naikequan"* (victory thereby is complete), so that the last character of the previous phrase is *"tian,"* and the last character of this phrase is *"quan,"* which were rhymes (*Shijia,* vol. 10, p. 16a).

In addition to Sun and Wu's discussion, the *Changduanjing* also records the beginning of this line as *"zhi di, zhi tian"* (vol. 9, "Tianshi" [*Hanhai congshu,* p. 1182]).

[9]This follows the discussion by Sun Xingyan and Wu Renji (*Shijia,* vol. 10, p. 16a).

THE NINE ZONES

1. The names for these nine zones all follow the self-descriptions given below in *Sun-tzu*. However, the interpretation of "susceptible zones" *("qingdi")* and "dominant zones" *("zhongdi")* necessitates explanation.

Regarding *qingdi* (lit., "light zones"), *Hanfeizi* pointed out that "the lack of power is *qing*."[1] Later on in the text *Sun-tzu* says, "Where the adversary's land is shallowly penetrated is *qing*" (p. 94). When troops are in this situation, their lack of sufficient combat power or depth of defense can allow them to be easily routed or defeated. Their condition is therefore vulnerable, so we interpret it accordingly.

Zhongdi (lit., "heavy zones") is the opposite of *qingdi*. Because it describes forceful positions, we interpret it accordingly.

Cao Cao thought that *qing* indicated "where soldiers could lightly desert," and scholars generally have followed his explanation. His interpretation, though, concerns training in military discipline rather than strategy.[2] Quite a few discrepancies exist between the nine zones' self-descriptions and Cao's explanations.

The seventh of these nine zones is "compartmentalized zones" *("pidi")*, which follows the later versions. This part is undecipherable in the Linyi text.[3]

---

[1]Vol. 7, "Yulao," p. 116.

[2]This opinion of Cao's probably was influenced by "Queries on the Nine Zones"; see Appendix 6.

[3]*Yinqueshan Hanmu zhujian "Sunzi bingfa"* (typeset edition, pp. 76 and 79) asserts that this reads *"fandi"* (lit., "floating zones"), but the string-bound edition of the same book (p. 132b) says, "In the bamboo-slat version this character is illegible." Hattori Chiharu's *Sonshi hyōhō kōkai* includes an appendix on the bamboo slats from the Han tomb at Linyi (p. 18); among the extant characters visible in this line is *di* (zones), but its preceding character is undecipherable, so the actual character cannot be determined.

2. "Where a lord conducts battles in his individual sector is separated" in the Chinese text reads *"zhuhou zhan qi di zhe wei san"* and follows the Linyi text.[4] *Zhan* (to conduct battles) in the later versions reads *zizhan* (to conduct their own battles). The line quoted in the *Shiji* (see below) is the same as that in the Linyi text, so we know this was the pre-Qin form.

Cao Cao noted, "Warriors and foot soldiers miss their [own] land; when the route [home] is near, they easily scatter." His explanation was possibly affected by the meaning of the character *san* (lit., "to scatter"), as well as the line later in this book, "with shallow positions come dispersion" (p. 101), so Cao was giving a strained interpretation.

But in fact, this line from *Sun-tzu* clearly states "where a lord conducts battles in his individual sector" and makes no mention of warriors and foot soldiers. In pre-Qin times, feudal lords commonly conducted joint military operations, but because of the terrain's containment in "separated zones" (*"sandi"*), the lords could not but conduct battle separately and were unable to synchronize. In this type of zone, armies were in danger of being individually destroyed by their common enemy. That is why the text later says, "with separated zones, do not battle" (p. 95), as attempting to form a united front is the primary task in such zones. The *Shiji*[5] records,

[Jing Bu] crossed the Huai [River] to assault Chu. Chu sent forces between the Xu and Tong [areas] in preparation for the battle. Three armies were formed; they planned to support each other in the conduct of irregular actions. Someone advised the Chu com-

---

The term *pidi* in the *Changduanjing* reads "sidi" (vol. 9, "Dixing" [*Hanhai congshu*, p. 1183]). *Si* here basically has two meanings: "water breaking on a bank and returning" and "a land-locked body of water" (*Shuowen*, 11 *shang*, p. 558). Jia Lin described this term of *Sun-tzu* as "destroyed by water," and Zhang Yu annotated it as "a water-logged area," both of which fit the *Changduanjing*'s reading. However, *Sun-tzu* described *pidi* as "where there is a maneuverable mountain forest, obstacle, or swamp, and the passes are difficult to forge" (p. 95), so *sidi* obviously is not compatible here.

Pi is defined as *hui* (broken) (*Shuowen*, 13 *xia*, p. 697); zones that have "broken" terrain are those with mountain forests, obstacles, swamps, and difficult passes, so we interpret this as "compartmentalized."

[4]In the later versions, the ensuing nine descriptions of the different types of zones all have the character *di* (zone) at the end of each line. However, from *Sun-tzu*'s sentence structure we can see that each line acts as a self-definition of that zone's characteristics. Since these describe their characteristics, the character *di* was not necessary, and so we do not follow the later versions here.

[5]Vol. 91, "Jing Bu Liezhuan," pp. 918–19.

manders, "[Jing] Bu is sophisticated at using forces; the people are always in fear of him. Moreover, the strategic book has 'where a lord conducts battles in his individual sector is a separated zone' ['zhuhou zhan qi di wei sandi']. Now we are separated into three (armies), so when he defeats one of our armies, the rest will flee. How would we be able to support each other?" This was not heeded. [Jing] Bu then in fact destroyed one of their armies, and their [other] two armies dispersed and fled.

This record proves that our discussion here is correct.

3. "Where a lord's land converges with many places" in the Chinese text reads "zhuhou zhi di sanshu." Shu means hui (to converge).[6] San (lit., "three") indicates many,[7] so "di sanshu" was another way of saying "a land converges with many places." Since the basic definition of qu in "qudi" (key traffic zone) is "where every place can be reached" ("sida"),[8] this gives us a better understanding of what sanshu means.

Whenever a zone is described as sanshu, it contains a large metropolis commonly frequented for business. This is the reason why at the end of this sentence in the text it is described as "if reached first will win major support among all the countries." However, Cao Cao interpreted this as meaning, "When we are equal with the enemy, and on the perimeter are other countries," while Mengshi said, "[This is] just as Zheng shares its borders with Qi, Chu, and Jin." These explanations not only ignore the ancient use of "three" to mean "many," but they also did not clearly ascertain the meaning of qu in qudi (key traffic zone).

4. "Where there is a maneuverable mountain forest, obstacle, or swamp and the passes are difficult to forge is compartmentalized" in the Chinese text reads "xing shanlin, xianzu, juze, fan nanxing zhi dao zhe wei pi" and follows the Shiyijia. The Linyi text has "maneuverable" (xing)[9] but not "obstacle" (xianzu); both the Wu-

---

[6]E.g., Mengzi records, "And then shu his aged people and inform them" (vol. 2, "Lianghuiwang" xia [Shisanjing, p. 5826]); Zhao Qi's note.

[7]Wang Zhong noted in his Shuxue, "When unable to fully express [something] using 'one' or 'two,' then signify it with 'three' to show that there are many." He also said, "This word is an abstract number" ("Neipian: Shi san jiu" shang, p. 2a); see Book 4, comment 5, footnote 13.

[8]Shuowen, 2 xia, p. 78.

[9]Our interpretation is based on the Shuowen: "Xing means people's gaits" (2 xia, p. 78).

jing and Sakurada versions have "obstacle" but not "maneuverable." They all have "the passes are difficult to forge" *("fan nanxing zhi dao")*.

"Mountain forests, obstacles, and swamps" can either be passed with great difficulty or impossible to pass at all; the character *xing* (maneuverable), though, points out that passes can exist, and it also acts as a response to "are difficult to forge." We therefore know that the *Wujing* and other versions overlooked the first character of this line, *"xing."*[10]

5. "Where fierce combat leads to survival but lack of fierce combat leads to destruction is lethal" in the Chinese text reads *"jizhan ze cun, bujizhan ze wang zhe wei si"* and follows the later versions.[11] The Linyi text reads *"ji ze cun, buji ze wang zhe wei si"* (where fierceness leads to survival and lack of fierceness leads to destruction is lethal) and omits the two *zhan* (combat) characters. Later on *Sun-tzu* says, "with lethal zones, conduct battles" *("sidi ze zhan")* (p. 96), so zones that are described as "lethal" are where combat must occur; therefore, the two *zhan* characters were erroneously dropped in the Linyi text.

6. "With dually traversable zones, do not leave gaps" in the Chinese text reads *"jiaodi ze wujue."* Cao Cao interpreted this as "mutually connected to each other." Since *jiaodi* are where the enemy may come, we should defend against their penetrating our gaps, as they would thereby block our troop connection and mutual support.

7. "With key traffic zones, strengthen diplomacy" in the Chinese text reads *"qudi ze hejiao"* and follows the *Wujing* and Sakurada versions. This line in the Linyi text is missing. The *Shiyijia* reads *hejiao* as *jiaohe*.[12] Cao Cao noted that *hejiao* meant "consolidating the feudal lords."

---

[10]Zhao Benxue noted, "In one edition is the character *'xing'* before *'shan'* [mountain], which is incorrect" (*Sunzi shu jiaojie yinlei, xia*, p. 22b), so his conclusion differs from ours.

[11]"Lethal" *(si)* here is not read "lethal terrain" *(sidi)*, since it has the same sentence pattern as the foregoing sentences; see also comment 2, footnote 4.

[12]Sun Xingyan and Wu Renji's criticism points out that *"jiaohe"* is incorrect (*Shijia*, vol. 11, p. 10b).

8. "Those who long ago were known as sophisticated at battle could make adversaries in conflict" in the Chinese text reads *"suowei gu shanzhanzhe, neng shi diren"* and follows the Linyi text.

8a. *"Shanzhanzhe"* ([those] sophisticated at battle) in the later versions reads *"shanyongbingzhe"* (those sophisticated at using forces), so its meaning is very similar. From the ensuing description in the text, however, we know that the situation under discussion concerns the conduct of conflict, thus the Linyi text is more accurate here.

8b. *"Diren"* (adversaries in conflict) is the same in every version. In modern Chinese this term means "enemy," but in *Sun-tzu* an enemy is referred to simply as *di*, not *diren*. The succeeding section's discussion concerns our engaging the enemy in battle, so we understand that *diren* was meant to indicate "the adversary who engages us in conflict."

9. "If the enemy is numerous and is advancing in well-ordered arrays" in the Chinese text reads *"dizhong yi zheng jianglai"* and follows the Linyi text. The later versions read *"dizhong zheng er jianglai"* (if the enemy is numerous, in well-ordered arrays, and advancing), so the meaning is similar.[13]

10. "The nature of forces" in the Chinese text reads *"bing zhi qing."* *Qing* here means "nature."[14]

---

[13]*Zheng* is written differently in the Linyi text and the later versions; in the Linyi text it literally means "straight," and in the later versions it literally means "even." These two characters were interchangeable in ancient times (see Zhu Junsheng's *Shuowen tongxun dingsheng*, "Ding" 17, "Zheng," p. 866). This term was used to describe a large army ready for battle, so it naturally meant "well-ordered arrays."

[14]E.g., the *Lüshi Chunqiu* has the line "this is called accommodating *qing*" (vol. 19, "Lisulan: Shangde," Gao You's note, p. 6a).

Following this phrase is *"zhusu"* (predominantly swiftness). *Su* (swiftness) in ancient times was also written as *shuo* (lit., "constantly," with the form of the character meaning "number"; the Linyi text follows this reading), and the two characters were interchangeable (*Erya*, vol. 2, "Shigu" *xia* [*Shisanjing*, p. 5593]).

11. "Invader" and "defender" in the Chinese text read, respectively, *"ke"* and *"zhu-ren"* (or *"zhu"*), which were archaic military terms.[15]

12. "And with death, how can our warriors' perseverance not be had?" in the Chinese text reads *"si, yan bude shiren jinli?"* Cao Cao read *"si yan bude"* (lit., "how could death not be had") as one part and *"shiren jinli"* (warriors will persevere) as another. If read this way, then what is *de* (had) here? And where does "warriors will persevere" come from? So, this must be read as a single sentence in order for it to be understood.

    Du Mu emulated Cao Cao's reading and noted, "This says the warriors will certainly die; how could victory thereby be impossible?" That is an improper reading, for military victory lies in the commanders' superior strategy and tactics, while warriors unafraid of risking death serve to develop combat power; these two matters cannot be confused. *Sun-tzu* later directly indicates this in the line, "And when they are launched into inextricable positions, the valor of great heroes will arise" (p. 98), which contains the same message as this line.

13. "Without other alternatives will fight" in the Chinese text reads *"budeyi ze dou"* and follows the later versions. The Linyi text here reads *"___ suowang se dou"* (the first part is missing); if this had at one time read *"wusuowang ze dou"* (in inextricable positions will fight), it repeats a previous line in this paragraph.

14. "Disciplined" in the Linyi text reads *"tiao,"* while the later versions read *"xiu."* Both *tiao* and *xiu* had the meaning of *zhi* (well managed),[16] so they were interchangeable and are interpreted here as "disciplined."

---

[15]E.g., the *Liji* has the line "[conflicts with] weapons and chariots will not rise; [it] should not be initiated by our side" (vol. 14, "Yueling: Mengchun" [*Shisanjing*, p. 2935]); Zheng Xuan's note, "To be a *ke* is disadvantageous and to be a *zhuren* is expedient." Kong Yingda annotated, "Raising forces to invade others is called *ke* [lit., 'guest']; when the enemy comes, those who stand against them are called *zhu* [lit., 'host']."

[16]E.g., the *Liji* has the paragraph "this month ordered musicians *xiu* the *tao* drums and the *bing* drums . . . *tiao* the *yu* ocarina and *sheng* ocarina" ("Yueling: Zhongxia" [*Shisanjing*, p. 2961]); Zheng Xuan's note: "*Xiu . . . tiao . . .* express the management of this equipment and the practice of these activities."

15. "Forbid superstition, dismiss apprehension" in the Chinese text reads "*jinxiang quyi.*" *Xiang* (superstition) is a belief in good or bad luck.[17] Superstition and *yi* (apprehension) here are both manifestations of soldiers' emotional instability.

16. "Unto death they will not desert" in the Chinese text reads "*zhisi wuosuozhi*" and follows the later versions. This part in the Linyi text is missing. *Zhi* is defined as *wang* (to go);[18] since it is used in a combat situation, we interpret it as "to desert." The *Shiyijia* has a note that says, "One other edition reads '*zhisi wusuozai*' [unto death they will not be harmfully influenced]." Of the two different readings, "unto death they will not desert" is manifestly preferable.

17. "Risk numerous deaths" in the Chinese text reads "*wuyusi*" and follows the Linyi text. *Si* (death) in the later versions reads *ming* (life). *Yu* means "abundant,"[19] so "*wuyusi*" implies "having not enough death," which portrays death repeatedly being faced. The meaning of this line in the later versions is "will have no long life" and also is acceptable, but it is not as moving as the Linyi's version.

18. "Tears" in the Chinese text reads "*ti.*" This character's ancient and modern definitions differ. Today this indicates nasal mucus, but in ancient times it meant "tears."[20]

19. "Great heroes" in the Chinese text reads "*Zhu Kuai.*" These were the given names of two ancient heroes—Zhuan Zhu and Cao Kuai[21]—who dared to risk their lives for a cause.

---

[17]*Shuowen,* 1 *shang,* "Xiang," p. 3; Duan Yucai's note. *Xiang* is today normally understood to mean "fortune."

[18]*Erya,* "Shigu" *shang* (*Shisanjing,* p. 5579).

[19]*Shuowen,* 5 *xia,* p. 224.

[20]*Shuowen,* 11 *shang,* p. 570; Duan Yucai's note.

[21]Zhuan Zhu assassinated Liao, the King of Wu, and claimed his throne for the princeling Guang, who became Helü, the King of Wu (*Shiji,* vol. 86, "Cike Liezhuan," pp. 879–80). Sun Wu later paid a visit to Helü (see the Introduction and Appendixes 1, 5, and 6).

20. "Those sophisticated at commanding battle arrays" in the Chinese text reads *"gu shanyongjunzhe"* and follows the Linyi text; later versions read *jun* (battle arrays)[22] as *bing* (forces).

Regarding the character *jun*, when the enemy is engaged, battle arrays are already in place. The ensuing passage about the serpent at Mount Heng illustrates how to operate battle arrays. The later versions' use of the character *bing* here does not give it the meaning of *yongjun* (commanding battle arrays) and confuses this passage's intent.

21. "A serpent at Mount Heng" in the Chinese text reads *"Hengshan zhi she ye"* and follows the Linyi text. The later versions all read *Heng* as *Chang* in order to avoid the taboo character *heng*, which was an emperor's given name in the Han, Tang, and Song dynasties.

22. "The middle of its body" in the Chinese text reads *"zhongshen"* and follows the Linyi text. The later versions read this as *"zhong"* without the character *shen* (body).[23]

23. "While navigating the same boat" in the Chinese text reads *"dang qi tongzhou er ji ye"* and follows the Linyi text. The later versions have after this line the phrase *"yufeng"* (encountered gales of wind). The ancients often used large bodies of

---

As for Cao Kuai, various accounts have been ascribed to him. *Guanzi* recorded that when the state of Qi invaded Lu, Lu sought a peace talk. Cao Kuai thereupon took up his sword and kidnapped Lord Huan of Qi, demanding that their land be returned, which it was when an agreement was made (vol. 7, "Dakuang," p. 107). *Guanzi* was written in Qi, so this is the Qi rendition.

The people of Lu, though, had a different version: the *Zhanguoce* records that the famous strategist Lu Lian, who was a native of Lu, once said, "Not even an army could compare with an enraged Cao Mo and his three-foot sword" (vol. 10, "Qice" 3, p. 206). Many later records on this have patterned themselves after Lu's description, such as in the *Heguanzi* (xia, p. 2a), *Shiji* ("Cike Liezhuan," p. 879), and *Wenxuan* (vol. 41, Li Lu's "Da Su Wu shu," p. 759).

Sun-tzu's description here is the same as that in *Guanzi*, which clearly shows that Sun Wu, as a native of Qi, emulated the Qi rendition.

[22] See Book 7, comment 12d.

[23] The *Zhanguoce* also uses a snake in an example: "when the *zhongshen* [middle of its body] was struck, the head and tail both came to its aid" (vol. 25, "Weice" 4, p. 503); the term *zhongshen* is used here exactly as in the Linyi text, so we know that this was a pre-Qin convention.

water as symbols of danger,[24] so the addition of "gales of wind" was not necessary for them "to help each other."[25]

24. "Joining horses and embedding cartwheels" in the Chinese text reads *"fangma mailun."* Cao Cao said, "*Fang[ma]* means to tie up the horses,[26] *mailun* shows that they no longer move. This says that concentrating on steadfastly digging in is not as suitable as flexible techniques. So, this means that *'fangma mailun'* are not at all dependable." His interpretation grasped the meaning here of *Sun-tzu.*

The *Chuci*[27] has the phrase "bury two wheels and hobble four horses" (*"mailianglunxi zhisima"*); this describes the conditions for fortifying arrays in a fight to the death and also is very similar to *Sun-tzu*'s description here.

25. "Gaining both rigidity and suppleness is the principle for terrain" in the Chinese text reads *"gangrou jiede, di zhi li ye."* In ancient Chinese, when "rigidity" *(gang)* and "suppleness" *(rou)* were used in reference to the land, this indicated the two fundamental classifications for its nature.[28] Cao Cao twisted this fact in a very odd way and created a forced explanation: "Strength and weakness become a unified power." This caused the readers who came after him to mistake "rigidity" and "suppleness" for the employment of forces.

[24]The most numerous examples can be seen in the *Yijing,* such as the line "advantage lies in crossing a great river" ("Xu diagram" [*Shisanjing,* p. 44]); its annotation says, "Danger lies ahead." Also the annotation to the "Song diagram" says, "Disadvantage lies in crossing a great river because there will be entrapment by a maelstrom" (*Shisanjing,* p. 45). Illustrations such as these clearly show the concept of danger at that time.

[25]The *Changduanjing* quotes this line from *Sun-tzu* as identical to that of the Linyi text (vol. 9, "Sheshi" [*Hanhai congshu,* p. 1209]). Also, *Deng Xizi* has the line "when crossing the sea in the same boat, gales of wind were encountered midway, so [they] united as one for deliverance from disaster" ("Wuhou," p. 5a); it appears that this line might have come from *Sun-tzu,* but it includes the phrase "gales of wind were encountered."

[26]The *Shuowen* records, "*fang* means joined boats" (8 *xia,* p. 408), so *fang* can be defined as "to join together." The *Guoyu* records, "*fang* boats and set plankings" (vol. 6, "Qiyu," p. 9b); Wei Zhao noted, "*Fang* means 'joined.'"

[27]Vol. 2, "Jiuge: Guoshang," p. 61.

[28]E.g., the *Liji* has the line "do not break the principles of the land" (vol. 14, "Yueling: Mengchun" [*Shisanjing,* p. 2935]); Kong Yingda annotated, "Land has rigidity and suppleness . . . [In the *Yijing*] the 'Shuogua' [note: vol. 9 (*Shisanjing,* p. 195)] says, 'Fulfilling the ways of earth are rigidity and suppleness.'"

26. "Concerns in commanding armies" in the Chinese text reads *"jiangjun zhi shi."* References to "commanders" in *Sun-tzu* always use the single character *jiang*, not the modern-day term for commanders, *jiangjun*,[29] so this term must mean something else. The ensuing text discusses the principles for commanding troops in battle, so we interpret *jiangjun* (*jun*, lit., "army") as "commanding armies."

27. "Scheming in impenetrability" in the Chinese text reads *"jing yi you."* In pre-Qin books the character *jing* (lit., "quiet"; "calmness") often was defined as *mou* (to deliberate; to scheme).[30] But Cao Cao overlooked this fact and noted, "This means calmness," and his interpretation greatly influenced later annotators; moreover, he also distorted this line so that it reads as concerning a commander's cultivation. If Cao was correct, then *"jing yi you"* would have no relationship with the following line, "having the capability to subjugate the eyes and ears of warriors and soldiers" (p. 100). Also, a commander's cultivation is a long-term undertaking; how could one be expected to discuss cultivation when one is about to lead troops into battle? Cao Cao's interpretation is therefore not used in favor of *Sun-tzu*'s *"jing"* in this line.

You means *yin* ("hidden," and so "impenetrable").[31]

28. "Having the capability to subjugate the eyes and ears of warriors and soldiers, making them suppress their senses" in the Chinese text reads *"neng yu shi zu zhi ermu, shi zhi wuzhi."*

    28a. *"Yu"* (subjugate) is today commonly understood to mean "to fool" or "a fool," but there is a gap between this modern interpretation and its basic meaning in pre-Qin times.[32] Commanding armies is not a matter of hood-

---

[29]See Book 1, comment 13a, and Book 7, comment 4.

[30]E.g., the *Shujing* records, *"jing yan* behaved traitorously" (vol. 2, "Yaodian" [*Shisanjing*, p. 256]); Kong Anguo's note.

[31]*Shuowen*, 4 *xia*, p. 160.

[32]*Yu* is defined in the *Shuowen* as *zhuang* (simple and honest; naïve) (10 *xia*, p. 514). Duan Yucai's note indicates that *yu* is the opposite of *zhi* (sense; perception). *Yu* is used here as a verb to mean that which makes someone this way or makes him not exercise his senses. That is why *Sun-tzu* then says this is "making them suppress their senses" *Laozi* has this: "Not by way of enlightening the people, but by

winking one's troops, but rather requires a complete calibration of action, so we interpret *yu* accordingly.

28b. "*Shi zhi wuzhi*" (making them suppress their senses) follows the later versions. The Linyi text reads "*shi wu zhi*" (*zhi*, lit., "of" or "to go"); the meaning remains unclear to us.

Wuzhi literally means "without senses or intellect," but since people have ears, eyes, and brains, how can their senses be removed? We therefore know that *wuzhi* here means making them suppress these senses.

29. "Making the people suppress their judgment" in the Chinese text reads "*shi min wushi*" and follows the Linyi text.[33] Although *shi* in ancient times often was defined as *zhi* (lit., "intellect"),[34] this is not the *zhi* having to do with "senses" (see comment 28b), but is the type of *zhi* that concerns "judgment,"[35] so we interpret it accordingly.

30. Following this line the *Shiyijia* has "burn boats and break cooking vessels" ("*fen-zhou pofu*"), but this was not recorded in either the Linyi text or the *Wujing* and Sakurada versions. This description was in fact taken from the *Shiji*.[36] Since this historical fact occurred for the first time at the end of the Qin Dynasty, it could not possibly have been recounted by Sun Wu.

---

way of *yu* [subjugating; not allowing to use one's own senses] them" (ch. 65, Wang Bi's edition, p. 17b); the meaning of the character here is the same.

Also, the *Shijing* has the term "*yuchuan*" (vol. 12, "Xiaoya: Jienanshan series: Qiaoyan" [*Shisanjing*, p. 974]); Mao Heng noted, "*Yuchuan* is a mastered dog and refers to hunting dogs." (Note: the *Shijing* originally used the character *yu* [lit., "to meet"] here. Yu Shengwu indicated that in ancient times it was interchangeable with *yu* [simple; naïve]; see *Zhuzi xinzheng*, vol. 2, under the line "*shi yi yuhan yuduo zhi min*," pp. 285–86.) When a dog does not follow its own senses, it can be said to be mastered, and this explanation assists us in approaching a more accurate interpretation of *yu* here.

[33] The later versions read *min* as *ren* to avoid a Tang Dynasty taboo character.

[34] *Shuowen*, 3 *shang*, "Shi," second definition, p. 92.

[35] The *Zhouli* records, "The first type of clemency is called 'not *shi*'" (vol. 36, "Zhouguan: Sici" [*Shisanjing*, p. 1901]); Zheng Xuan noted, "*Shi* means 'discernment,'" which is perception of the object. Zhu Junsheng indicated that "discriminating between right and wrong is called '*shi*'" (*Shuowen tongxun ding-sheng*, "Yi bu" 5, p. 227).

[36] Vol. 7, "Xiang Yu benji," p. 110. This criticism was initially made by Zhao Benxue (*Sunzi shu jiaojie yinlei, xia*, p. 39b).

31. The above paragraph on the six terrains (from "where away from the country" to "lethal areas") ought to be a segment from Book 8, "Nine Adaptations."[37] The Linyi text describes a lethal area as "the rear is blocked and enemies are in front" (*"hou gu qian di"*), which is different from the later versions. Also, following lethal zones in the Linyi text is the line "where inextricable positions lie is a *qiongdi* [futile zone]," but in the later versions this reads *"sidi"* (lethal zone). We can see that since ancient times the characters in this paragraph have been jumbled. Because the beginning and ending of these lines are damaged in the Linyi text, we follow the later versions here.

32. "With susceptible zones we will urge them to advance swiftly" in the Chinese text reads *"qingdi, wujiang shizhi lou"* and follows the Linyi text. The later versions read *lou* as *shu* (lit., "to join"). *Lou* was of the ancient Qi dialect and indicated "to immediately do or go."[38]

   The later versions' use of *shu* has this interpretation by Cao Cao: "Make them mutually contact." Since the foregoing text of this book describes susceptible zones as "where the adversary's land is shallowly penetrated" (p. 94), and says "with susceptible zones, do not halt" (p. 95), we can see here that "advance swiftly" (p. 102) means to make a quick surge into enemy territory. Thus, a deep penetration of enemy land is the express goal for the operation, so we should follow the Linyi text.

33. "With contended zones we will rapidly approach them from their rear" in the Chinese text reads *"zhengdi, wujiang qu qihou"* and follows the later versions. The Linyi text reads *"zhengdi, wujiang shibuliu"* (with contended zones we will cause no lingering); this description actually corresponds to the admonition for "severable zones" in Book 8, "The Nine Adaptations": "never linger in severable

---

[37]See Book 8, comment 4. In this section, *qudi* (key traffic zones) are described in the Linyi text as *siche* (where every place can be reached); in the later versions the character *che* was changed to *da* to avoid a taboo character in the emperor Han Wudi's given name. These two characters were interchangeable.

[38]E.g., the *Gongyangzhuan* records, "madame did not *lou* [him]" ("Zhuanggong ershisinian" [*Shisanjing*, p. 4855]); He Xiu noted, "*Lou* means *ji* [a swift action] in the Qi dialect. . . . [it means] madame halted, unwilling to immediately obey." Sun Wu was a native of Qi, so the character *lou* used in this way was of his dialect.

zones'' (p. 75). After this line the Linyi text also has ''____ *di, wujiang qu qihou*'' (with ____ zones we will rapidly approach them from their rear), a description that corresponds with contended zones in the later versions. However, since a character is missing, we are uncertain what type of zone is being discussed in the Linyi text here.

34. ''With dually traversable zones we will fortify their junctures'' in the Chinese text reads ''*jiaodi, wujiang gu qijie*'' and follows the Linyi text. ''*Gu qijie*'' in the later versions reads ''*jin qishou*'' (be cautious of their defenses).[39]

35. ''With key traffic zones we will be diplomatic in our alliances'' in the Chinese text reads ''*qudi, wujiang jin qishi*'' and follows the Linyi text. ''*Jin qishi*'' in the later versions reads ''*gu qijie*'' (fortify their junctures).[40] Earlier in this book it says ''with key traffic zones, strengthen diplomacy'' (p. 95), so we define *shi* (lit., ''reliance'') as ''alliances.''

36. ''The nature of forces is: when within range, defend; when without other alternatives, fight; and when superior, hunt for them'' in the Chinese text reads ''*gu bing zhi qing*:[41] *dai ze yu*,[42] *budeyi ze dou, guo ze cong*.'' The character *qing* in ''*bing*

[39]All of the Tang Dynasty sources—e.g., the *Tongdian* (vol. 159, ''Bing'' 12, p. 839), Du You's note (*Shijia*, vol. 11, p. 28a), and the *Changduanjing* (vol. 9, ''Dixing,'' in the annotation to ''*jiaodi*'' [dually traversable zones; Zhou Guangye's edition, p. 266])—quote this line identically to that in the Linyi text.

[40]The *Tongdian* (vol. 159, ''Bing'' 12, p. 839) quotes this line as ''*jin qishi*'' (substituting *shi* [lit., ''market''] for *shi* [lit., ''reliance'']; the *Shuowen tongxun dingsheng* says that these two characters were pronounced the same and were interchangeable [''Yibu diwu,'' p. 208]), so it is in fact the same as the Linyi text. Comment 34 also shows that the Linyi text's rendering of this line is correct.

[41]This reading follows the later versions. The Linyi text reads ''___ *hou zhi qing*.'' This line, then, probably ought to read ''*gu zhuhou zhi qing*'' (the nature of feudal lords).
''Feudal lords'' should have been used here to symbolize different countries' armies, as in the foregoing line, ''where a lord conducts battles in his individual sector is separated'' (p. 94). The use of ''lord'' in that line does not indicate the battles of a single person, but rather the troops of his which are engaged in battle; the usage is the same in both lines. If the Linyi text in fact read ''the nature of feudal lords,'' its meaning would not have been that different from the later versions' ''nature of forces.''

[42]This reading follows the Linyi text. The later editions read ''*wei ze yu*'' (when surrounded, defend). If the enemy has already ''surrounded'' us, it is too late to begin a defense, so we do not follow this.

zhi qing'' means ''nature.''[43] *Dai* in ancient times was defined as *ji* (''what can be reached,'' so ''within range'').[44]

The most difficult character to interpret in this line is *guo. Guo* is the same position in this phrase as the foregoing *dai* (within range) and *budeyi* (without other alternatives), so we know that this describes the situation that forces have to handle. Cao Cao said it meant ''overly trapped, then follow plans.'' He defined *guo* as ''overly'' and added his own explanation ''trapped''; the meaning, therefore, was misconstrued and cannot be accepted. Li Quan's annotation reads, ''*Guo* and be careful about movement.'' He did not explain what *guo* meant, although we might guess that he could have intended it to mean ''cross over the enemy's border.'' The meaning of *cong* was not discussed by him either.

The meaning of *guo* lies in the meaning of *cong. Sun-tzu's* use of *cong*—other than in this instance—has mainly indicated our response to where the enemy's strength is insufficient. For example, Book 7, ''Armed Contention,'' says, ''with a deceptive retreat, do not hunt for *[cong]* them'' (p. 74). Also, Book 10, ''Terrain,'' says, ''with gorge-path terrain . . . if the enemy first situates in it and is ready at the gorge mouth, do not hunt for *[cong]* them; if not, hunt for *[cong]* them'' (p. 89) and ''with obstacled terrain . . . if the enemy first situates in it, conduct a withdrawal; do not hunt for *[cong]* them'' (p. 89). And finally, Book 12, ''Attacks Using Fire,'' says, ''Let the fire inflict the severest damage; hunt for *[cong]* them when huntable; halt when not huntable'' (p. 108). The character *cong* in this line, therefore, should not have a different interpretation.

We know from *cong's* meaning that *guo* can be seen to plainly indicate our ''surpassing of the enemy'' or ''being superior.''[45]

37. ''Of these several things, if a single one is not known, an overlord's forces cannot be realized'' in the Chinese text reads ''*siwu zhe, yi buzhi, fei wangba zhi bing ye.''*

> **37a.** ''Of these several things'' in the Chinese text reads ''*siwu zhe''* (lit., ''the four or five''). This was a pre-Qin term that indicated ''several things'' in

[43]See comment 10.

[44]*Guangya*, 5 *shang*, ''Shiyan,'' p. 12b.

[45]E.g., in the *Yijing*, Kong Yingda annotated: ''*Guo* is the *guo* [lit., ''over''] of *guoyue* [to surpass]'' (vol. 3, ''Daguo diagram'' [*Shisanjing*, p. 82]). When we withstand the enemy, what we can surpass is naturally the enemy.

a general manner.[46] Later generations were unaware of this practice, as Cao Cao and Zhang Yu had interpreted this as ''four'' plus ''five'' equals the ''nine terrains,'' which was merely a speculation.

37b. ''Overlord'' in the Chinese text reads ''*wangba*'' and follows the Linyi text. The later versions read ''*bawang*.'' In the pre-Qin era, *wang* and *ba* were originally two terms that indicated the ones whose influence could rule intercountry order: the one who subordinated all of the countries was a *wang*, and directly under the level of *wang* was the *ba*.[47] Both *wang* and *ba* would be similar to a ''superpower'' today. Since *wang* and *ba* have their own specific meanings, the term can be written either *wangba* or *bawang*.[48] We follow the Linyi text here in order to avoid any possible misunderstanding.

38. ''By competing for worldwide alliances and developing worldwide influence'' in the Chinese text reads ''*shigu, pizheng tianxia zhi jiao, piyang tianxia zhi quan*'' and follows the *Wujing* and *Shiyijia* versions.[49] The two *pi* (now read *bu* [lit., ''no''])

---

[46]*Sun Bin bingfa* has the line ''the legions of the three armies can be divided into *siwu*.'' *Mozi* also employed this term in ''*siwu* states'' and ''*siwu* people'' (vol. 5, ''Feigong'' *zhong*, p. 84). Their usage of *siwu* is the same as that in the line under discussion here. In modern Chinese a similar application can be found in the term *sanwu* (lit., ''three five'').

[47]The *Zuozhuan* says that a *wang* was one who regulated all of the countries' lands and brought them advantages, while the *ba* established moral influence and satisfied general aspirations (vol. 25, ''Chenggong ernian'' [*Shisanjing*, pp. 4111–12]), so annotators defined *wang* as the lord of all the countries and *ba* as the one who controlled the *wang*'s policies and influence (ibid., Kong Yingda's annotation; also, Takezoe Kokou, *Sashi kaishen*, under the line ''*wubo zhi ba*'' [vol. 12, ''Cheng er,'' p. 22]).
Guanzi said, ''He who wins the people of all the countries is a *wang*; he who wins half of this is a *ba*'' (vol. 9, ''Bayan,'' p. 142). And *Mengzi* noted, ''One who wields power to aid benevolence is a *ba*; one who wields moral influence to achieve benevolence is a *wang*'' (''Gong Sunchou'' *shang*, vol. 3 *xia* [*Shisanjing*, p. 5843]).

[48]In ''Chenggong ernian,'' *Zuozhuan*, it first says *wang* and then *ba* (vol. 25, *Shisanjing*, pp. 4111–12). Yet, ''Mingong yuannian dong,'' *Zuozhuan*, has Zhong Sunqiu giving it as *bawang* (*Shisanjing*, p. 3874). *Mengzi* first says *ba* and then *wang*; see footnote 47. *Xunzi* has the chapter title ''Wangba'' (vol. 7, p. 1a). So, we know that there was no set pattern for this during the Spring and Autumn and Warring States periods.

[49]The *Shiyijia* noted that *piyang* in one other edition reads *pishi* (''to work on''; *pi* acts as a mood word). The Sakurada version is the same, except that it reads *duo* (to snatch) for *yang*. The Linyi text has only the characters ''*shigu pi*'' (therefore, *pi*) still extant, so it appears basically similar here to the later versions.

characters here act as mood words and do not have any actual meaning,[50] which was a special usage for *pi* in the pre-Qin period. If we read *pi* as a negative, *Sun-tzu*'s meaning would be confounded.[51]

39. "Thus, their city may be occupied and their country toppled" in the Chinese text reads *"gu qi cheng keba, qi guo keduo"* and follows the later versions. The Linyi text only has extant "_____ *keba ye, cheng keduo ye"* (note: the missing characters were probably *"gu guo"* [thus, country]).[52] So, the positions of "city" and "country" are flipped in the Linyi text and the later versions, and the Linyi text does not have the two *qi* (their) characters.

40. "Transcend rules when conferring rewards; transcend policy when issuing orders" in the Chinese text reads *"wufa zhi shang, wuzheng zhi ling"* and follows the Linyi text. The two *zhi* (lit., "of") characters are defined as *yi* (to use; to issue; to confer). The later versions have the character *shi* (to conduct; to grant) before the first line and *xuan* (to hang) before the second.[53]

41. "Direct" in the Chinese text reads *"fan"* (lit., "to invade"; "to force").[54] It is difficult to match the meaning of this character with the sentence's intent, so we

[50]Examples of this can often be seen in ancient writings. E.g., the *Shijing* records, "the Zhou is glorified [*pixian*]; the divine lord's care is here [*pishi*]" (vol. 16, "Daya: Wen Wang series: Wenwang" [*Shisanjing*, p. 1083]); Mao Heng's note.
Wang Yinzhi said that in the ancient classics *pi (bu)* can act as an "initial vocalization" that has no inherent meaning, and he gives dozens of examples (*Jingyi shuwen*, vol. 32, pp. 762–63).

[51]With such a reading, what would be the meaning of the preceding text's "with key traffic zones we will be diplomatic in our alliances" (p. 102) and the following text's "by not knowing other lords' minds, one cannot secure allies" (p. 103)? (This paragraph also appears in Book 7.)

[52]The *Taiping yulan* records this line as *"gu qi guo keba er qi cheng keduo ye"* (vol. 304, "Bing bu" 35, p. 1400), so it is similar to the Linyi text here.

[53]For *zhi*, see Pei Xuehai's *Gushu xuzi jishi*, vol. 9, eleventh definition, p. 736.
In ancient times, the character *ling* (orders) was used in combination with such verbs as *chu* (to give), *fa* (to issue), or even *shi* (to grant). Only *fa* (law; rule) used the verb *xuan* (to hang or post [as an announcement]), so the later versions' character use is questionable.
The *Taiping yulan* records these two lines as *"wufa zhi xuan, wugong zhi ling"* ([previously] posted no rules, [previously] regulated no [grades of] merit) (vol. 304, "Bing bu" 35, p. 1400); although their meaning differs slightly from all other versions, they do not have the characters *shi* and *xuan* at the beginning of the lines and so are in this way similar to the Linyi text.

[54]*Shuowen*, 10 *shang*, p. 479. Also, the *Guoyu* has the line *"fan* shook the Wu state's troops" (vol. 19, "Wuyu," p. 4b); Wei Zhao's note.

know that *fan* here actually was intended to be read as another interchangeable character, *fan* ("to rule"; therefore, "to direct").[55]

42. "Direct them into hazardous situations without revealing other prospects" in the Chinese text reads *"fan zhi yi hai, wugao yi li"* and follows the Linyi text. The later versions read *"fan shi yi li, wugao yi hai"* (direct them for advantages without revealing hazards). The way in which forces are used is as it was described earlier in this book: "concentrating all the armies' legions and launching them into danger" (p. 100); where is the *"li"* (advantage; opportunity) there? If *"wugao yi li"* (without revealing opportunities) is used as a precept in military operations, the troops will not become opportunistic.

43. "Warily scrutinizing the enemy's intent, concentrating against the enemy toward one goal, and trouncing their commanders over a thousand miles" in the Chinese text reads *"shenxiang di zhi yi, bingdi yixiang, qianli shajiang."* This reading follows the later versions.

    43a. In "warily scrutinizing the enemy's intent" (*"shenxiang di zhi yi"*), the character *shen* (commonly read *shun* and meaning "to follow") in ancient times was interchangeable with *shen* (awareness; warily).[56] *Xiang* (to examine; to scrutinize) was defined as *shen*.[57]

[55]E.g., the *Yijing* records, "*fanwei* the changes of heaven and earth" (vol. 7, "Xici" *shang*); Ruan Yuan's (Qing, 1764–1849) critical notes ("Jiaokanji" [*Shisanjing*, p. 173]).
    Cao Cao defined this *fan* as *yong* (to use), but we do not know his source. (Qing) Bi Yixun noted in his *Sunzi xulu*, "The character *fan* does not have the primary meaning of *yong* [to use]" (p. 13b). Although this is correct, Bi then went on to interpret *fan* as *dong* (to move), which does not seem to be a suitable definition either.

[56]E.g., the *Yijing* notes, "step on frost and hard ice will come; this refers to *shun*" (Benyi edition, vol. 7, "Wenyanzhuan: Kun diagram," p. 411). Zhu Xi's (Song, 1130–1200) annotation reads, "The ancient characters *shun* and *shen* were interchangeable."

[57]E.g., in *Xunzi*, the line "to clutch firmly and *xiang*" (vol. 1, "Xiushen," p. 9b); Yang Jing noted, "*Xiang* means to scrutinize matters." Also in *Xunzi*, it again reads "to clutch firmly and *xiang*" (vol. 3, "Zhengni," p. 15b); Yang Jing noted, "Carefully retain one's duty and *xiangming* [scrutinize] regulations."
    Both Cao Cao's and Mei Yaochen's notes define *xiang* as *yang* (deception; to deceive), but neither mentions *xiang*. (*Yang* and *xiang* were interchangeable in ancient times; see Dai Tong's *Liushu gu*, vol. 8, "Yang.") We therefore know that since antiquity there have been two renderings for this line. However, from the following discussion in this comment we can plainly see that the character *yang*, which is read to be *shenyang*, was actually an interchangeable character for *xiang* and should never be interpreted as "deception."

What *Sun-tzu* discusses here is basically the same as in a line in Book 9, "Troop Maneuvers": "With forces, many are not necessarily ideal; just do not advance boldly, be able to concentrate strength decisively, anticipate the enemy, and annihilate the adversary—that is all" (p. 86). "Concentrating against the enemy toward one goal" (*"bingdi yixiang)"* is similar to the term "concentrate strength" (*"bingli"*). Moreover, "trouncing their commanders over a thousand miles" (*"qianli shajiang"*) is much like "annihilate the enemy" (*"quren"*), and therefore "warily scrutinizing the enemy's intent" (*"shenxiang di zhi yi"*) is equivalent to "anticipating the enemy" (*"liaodi"*).

43b. "Trouncing" in the Chinese text reads *"sha."* Cao Cao defined this as "even over a thousand miles one is able to *qin* [capture] their commanders." We too do not directly translate *sha* here, using its literal meaning of "to kill."[58]

44. "This is called adeptly achieving a mission" in the Chinese text reads *"shiwei qiaoneng chengshi"* and follows the *Wujing* and Sakurada versions.[59]

45. "Bolt the border gates, sunder the passes" in the Chinese text reads *"yiguan zhefu."* *Guan* indicates the gate bolts,[60] so *yiguan* has the basic meaning of "to fasten the gate bolts," and this is a complementary phrase to "sunder the passes" (*zhefu*). However, a direct translation here would not provide a clear enough meaning, so we interpret it accordingly.

Regarding the term "passes" (*fu*), in ancient times, all people going into a federation or country had to receive an official permit that allowed them entry,[61] so we interpret this accordingly.

---

[58]See Book 2, comment 15.

[59]The Linyi text reads *"ci wei qiaoshi"* (this is called being adept at a mission). The *Shiyijia* version reads *"ci wei qiaoneng chengshi zhe ye"* (this is called one who is adept at achieving a mission).

[60]Gu Yanwu, *Rizhilu*, vol. 32, "Guan," p. 765.

[61]E.g., the *Zhouli* records, "The gateways use *fujie*" (vol. 15, "Diguan: Zhangjie" [*Shisanjing*, p. 1593]); Zheng Xuan's and Jia Gongyan's annotations.

46. "Take effective actions in the court departments to manage their duties" in the Chinese text reads *"li yu langmiao zhi shang yi zhu qi shi."* Li (to take effective actions) takes its meaning from *mian* (to commit all efforts).[62] *"Langmiao"*[63] (the court departments) was a common term in the pre-Qin period. *Miao* in this term means "the court."[64] *Lang* indicates the east and west wings placed to the left and right of the court for conducting the government's various departmental affairs.[65]

As for *zhu* (to manage),[66] Du Mu pointed out that one other edition reads this as *mou* (to deliberate; to plan), which has a similar meaning.

47. "Has a breach" in the Chinese text reads *"kaihui"* (lit., "to open a district gate")[67] and follows the Linyi text. The later versions read this as *"kaihe"* (to open a single door).[68] Cao Cao said that this phrase indicated that "the enemy has a gap," which is precisely *Sun-tzu's* meaning here.

48. "Secretly take actions toward joint operations" in the Chinese text reads *"wei yu zhi qi."* Du Mu said that *wei* meant *qian* ("sneakily," thereby "secretly"). *Yu* (commonly understood to mean "to be with") in ancient writings was often

[62]Wang Niansun, *Dushu zazhi,* VIII-3, under the line "*qinshu,*" p. 17b.

[63]The Linyi text reads *"lang"* without the character *miao,* which probably was an abbreviated form.

[64]See Book 1, comment 27b.

[65]The *Shuowen* says, "*Lang* are the east and west annexes" and "wings are *lang*" (Cheng Changzhi wood-block edition, 9 *xia,* p. 193). We therefore know that *lang* were the two wings on the east and west. (It was the ancient practice to place imperial courts in the north and facing south, so the *lang* were on the eastern and western sides.)
Also see (Han) Yan Yannian's poem "Kongshi pi langsi" (*Wenxuan,* vol. 22, "Jujia xing Jingkou, shiyou Suanshan," p. 411), about which Li Shan noted, "*Lang* . . . are where the imperial courts are." Because the Han Dynasty complied with pre-Qin procedures, *lang* was also used in referring to governmental offices.

[66]*Zhu* (lit., "to punish") had the archaic definition of *zhi* (to manage); Cao Cao noted this definition, which was often used in ancient writings.

[67]For *hui,* see the *Shuowen,* 12 *shang,* p. 594.

[68]For *he,* see the *Shuowen,* 12 *shang,* p. 594. *He* also has the meaning of "to close," which often caused some annotators to mistakenly guess that this meant the period of time before the enemy has decided its own course of action.

interchangeable with *ju* (lit., "to lift"; "to raise").[69] When *ju* is used in reference to dealing with the enemy, we know that this means "to take actions." *Zhi* (lit., "of") is here defined as *yu* (toward).[70] For *qi*, see Book 9, comment 18.

49. "Follow the enemy as a carpenter's chalk" in the Chinese text reads *"jian*[71] *mo sui*[72] *di."* Our interpretation follows the reading of these four characters as a single sentence.

Cao Cao said that this line meant "proceed in accordance with *guiju* [lit., "rule"; here, possibly "policy"] but be flexible" *("xing jian guiju, wuchang ye"),* which roughly means that one should faithfully carry out policy but be adaptable to circumstances. Cao's reading would therefore have been *"jianmo, suidi."* Although when read this way this line has a certain value and quite a few scholars have emulated it, we are not certain what *guiju* indicated.

[69]Wang Yinzhi, *Jingyi shuwen,* vol. 19, under the line *"guanjun ju chunchen"*; Wang's note, p. 450.

[70]Pei Xuehai, *Gushu xuzi jishi,* vol. 9, "Zhi," eighteenth definition, p. 745.

[71]The *Shiyijia* indicates that in another edition *jian* reads *chan* (to eliminate); Jia Lin followed this reading and noted, "Victory is obtained in whatever way is expedient; one cannot hold to a definite procedure."

[72]*Sui* is given as *xun* in the *Taiping yulan* (vol. 270, "Bing bu" 1, p. 1264); these two characters were interchangeable (see Book 12, comment 11, footnote 22).

ATTACKS USING FIRE

1. "Attacks using fire" in the Chinese text reads *"huogong."* Cao Cao explained, "Conform to fire in attacking the enemy." We follow both this and the character meanings of *huogong* (*huo* means "fire" and *gong* means "to attack") for our interpretation.

2. "Attack fires" in the Chinese text reads *"gonghuo"* and follows the Linyi text. The later versions all read this as *"huogong"* (attacks using fire). The ensuing discussion in *Sun-tzu* merely introduces the purposes for which fires are used, rather than describing how the fires are used in coordination with strikes on the enemy. Therefore, the Linyi text makes better sense.

3. "The burning of transport lines" in the Chinese text reads *"huosui"* (*huo* acts as a verb here). *Sui* is in the form now pronounced *dui;* this *dui* (lit., "arrays") in ancient times was interchangeable with *sui* (lit., "route").[1] Jia Lin wrote, "*Sui* means *dao* [way]—to burn the provision route and supply transport." We interpret it accordingly.[2]

---

[1]The *Shiyijia* noted that "another version of *dui* is *sui.*"

[2]Alternately, Du Mu interpreted this as "burn their battle columns." This, though, was already included in the "burning of adversaries." On the other hand, Li Quan wrote, "Burn their banners, accoutrements, and weapons," but these are included in "the burning of stockpiles" and "the burning of arsenals." The strangest reading of all was Du You's rendering of *dui* as *zhui* (lit., "to fall") (*Shijia*, vol. 12, p. 3b); this misled readers into believing this term meant "to use incendiary missiles." From *Sun-tzu*'s sentence pattern in the preceding lines we can see that *huo* (to burn) is immediately followed by its object, and *zhui* (to fall) is not a noun, showing that Du You's interpretation is obviously problematic.

4. "The operation of fires requires proper conditions, and these conditions must exist beforehand" in the Chinese text reads *"xinghuo you yin, yin bi su ju"* and follows the Linyi text.[3] The later versions read "the operation of fires must have proper conditions, and smoky fire must exist beforehand" (*"xinghuo biyou yin, yanhuo*[4] *bisuju"*).

Zhang Yu said, "Generally, attacks using fire all take advantage of dry weather; the camp should be located amid tall grasses and bamboo with accumulated fodder and gathered provisions. Their living quarters should be near grassy areas. Conform to the wind and burn them." Moreover, fire attack in *Sun Bin bingfa*[5] records the following:

The method for using fire in battles: [when the enemy is] downwind and in a low, flat, brush-covered area, and the warriors in all their armies have no place to run, under these conditions one can set fire. In gales of wind with grass growing everywhere, when their firewood and grasses are piled up and the enemy camp has lax guards, then one can set fire. Use this fire to disrupt them, then rain arrows down on them. At this time sound the drums and yell war cries to spur the attack. Use the fire's power as a support. This is the way of using fire in battles.

Therefore, we know that *yin* indicates the various proper conditions for using fire.[6]

"Beforehand" is read *su*.[7]

---

[3]The first character of this line, "*xing,*" is missing in the Linyi text, so the later versions were used to amend it.

[4]Some Qing Dynasty scholars held that the term "smoky fire" (*yanhuo*) in the later versions ought to read "flames" (*biaohuo*). (*Mozi* has the line "make a *yan* [lit., 'smoke'] arrow for shooting fire onto city gates" [vol. 14, "Beichengmen," p. 306; Sun Yirang's annotation].) But reading this as "flames" is still unacceptable, for how could an army possibly lack means for starting a fire? (Of course, reading *biaohuo* as meaning "incendiary weapons" does make much sense; however, this is just a conjecture based on this quote from *Mozi* and lacks any concrete proof.) In "Attacks Using Fire," the most important factor is the grasp of proper conditions; we therefore know that the Linyi text is correct here.

[5]*Xia,* "Shizhen," p. 85.

[6]*Yin* was interpreted by Cao Cao as "take advantage of our undercover agents." Chen Hao has pointed out that Cao's opinion was incorrect: "[One] must have expedience, not just undercover agents."

[7]The *Guoyu* records, "Planning must *su* forecast its achievements" (vol. 19, "Wuyu," p. 1a); Wei Zhao's note.

5. "These four" in the Chinese text reads "*ci si zhe*" and follows the Linyi text.[8] The later versions read "*ci zixiu zhe*" (these four constellations). However, the preceding text says, " 'specific days' are when the moon is aligned with the constellations Qi [in the Western constellation Sagittarius], Bi [in Andromeda], Yi [in Crater], and Zhen [in Corvus]" (p. 108). So, the days the "gales will blow" are not due to these four constellations, but because the moon is aligned with certain stars. We therefore follow the Linyi text here.

6. "When fire is set and their forces are calm, cancel the attack" in the Chinese text reads "*huo fa qi bing jing, er wugong*" and follows the Linyi text. *Qi* indicates "if the condition is thus."[9] *Er* is read to mean *ze* (then).[10]

   The later versions read this line as "*huo fa bing jing zhe, dai er wugong*" (if fire is set [when their] forces are calm, wait and do not attack); this reading has dissimilarities since "fire is set" is a predetermined condition and "their forces are calm" indicates a surprise condition. The deduction is that they must have preparations, so what is there to wait for? Therefore, the later versions of this line are not logical.

   The *wu* in *wugong* expresses a prohibitory mood, so in following the text's meaning we have interpreted it as "cancel."

7. "Let the fire inflict the severest damage; hunt for them when huntable; halt when not huntable" in the Chinese text reads "*ji qi huoyang, kecong er cong zhi, bukecong er zhi.*"[11]

---

[8]The beginning of this line has "*yue zai*" (when the moon is aligned with), which follows the later versions. This part in the Linyi text is missing. However, Sun Xingyan and Wu Renji quoted this phrase as "*xiu zai*" (lit., "the constellations are in") (*Shijia*, vol. 12, p. 4b) by following the *Tongdian* (note: vol. 160, "Bing" 13, p. 847) and the *Taiping yulan* (note: vol. 321, "Bing bu" 52, p. 1475); moreover, Du Mu (who incorrectly believed that *xiu* meant "where the moon was staying"), Mei Yaochen, and Zhang Yu all followed this reading of *xiu zai*.

Constellations in ancient times were referred to as *xiu*, and the moon's alignment with certain constellations presaged unusual changes in the wind or rain. The pre-Qin classics contain extremely clear records of this (see Book 1, comment 10a, footnote 29), so altering this phrase to read "*xiu zai*" is unacceptable.

[9]Yang Shuda, *Ciquan*, vol. 4, "Qi," fourth definition, p. 40.

[10]Wang Yinzhi, *Jingzhuan shici*, vol. 7, "Er," sixth definition, p. 146.

[11]The five characters "*zhi, bukecong er*" are missing in the Linyi text.

7a. In the phrase *"ji qi huoyang"* (let the fire inflict the severest damage),[12] which follows the Linyi text, the later editions read *huoyang* as *huoli* (lit., "the fire's power"). Two explanations have been given for this line: that the fire burns to its extreme power, or the fire burns out.[13] Fire is used in an attack in order to cause disaster and turbulence, which in turn allows the attack to be irresistible. So, the later versions of this line are not as clear as the Linyi text.

7b. *"Zhi"* (halt) in the Linyi text originally read *"zhi zhi"* (lit., "halt it"), while the later versions read *"zhi."* Having the second *zhi* (it) character here is either inappropriate[14] or might have been used to end the sentence.[15]

8. "Diurnal winds are forceful; nocturnal winds are gentle" in the Chinese text reads *"zhoufeng jiu, yefeng zhi."* Most annotations have dissimilarities here because the common definitions for *jiu* and *zhi* are "to be long" and "to cease." However, diurnal winds are not necessarily long, and nocturnal winds do not necessarily cease.

---

[12]*Yang* (lit., "middle") is a substitute character for *yang* (damage). The Mawangdui silk text of the *Jingfa* contains many proofs of this; examples can be found in the "Sidu," "Wanglun," and "Mingli" parts (*Boshu zhujian*, pp. 16–23), so this must have been a common pre-Qin practice.

Yang means *hai* (damage; disaster) (e.g., *Guoyu*, the line "their people were unable to bear the *yang* of hunger and exhaustion" [vol. 19, "Wuyu"; Wei Zhao's note]), so *huoyang* indicates the damage caused by fire.

[13]Du Mu annotated this as "wait until the fire has burned out."

[14]In both Book 11, "The Nine Zones," and later here in Book 12, "Attacks Using Fire," the same line is repeated: *"heyu li er dong, buheyu li er zhi"* (act when advantageous; halt when not advantageous) (pp. 96 and 100; see comment 13); the sentence structure is identical to that of this line, and at the end of neither of these lines is the character *"zhi"* (it).

Moreover, in the *Lunyu* when Zigong asked about how to treat a friend, Confucius answered, "Loyally advise and faithfully guide him; if not possible, halt" (*"zhonggu er shandao zhi, buke ze zhi"*) (vol. 12, "Yanyuan" [*Shisanjing*, pp. 5438–39]); the sentence pattern here is likewise similar to this line of *Sun-tzu* in that it also does not have the object *zhi* (it) after *zhi* (halt).

[15]See Pei Xuehai, *Gushu xuzi jishi*, vol. 9, "Zhi," twenty-eighth definition: *"zhi* is as if saying *ye*," p. 751.

Jiu had the ancient meaning of *ju* ("buffeting," so "forceful").[16] *Zhi* indicates "not in a wild manner,"[17] so we interpret it as "gentle."

9. "Take defensive measures against them" in the Chinese text reads *"yi shu shou zhi."* The basic definition of *shu* is "to calculate." Because the process of calculation has a definite procedure, it also is defined as "means."[18] By observing the characteristics in these definitions of *shu*, as well as the succeeding text's phrase "to guard against them" (*"shou zhi"*), we have interpreted it as "defensive measures."[19]

10. "Attack supported by fire is indefensible" in the Chinese text reads *"gu yi huo zuo gong zhe ming."* *Gu* here acts as a mood word,[20] and *ming* (lit., "bright") should be interpreted as *qiang* (dynamic; strong; indefensible).[21]

11. "When battles gain victories and attacks achieve occupations, yet these successes are not followed up, it is disastrous. This is known as 'persisting turmoil' " in the

---

[16]*Shuowen*, 5 *xia*, "Jiu"; Duan Yucai's note, pp. 239–40.

[17]E.g., *Xunzi* records, "To be appointed, then will be courteous and *zhi*" (vol. 2, "Bugou," p. 3a); Yang Jing's note.

[18]*Shuowen*, 3 *xia*, p. 124. Also, *Guangya*, 5 *xia*, "Shiyan," p. 13b.

[19]Du Mu annotated this line as "must reckon the numbers of the stars' movements and wait for the days of rising winds, then one can set fire; this cannot be done at any time." Some have emulated his position. However, Du Mu here is unreliable.

Sun-tzu in the preceding text has already discussed this, so it need not be repeated. Furthermore, the requirements for "attacks using fire" lie not only with the celestial alignments; humidity and operational conditions all are important.

In fact, this line of *Sun-tzu* does not discuss attacking the enemy, but rather defense. Zhang Yu therefore noted, "It is not enough to know the use of fire in attacking the enemy; also take care to defend against the enemy attacking oneself." We follow his view to interpret *Sun-tzu's* counsel in this line.

[20]Yang Shuda, *Ciquan*, vol. 3, "Gu," eighth definition, p. 16.

[21]Wang Yinzhi, *Jingyi shuwen*, the line *"zhengming,"* which quotes Wang Niansun: *"Ming* is as if saying *qiang"* (vol. 19, p. 475).

Mei Yaochen wrote that this meant "clearly and easily will be victorious," and Zhang Yu added that this described "brightly able to win victory." Both of these are forced interpretations. What relationship does brightness or clarity have with victory?

Chinese text reads *"fu zhansheng gongqu, er busui*[22] *qi gong zhe, xiong; ming zhi yue 'bi*[23] *liu'"* and follows the Linyi text.

Cao Cao interpreted these lines as "like the flow of water, it does not return." We do not know if he is referring to *gong* (success) or *bi* (lit., "waste"; "outlays"). Cao also noted, "Some say the rewards are not punctual, just *biliu*. Reward good deeds; do not wait for another day." But what does *biliu* refer to here? And how can this matter be *xiong* (disastrous)? Cao does not explain.

To interpret this line properly one must first understand what *"sui qi gong"* (lit., "to follow up these successes") means. Evidence can be found in the following line: "an enlightened lord considers these and distinguished commanders follow them" (p. 109). So, *"sui zhi"* indicates following the lord's deliberations that concern both the country and politics.

Since this line states that the battle is victorious and the attack is successful, armed conflict thus has been concluded. Needless to say, it is in the country's interest to grade fealty and reward efforts in battle; this is what an enlightened lord considers.

Moreover, the Mawangdui silk text of the *Jingfa*[24] records, "After the blades of the military, follow them with *wen* (political management); only then will this be successful." What is meant by success is therefore not achieved through military power but must be sought through politics. Military power can do no more than act as an effective support—not "succor," according to *Sun-tzu*—for a country's political strategy. Therefore, armed conflict is guided by assured victory within the political considerations, and as soon as a mission is fulfilled, a political resolution must be turned to before the country can achieve complete success. This is our understanding of *"sui qi gong."*

The *bi* in *"biliu"* was in pre-Qin times the equivalent of *bei*.[25] *Bei* means *ni*

---

[22] *Sui* in the later versions reads *xiu* 修 In the ancient classics, *xiu* generally was written as 脩 (*Shuowen*, 4 *xia*, p. 176; Duan Yucai's note). *Xiu* in this line of *Sun-tzu* actually was mistaken for *xun* 循 Sun Yirang explained that "*xiu* and *xun* had similar forms in the clerical script [*lishu*], so the two characters were often erroneously copied" (*Zhayi*, vol. 5, "Shangzi," under the line *"yu min buxiu fa, ze wen faguan,"* p. 263).
Xun was a synonym for *sui* in the Linyi text.

[23] This character is read *fei* today, but it was read *bi* in ancient Chinese.

[24] "Sidu" (*Boshu zhujian*, p. 17).

[25] E.g., *Liji*, the line *"kou bi er fan"* (vol. 55, "Ziyi" [*Shisanjing*, p. 3578]); Zheng Xuan's note.

(turmoil).[26] So, *biliu* here means *beiliu* (persisting turmoil), and if an unsettled situation still remains, this sooner or later will be the source of great discord; this is therefore called *xiong* (disastrous).

The character *ming* (lit., "to order") in *"ming zhi yue"* is read as meaning *ming* (lit., "to be called").[27]

12. "Armies" in the Chinese text reads *"jun"* and follows the Linyi text. The later versions read *"shi"* (troops).

13. "Act when advantageous; halt when not advantageous" in the Chinese text reads *"heyu li er dong, buheyu li er zhi"* and follows the later versions. The Linyi text reads *"heyu li er yong, buhe er zhi"* (utilize when advantageous; halt when unsuitable). Because this repeats a line in Book 11, "The Nine Zones" (p. 96), they should have the same form, so we do not follow the Linyi text here. Furthermore, it was the ancient practice to use *dong* (to act) and *zhi* (to halt) as complementary verb pairs; the Linyi text's reading of *yong* (to utilize) with *zhi* seems, then, inaccurate.

14. "But annihilated countries may never exist again, nor may the dead ever live again" in the Chinese text reads *"wangguo buke fucun, sizhe buke fusheng."* This line is missing in the Linyi text; in the later versions *ke* (may) is read *keyi; keyi* is an example of later Chinese and could not have been part of the original text. The *Zhanguoce* records that the renowned Qin commander Bo Qi once said, *"Po-guo buke fuyuan, sizu buke fusheng"* (destroyed countries may never be complete again, nor may dead soldiers ever live again).[28] He was citing *Sun-tzu* here, and in both places he used *ke*, not *keyi*.

[26]E.g., *Liji*, the line *"jiangzhu tiandi er bubei"* (vol. 53, "Zhongyong" [*Shisanjing*, p. 3544]); Kong Yingda's annotation.

[27]E.g., the *Zuozhuan*, the line *"ming* him with the name Chou" (vol. 5, "Huangong ernian" [*Shisanjing*, p. 3782]); Ruan Yuan in his critical notes ("Jiaokanji") indicated that *ming* (to order) is the same as *ming* (to call; to be called).

[28]Vol. 33, "Zhongshan ce," p. 678. The *Taiping yulan* also quotes this line from *Sun-tzu* using *ke* rather than *keyi* (vol. 272, "Bing bu" 3, p. 1274).

COMMENTS ON BOOK 13

ESPIONAGE

1. "Advancing out of the country for conflict over thousands of miles" in the Chinese text reads "*chuzheng qianli*"[1] and follows the later versions. This line in the Linyi text is missing. *Chu* (lit., "to go out") is in reference to a country. *Zheng* here follows its basic meaning of *xing* (lit., "to go"; "to advance").[2]

2. "Both sides stalk each other over several years" in the Chinese text reads "*xiangshou shunian.*" *Xiang* here means "mutually" or "each other." *Shou* (lit., "to guard"; "to defend") is interpreted here as "to stalk."[3] When two countries conduct armed conflict against each other over several years, they cannot be said to simply "guard" or "defend" against each other; they must stalk chances to attack and defeat their opponent, which is why this line concludes, "to contend for victory in a single day" (p. 111).

---

[1]"*Chuzheng*" in the *Shijia* reads "*chubing*" (to dispatch forces); the *Taiping yulan* quotes this line as "*chushi*" (to dispatch troops) (vol. 292, "Bing bu" 23, p. 1348).

In addition to its archaic definition of *xing* (to go) (see footnote 2), the character *zheng* had the definition of "superiors attacking inferiors," especially among the Confucianists (e.g., *Mengzi*, vol. 14 *shang*, "Jinxing" *xia* [*Shisanjing*, p. 6028]). Both the *Shijia* and the *Taiping yulan* possibly made their changes because of this influence.

[2]*Shuowen, 2 xia*, "Zheng," p. 71; Duan Yucai's note indicates that in a "Shiyan" (note: in the *Erya*, vol. 3 [*Shisanjing*, p. 5610]), *zheng* is defined as *xing* (to go).

[3]*Shou* (to guard) can be read here as *shou* (to hunt). Many examples exist of these two characters being used interchangeably; see Yu Shengyu, *Zhuzi xinzheng*, vol. 2, "Lüshi Chunqiu xinzheng," under the line "*yi qi shou* [lit., "animal"] *zhe xian zhi, suoyi zhong zhi ye*," p. 331. Also, Yang Shuda indicated that *shou* (to guard) had the ancient definition of *qiu* (to seek; to search for) (*Jiweiju dushuji*, "Du Zuozhuan," under the line "the lord of Lu *shou* Qi for three years but achieved nothing," p. 70). Both of these explications referred to this line of *Sun-tzu*, so *shou* is defined as "to stalk" here.

3. "To be parsimonious" in the Chinese text reads *"ai"* (today lit., "to love"). In pre-Qin usage this character indicated "parsimony,"[4] and its meaning differed from its modern definition.[5]

4. "It must be gained from what is learned by men" in the Chinese text reads *"bi qu yu ren zhi zhe"* and follows the Linyi text. The later versions read, *"bi qu yu ren, zhi dizhiqing zhe ye"* (it must be gained from people who know the enemy's status).[6] "Those who know the enemy's status" are without a doubt extremely valuable. But, the collection of information on the "enemy's status" is not limited only to such people, nor do these people necessarily completely comprehend the enemy's situation. In other words, espionage is very broad, and what "those who know" can provide is only one part of the puzzle that is "the enemy's status." The later versions' reading, then, cannot be considered incorrect; it just is not as comprehensive as that of the Linyi text.

5. "Turned agents" in the Chinese text reads *"fanjian."*[7] *Sun-tzu* later in the text defines "turned agents" as ones obtained from among enemy agents who are plied with advantages and instructed by us. So, in other words, the loyalty of these agents is turned to our side, and we interpret this term accordingly.

6. "Covert mastery" in the Chinese text reads *"shenji."* Regarding *shen* (lit., "deity"), *Sun-tzu* uses this term as a noun twice in the entire work: the first is in Book 6, "Superiority and Inferiority," where we interpret it as "supreme" (p.

---

[4]*Yi Zhou shu*, the line "miserly in giving is called *ai*" (vol. 6, "Shifa," p. 99). Also *Mengzi* has the line "people all thought my lord was *ai*" (vol. 1 *xia*, "Liang Huiwang" *shang* [*Shisanjing*, p. 5802]); Zhao Qi noted, "*Ai* means *se* [parsimonious]."

[5]In the pre-Qin period, the character that meant "to love" was *ai* 悉, and later the modern form, 愛, took its place (see *Shuowen*, 10 *xia*, "Ai," p. 510; Duan Yucai's note).

[6]The Sakurada version reads *"bi qu yu ren er zhi di zhi qing ye"* (it must be gained from people, and they know the enemy's status).

[7]*Fanjian* defined as "turned agents" is a term unique to *Sun-tzu*. In modern times it has been translated as "double agents," which is incorrect. The loyalty of double agents lies with only themselves, as they work for two opposing enemy sides. The general Chinese concept of *fanjian*—other than that in *Suntzu*—is that they are those spies working to undermine enemy unification.

68), and the second place is here. We follow the preceding text to this line, "none can penetrate their ways" (p. 112), in interpreting *shen* as "covert."[8]
  Ji means "mastery."[9]

7. "Agents-in-place" in the Chinese text reads *"yinjian"* and follows the later versions. The Linyi text has *"shengjian"* (mobile informants) in this position, so we know that its order is erroneous.

8. "Hidden provocation agents, when a sham is constructed externally, then apprise our agents and disseminate it among the enemy" in the Chinese text reads *"sijian zhe, wei kuangshi yu wai, ling wujiang zhi zhi, er chuan yu di jian zhe ye."*[10]

8a. Regarding *"sijian"* (hidden provocation agents), Du You, Du Mu, Mei Yaochen, Wang Xi, and Zhang Yu all said that because the outcome of a matter will prove that our agents deceived the enemy, the enemy will certainly terminate our agents, which is why *Sun-tzu* refers to hidden provocation agents as *sijian* (lit., "dead agents").

8b. For *"chuan yu di jian"* (disseminate it among the enemy), Li Quan suggested that *chuan* (disseminate) should read *dai* (to stay),[11] which is problematic.

---

[8]*Xunzi* noted, "Their activities are not seen; only their achievements are seen—this is called *shen*" (vol. 11, "Tianlun," p. 10a). This agrees with *Sun-tzu*'s description.

[9]E.g., the *Shijing* records, "Gangji all areas" (vol. 16, "Daya: Wenwang series: Yupu" [*Shisanjing*, p. 1108]); Kong Yingda annotated that *ji* indicates "managing even the minuscule, attaining with utmost thoroughness," so we know that *ji* is a complete and thorough mastery of something.

[10]The Sakurada version's description of *"sijian"* (hidden provocation agents; lit., "dead agents," see comment 8b) is that they *"wei di ye"* (are given up to the enemy).

[11]Also, Yu Chang supported this interpretation and pointed out that the *Tongdian* (note: vol. 151, "Bing" 4, the line *"dai yu di jian zhe ye,"* p. 791) and the *Taiping yulan* (note: vol. 292, "Bing bu" 23, the line *"dai yu di ye,"* p. 1348) both use *dai* instead of *chuan*. Yu also explained that "these types of agents often *dai* [stayed] among the enemy and did not return, so were therefore called *sijian* [dead agents; *si* also means 'immobile']," as well as noting that these agents had as their mission "the sending of reports" (*Xiangcao xujiaoshu*, "Sunzi," p. 450). What Yu was actually describing here were deep-cover agents, and these have been greatly used ever since ancient times. However, later in the text *Sun-tzu* says that *"sijian*, when a sham is constructed externally, then apprise our agents and disseminate it among the enemy" (p. 113), which clearly shows that Li Quan's and Yu Chang's explanations are not representative of Sun-tzu's meaning.

9. "Of those close to the armies, none are closer than agents" in the Chinese text reads "*gu sanjun zhi qin, moqin yu jian*" and follows the Linyi text. The *Wujing* and *Shiyijia* read this as "*gu sanjun zhi shi, moqin yu jian*" (of armies' affairs, none are closer than agents).[12] This section discusses the relationship between the armies and agents, so reading this as "armies' affairs" (*sanjun zhi shi*) is incorrect.

10. "Humanity" in the Chinese text reads "*ren*" and follows the Linyi text. The later versions read this as "benevolence and justice" ("*ren yi*"). This term was first used by Mencius, who lived about a hundred years after Sun Wu, so the book *Sun-tzu* could not have implemented it.

11. "Thorough observation" in the Chinese text reads "*weimi.*" This section is missing in the Linyi text, while the later versions read this as "*weimiao.*" We follow materials from the Tang Dynasty[13] and the succeeding text to determine the text here. The later versions give this as "*weizai, weizai,*" while the Linyi text reads "*mizai, mizai.*" *Mi* is defined as "to scrutinize," and so "to observe" (*shen*).[14] *Miao* means "minuscule" (*wei*).[15] Therefore, *weimi* indicates thorough observation, while *weimiao* indicates infinitesimal. Of these two terms, "thorough observation" (*weimi*) makes more sense in relation to the text.

---

[12]Sun Xingyan and Wu Renji's criticism follows both the *Tongdian* (note: vol. 151, "Bing" 4, p. 791) and the *Taiping yulan* (note: vol. 292, "Bing bu" 23, p. 1348) in giving "*sanjun zhi qin*" as the correct text of *Sun-tzu* here (vol. 13, p. 10b). The *Changduanjing* (vol. 9, "Wujian" [*Hanhai congshu*, p. 1192]) quotes this in the same way as the Linyi text. Moreover, Du You's and Zhang Yu's annotations follow versions that also are identical to the Linyi text here.

The Sakurada version is similar, but "none are closer than agents" is read "in association, none is closer than that of agents."

[13]Such Tang dynastic records as the *Tongdian* (vol. 151, "Bing" 4, p. 791), *Changduanjing* (vol. 9, "Wujian," where the text reads "*miwei*" [*Hanhai congshu*, p. 1192]), and the version used by Du You (note: his annotation first addresses *wei* and then *mi*, so we know the text he followed), as well as the early Song's *Taiping yulan* (vol. 292, "Bing" 23, "Yongjian," p. 1348), all read this term as *weimi*. *Weimiao* is first seen in the later versions written after the early Song Dynasty, so we also can see that in the text of *Sun-tzu*, *weimi* is more credible than *weimiao*.

[14]E.g., the *Zhouli* has the line "wielders then *mi*" ("Kaogongji: Luren" [*Shisanjing*, p. 2003]); Zheng Xuan's note, as well as Sun Yirang's notes (*Zhouli zhengyi*, vol. 82, pp. 3409–11).

Moreover, under the line "no activities are observed [*mi*] more than those of agents" (p. 113), the *Shiyijia* has the note, "*Mi*: another edition reads *shen* [to scrutinize]" (*xia*, p. 46a). We therefore know that *mi* and *shen* had the same meaning and were interchangeable.

[15]E.g., the *Lüshi Chunqiu* records, "What is known is *miao*" ("Shenfen," vol. 17, p. 3b); Gao You's note.

12. "Observe, observe!" in the Chinese text reads *"mizai, mizai!"* and follows the Linyi text.[16] The later versions read this as *"weizai, weizai!"* (lit., "minuscule, minuscule!").

Mizai indicates that the truth of a matter must be observed, so the next line reads, "there are no events where agents are not utilized" (p. 114). If it is read as meaning "minuscule, minuscule!" it has no connection with the succeeding line (see comment 11).

13. "Before an agent's activity is under way, if it is leaked, none of the agents nor those informed may live" in the Chinese text reads *"jianshi weifa, er xianwen, jian yu suogaozhe, jiesi"* and follows the *Wujing* and *Shiyijia*. The Linyi text has only the extant characters "_____ *shi weifa, wen jian* _____" (__ activity is under way, hear agent __). Zhao Benxue noted, "One edition reads 'the one who heard it and those he told must both die' ['*wen yu suogaozhe jiesi*'], which is not right." He also wrote, "Execute those agents who leaked information and execute those who heard it in order to seal their mouths."[17]

14. "Be certain to ferret out the enemy agents who come to spy on us" in the Chinese text reads *"bi suo dijian zhi lai jian wo zhe"* and follows the *Wujing*. This part is missing in the Linyi text. Both the *Shiyijia* and Sakurada versions read *dijian* (enemy agents) as *diren zhi jian* (today, "agents of the enemy"). Sun-tzu's references to the enemy are given as *di*, not *diren*,[18] so we do not accept the *Shiyijia* and Sakurada versions of this line.[19]

15. "Regarding the five agents' activities, the lord must know them" in the Chinese text reads *"wujian zhi shi, zhu bi zhi zhi"* and follows the later versions. The Linyi text reads *"wujian zhi shi, bi zhi zhi"* (regarding the five agents' activities, they

---

[16]From Zhang Yu's annotation, which explained *mi* but not *wei*, we know that the text he followed during the Song Dynasty was the same as that used in the Tang records.

[17]*Sunzi shu jiaojie yinlei, xia*, p. 81b.

[18]See Book 11, comment 8b.

[19]Both the *Tongdian* (vol. 151, "Bing" 4, p. 791) and *Taiping yulan* (vol. 292, "Bing bu" 23, p. 1348) quote this line of *Sun-tzu* in the same way as the *Wujing*, except that they do not have the two characters *bi suo* (be certain to ferret out). Du You, Wang Xi, and Zhang Yu's annotations all use the term *dijian*, so we know they followed the same text as the *Wujing*.

must be known), with the character *zhu* (lord) apparently overlooked, and both the preceding and succeeding lines missing.

16. After this section the Linyi text also has the damaged line "__ [*zhi xing ye,*] *Shuaishibi zai Jing; Yan zhi xing ye, Su Qin zai Qi*" ([the rise of __] was due to Shuaishibi in the Jing state; the rise of the Yan sovereign was due to Su Qin in the Qi state); these refer to occurrences during the Warring States Period, which was much later than Sun Wu's time, so we do not include them in our text.

17. "These are the precepts for military affairs and are the guides for the armies' operations" in the Chinese text reads "*ci bing zhi yao, sanjun zhi suo shi er dong ye.*" Because this is mentioned along with *sanjun* (the armies; see Book 7, comment 4), we understand that *bing* here does not indicate forces or military operations, but military affairs.

PART 3

APPEN-DIXES

The first five of these appendixes were discovered as part of the Linyi text in 1972 at Yinqueshan, Linyi. The sixth appendix, "The King of Wu's Queries on Strategic Zones," appears in the *Shiyijia* version. It is our opinion that these are all apocrypha and were written during the Warring States Period by members of the Sun-tzu School. They are therefore valuable references but not part of *Sun-tzu* itself.

Finally, in the seventh appendix we have included a chronology of the Chinese dynasties.

THE KING OF WU'S QUERIES

INTRODUCTION

This record is presumed to be a dialogue between the King of the Wu state and Sun Wu regarding the state of Jin. With the Jin state as the topic here, we can see three main considerations:

First, its geographical location. Jin was the leading state of the central Chinese bloc and was located in modern-day Shanxi Province. To its west was the representative of the western powers, the Qin state (in modern-day Shaanxi Province); to its southeast was the Zheng state (in modern-day Henan Province), which acted as the frontline for the Chu state (in modern-day Hubei and Hunan provinces), the representative of the southern powers.

Second, the political climate of China at that time. During the Spring and Autumn Period (770–404 B.C.), such a political situation was brewing in China mainly due to the weakening power of the Zhou Dynasty's emperors. Powerful feudal lords became leaders out of necessity in order to maintain general stability. In the early Spring and Autumn Period, this power base was mainly located to the south of the Yellow River in Qi, while during the middle and late Spring and Autumn Period this shifted to Jin.

Third, political systems and culture. The Jin state comprised the mainstream of China's political systems and culture at that time. The Qin state to the west was colored by the Yi tribes, while the Chu to the south was considered Man, or barbarian. The superior political system and culture of central China gave rise to an exclusiveness that particularly emphasized the Jin's protective capacity.

It was because of these three factors that the Jin state became the nucleus of the Spring and Autumn Period. By 454 B.C., when the Jin state officially started to splinter,

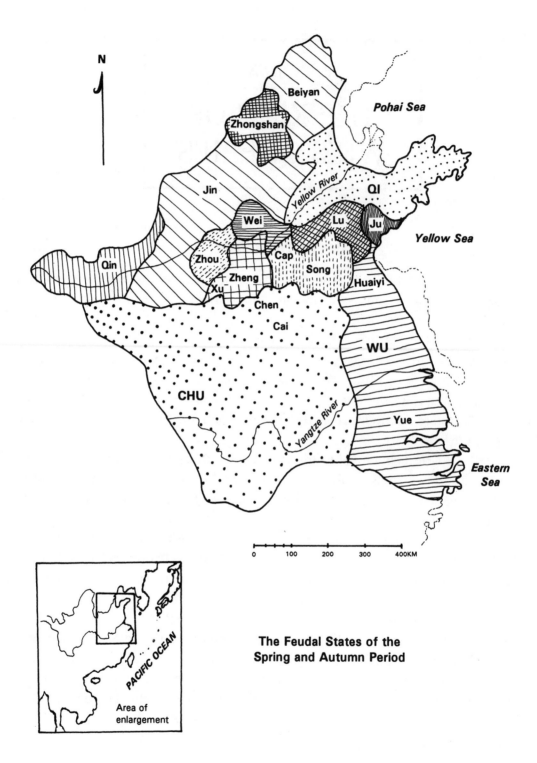

The Feudal States of the
Spring and Autumn Period

the Spring and Autumn Period began its decline and the seeds for the Warring States Period were sown.

More than a hundred years before that happened, though, in 584 B.C., the Jin state dealt with Chu by sending the exiled Chu officer Wuchen to the state of Wu (in modern-day Jiangsu Province), which was located to the southeast of Chu. Wuchen's mission was to act as a military adviser to train the Wu people in the skill and tactics of chariot driving and battle arrays in order to sharpen the military abilities of Wu against Chu. For this reason the discussion here has Jin looking upon the King of Wu as its ally to the south, and the Jin state is also considered the most powerful rival to Wu's future expansion into the Chinese heartland. What is examined is the predicted rise and fall of the six major powers within the Jin state, as well as analyses of the reasons for this vicissitude.

Regarding these political powers, the record mentions that the Fan and Zhongxing clans first degenerated, then the Zhi clan; both comments are historically factual. This discussion then predicts that the Han and Wei clans would then decline, after which the Jin state would completely be the domain of the Zhao clan, but this does not accord with the fact that the Han, Zhao, and Wei clans divided the Jin state among themselves. This shows that the discussion here was recorded in the fifty years between 454 B.C., when the Zhi family degenerated in the Jin state, and 403 B.C., when the Zhou emperor officially granted the Han, Zhao, and Wei clans feudal lordship.[1]

The reasons this record gives for the waxing and waning of these political powers are the size of the tax burden, the amount of forces supported by the state, whether its lord is arrogant and its officers extravagant, and whether it lightly initiates armed conflict. This even sets forth a formula for decline: heavy taxes lead to a rich government, which leads to arrogant lords, extravagant officers, and massive numbers of supported troops, which leads to lightly initiated armed conflict, and which in turn leads to destruction. It then says that if the six powerful Jin clans are measured against this formula, the order of decline would be the Fan, the Zhongxing, the Zhi, the Han, and the Wei, with only the Zhao distancing itself from this and thereby surviving.

This record of course is a valuable reference in understanding this school of Suntzu thought. However, two points bear consideration:

First, historical documents show that this record's predictions for the termination

---

[1] *Yinqueshan Hanmu zhujian "Sunzi bingfa,"* p. 144; in the appendix Wu Shuping's selected writings also hold this viewpoint.

of the Han, Wei, and Zhao clans were erroneous, which proves that using a single deductive formula to predict the complicated rise and fall of political powers is precarious. Such a profound and lucid master of strategy as Sun Wu would not have made such a bold prediction.

Second, for a country's military outlays one must observe the status of that country and its enemy in order to determine the least amount necessary. *Sun-tzu*'s Book 1, "Surveying," and Book 2, "Mobilizing for Armed Conflict," clearly explicate this. So, although "low taxes and a prosperous people" as a political ideal cannot be denied, political facts have not been considered here. Because of this, the argument lacks the comprehensiveness of *Sun-tzu*'s text. What is discussed in this record, then, did not originate with Sun Wu—although his age might have allowed him to see these historical events personally (see Introduction, note 5)—but should be considered an axiom of the Sun-tzu school of thought.

TEXT

The King of Wu asked Sun-tzu, "Of the six generals who separately govern in Jin, which one will decline first, and which one will be stable and prevail?"

Sun-tzu said, "Those of the Fan and Zhongxing clans will decline first."

"Which one will be next?"

"The Zhi clan will be next."

"Which one will be next?"

"The Han and Wei will be next. If the Zhao do not lose their traditional rules, all of Jin will belong to it."

The King of Wu asked, "May I know the reason for your words?"

Sun-tzu said, "Yes. The farm systems of the Fan and the Zhongxing use eighty strides for one *yuan* unit and one hundred sixty strides for one *mou* unit; moreover, the tax on these is one-fifth [twenty percent]. Their . . . paddies are narrow, [but they] support many active troops. With a tax of one-fifth, the government is rich. When the government is rich, many active troops are supported. Their lords are arrogant, their officials extravagant; they presume to have merit and constantly desire armed conflict. Thus I said they would be first.

. . . "[The Zhi clan's] government is wealthy, they have many active troops, their lords are arrogant, their officials are extravagant, and they presume to have merit and constantly desire armed conflict. Thus they will follow the Fan and Zhongxing clans.

"The farm systems of the Han and the Wei use one hundred strides for one *yuan* unit and two hundred strides for one *mou* unit; moreover, the tax on these is one-fifth. Their . . . paddies are narrow, but they support many active troops. With a tax of one-fifth, the government is rich. When the government is rich, many active troops are supported. Their lords are arrogant, their officials are extravagant; they presume to have merit and constantly desire battles. Thus I said they would follow the Zhi clan.

"The farm system of the Zhao uses one hundred twenty strides for one *yuan* unit and two hundred strides for one *mou* unit; the government appropriates no tax. The government is poor and supports few active troops. Their lord is modest and their officials are dutiful in administrating a wealthy populace. So I said that their territory is stable and that Jin will finally belong to them."

The King of Wu said, "Exactly. That is the proper way for a sage ruler. . . . kindly administrate their populace."

THE FOUR ADAPTATIONS

INTRODUCTION

This record is related to Book 8, "The Nine Adaptations," and its discussion provides operational guidance for "some routes need not necessarily be taken, some armies need not necessarily be struck, some cities need not necessarily be besieged, some land need not necessarily be contended, and some lords' orders need not necessarily be accepted" (pp. 75–76). The general rules followed here are "do not consider only immediate gain" but "achieve maximum future gain and minimum future harm," so it serves as an instructive resource. However, this record does contain inconsistencies:

First, its principles for adaptation are too explicit. We will use "some cities need not necessarily be besieged" as an example. In addition to the principle cited in this record, Sun Bin has one chapter[1] that expressly discusses how a city's attackability is completely determined by the positioning of the mountain or river terrain that supports it. Also, Cao Cao's annotation that "a city which is small and secure with ample provisions is not attackable" relies on a defensive condition. These examples clearly show that a strategic rule can actually be subject to various considerations. This fact also helps us realize why the text of *Sun-tzu* always discusses general principles and does not give individual conditions as illustrations: It was so that strategists could apply these principles to any situation they faced and thus make their appropriate refinements.

Second, the standpoint in this record regarding "some lords' orders need not necessarily be accepted" is unscrupulous, for *Sun-tzu* says very clearly in Book 10, "Terrain," that "when the ways for battle are definitely victorious, even if the lord orders no battle, the battle may still be waged; when the ways for battle are not victorious,

---

[1] *Sun Bin bingfa, xia,* "Xiong pin cheng," p. 115.

even if the lord orders a battle, the battle may still not be waged" (p. 92). "Lords' orders" in ancient times were the equivalent of "national directives." To "not accept" them was to be guilty of treason, a very serious matter.

From this it is very clear that the view provided in this record is to be regarded only as a reference, not as strategic gospel. So, then, at no time other than the moment of determining victory itself may tenets be allowed to challenge national directives. Strategy causes victory, but it is not victory itself. There is a Buddhist saying that when a hand points at the moon, its purport is the moon, not the hand. Obdurate belief in this record's "some lords' orders need not necessarily be accepted" causes one to focus on the hand and disregard the moon, thereby missing *Sun-tzu*'s original intent.[1]

[1]See Appendix 5.

TEXT

. . . [Some routes need not necessarily be taken, some armies need not necessarily be struck,] some cities need not necessarily be besieged, some land need not necessarily be contended, and some lords' orders [need not necessarily be carried out].

Why some routes need not be taken: With shallow penetration, previous activities cannot be continued; with deep penetration, subsequent gains will be disconnected. And actions will cause harm; immobility will bring entrapment. Such ones should not be taken.

Why some armies need not be struck: When two armies set up bases in coordination with the order of battle, in our surveys, our strengths are sufficient to destroy their army and capture their commanders. However, if we make long-range surveys, there are better ways to exercise power irresistibly and skill flexibly; then the army . . . commander. In such cases, even though an army is attackable, it need not be struck.

Why some cities need not be besieged: In our surveys, our strengths are sufficient for occupation, but the occupation cannot further what we have gained. Also, once taken, we cannot protect it. If strength . . . to it, the city will certainly not be occupied. As a consequence of our previous accomplishments, when our advantages are gained, [the city] will surrender of itself. If we fail, this will not adversely affect the outcome. In such a situation, even though the city can be besieged, do not besiege it.

Why some land need not be contended: water [? grasses] . . . in mountain valleys that cannot supply our needs . . . and . . . vulnerable. In such a situation, do not contend it.

Why some lords' orders need not be carried out: when a lord's orders countermand the above four adaptations, they cannot be carried out. . . . carried out. Activities . . . adapted, then know how to use forces.

APPENDIX 3

THE YELLOW EMPEROR'S ATTACK ON THE RED EMPEROR

INTRODUCTION

This record uses brilliant historical emperors—the Yellow Emperor, King Tang of the Shang, and King Wu of the Zhou—to illustrate two matters:

First, that a successfully working internal government is the necessary foundation for military action.

Second, the rules for effective battle arrays are that these need to be to the right of lowlands, have perpendicular arrays, and possess a main route to the rear. Since in ancient times the locus of forces was in the right flank, lowlands acted to block the enemy's main forces and allowed one's main forces to occupy higher ground. Perpendicular arrays augmented the depth of defense, while a main route to the rear made the supply line accessible and at the same time prevented it from being cut off by the enemy. All of these rules complement the text of *Sun-tzu*.

Not only do very early Chinese historical records exist on ancient troop use, but most of these records are copious. For this reason we are still able to have a general idea of what important military campaigns were like three to four thousand years ago. These materials show at least that what this record discusses regarding the battles of the King of the Shang against the Xia and the King of the Zhou against the Shang is not factual.[1]

In this record, the use of the five colors to correspond with the five directions of "east, south, center, west, and north" clearly demonstrates that this is an interpretation from after the middle Warring States Period.[2] Also, referring to great individuals

[1]See *History of Wars in China*, Book 1, and *Zhongguo junshishi*, vol. 2, "Binglue" *shang*.
[2]See Wang Men-ou, *Zouyan yishuokao*, ch. 4 and 6.

from ancient history to give weight to a theory was a convention of Warring States Period scholars.

TEXT

Sun-tzu said . . . [The Yellow Emperor attacked the Red Emperor in the south. He reached] . . . The battle occurred on the Banshan plain. He positioned to the right of the lowlands, had perpendicular arrays, and had a main route to his back. He annihilated and conquered the enemy. Over . . . [years] relieved the people from public labor . . . developed agriculture, and pardoned prisoners.

Then he attacked the . . . [Green] Emperor in the east. He arrived in Xiangping. They fought at Bing . . . [He positioned to the right of the lowland], had perpendicular arrays, and had a main route to his back. He annihilated . . . [and conquered the enemy]. Over . . . years he relieved the people from public labor, developed agriculture, and pardoned prisoners.

Then he attacked the Black Emperor in the north. He arrived in Wusui. . . . [They fought at] . . . [He positioned to the right of the lowland, had perpendicular arrays, and had a main route to his back. He annihilated and conquered the enemy. Over . . . years he relieved the people from public labor, developed agriculture, and pardoned prisoners.] . . .

. . . [Then he] attacked the White Emperor in the west. He arrived in Wugang. They fought at . . . [He positioned to the right of the lowland, had perpendicular arrays, and had a main route to his back. He annihilated and conquered the enemy.] . . .

. . . [He] had defeated four emperors and had conquered all of China. The tyrants . . . brought progress to China, and all of China obeyed him in every land.

Tang [the King of the Shang] attacked Jie [the King of the Xia] . . . [He arrived in] . . . They fought at Botian. He positioned to the right of the lowlands, had perpendicular arrays, and had a main route to his back. He annihilated and conquered the enemy.

King Wu [of the Zhou] attacked Zhou [the King of the Shang]. He arrived in Chinsui. They fought on the field of Mu. . . . [He positioned] to the right of the lowlands, had perpendicular arrays . . . [and had a main route to his back. He annihilated and] conquered the enemy. This one emperor and two kings all knew [how to] take advantage of the way of heaven . . . of . . . and the people's needs, therefore . . .

APPENDIX 4

TERRAIN II

INTRODUCTION

The use of terrain is an important topic in military operations and it also is extremely complex. So, although not much is left of this record, what is extant still retains a certain research value. Decay has made interpretation difficult. From the remaining characters on these bamboo slats we can discern the correlation between directions and both the left and right; it assists us in understanding that the optimum direction in ancient arrays was south-facing. The remaining portions regarding the nature of the ancient study of terrain and its use in deployment arrays provide clues for researchers.

What is especially worth discussing here is the inscription regarding the array rule "have their rear-right against hills, and their front-left against water or a swamp" ("*youfu qiuling, zuoqian shuize*"). This rule was similarly noted in the *Shiji*,[1] so we can see how it broadly influenced ancient China.

[1]Vol. 92, "Huailinghou liezhuan," p. 923.

TEXT

. . . In terrain, the east is left and west is [right] . . .

. . . *shou* [lit., "head"; "to head toward"], if the terrain is flat, emphasize the left; army . . .

. . . terrain. When engaging [armies in] a water [swamp] . . .

. . . *zhe,* is the lethal terrain. Where grass grows . . .

. . . terrain is rigid, do not . . . *ye* . . .

. . . *tianli* [Gigantic Coop], *tianjing* [Gigantic Pit], *tianwan* [Gigantic Bowels][2] . . .

. . . is called the Great Advantage; a position at its front is called the Concrete Defense; a position at its right is called the Supreme Firmness; a position at its left is called . . .

. . . a situation on high ground, is called The Established Hall; . . . is called . . . ; the accommodation of water on the left is called Advantage; water on the right is called Obstruction . . .

. . . the fifth lunar month *du* [to cross] . . . land, the seventh lunar month . . .

. . . the armies set their battle arrays regardless of the morning or the evening; have their rear-right against hills, and their front-left against water or a swamp. The perpendicular ones . . .

. . . the principles of the nine zones, psychological reactions, must never [be taken lightly] . . .

[2]See Book 9, comment 12.

AN AUDIENCE WITH THE KING OF WU

INTRODUCTION

This record describes a story of how Helü, the King of Wu, tested Sun Wu's military abilities. Of all the material still available today on the man Sun Wu, this story is the most complete[1] and has achieved the broadest dissemination, but its reliability is questionable.

First, the King of Wu ordered Sun Wu to train two arrays of palace ladies (one version says 180 palace ladies) into battle-ready troops. Three times Sun Wu acted on these orders, but the palace ladies only laughed and disobeyed. When this happened, Sun Wu disregarded the King of Wu's interdiction and applied military law in having the two array chiefs—who were beloved concubines of the king—executed. After that the palace ladies not only became totally obedient but were immediately considered well-trained soldiers. A messenger was dispatched to the King of Wu to tell him that this army of palace ladies could be used in battle. The king was unwilling to go see them, so Sun Wu reproached him as being one who talks but doesn't act.

That this story is absolutely ridiculous goes without saying. Only if we compare the troop training used here with that in the text of *Sun-tzu* do their differences become obvious. In this record Sun Wu's way for training his troops is very simple: he terrifies

---

[1]In addition to the Linyi text's version, both the *Shiji* and the *Wu Yue Chunqiu* record this with only slight variations. A translation of the *Shiji*'s version is included in the Introduction, note 10. The Linyi text suffered considerable damage in this portion, and where it was considered important, descriptions were added from the *Shiji* and the *Wu Yue Chunqiu*. The places where the characters are still extant but their meaning is uncertain were eliminated; we have marked these places with an ellipsis and asterisk (. . . *). Brackets [ ] are used to mark additions by the author.

them; when the troops are terrified, then an army is immediately formed; when the troops are terrified, the army immediately has combat power. However, in Book 9, "Troop Maneuvers" (pp. 86–87), *Sun-tzu* says,

> When there is no bond with the soldiers but punishments are meted out, they will be disobedient; if disobedient, they will be difficult to use. When there is a bond with the soldiers but punishments cannot be meted out, they still will be useless. So, unite them through benevolence and regulate them through strictness—these ensure internalized discipline. Establish the ingrained execution of orders in training one's people, and then the people will follow. Fail to establish the ingrained execution of orders in training one's people, and then the people will not follow. The ingrained execution of orders comes from being in accord with the legions.

Book 10, "Terrain," also says, "View soldiers as infants and thus be able to lead them into ravines. View soldiers as beloved sons and thus be able to lead them unto death" (p. 92). *Sun-tzu*'s method in the text is to use compassion and fraternal bonds as the foundations for cultivating soldiers' ingrained obedience, then to use discipline in training the soldiers' ability to carry out orders. Where in this record, then, is there the faintest shadow of these principles of *Sun-tzu?*

Second, when Sun Wu ordered the execution of the king's two concubines, he rejected the king's request for clemency by saying, "When commanders are commissioned an army, some lords' orders need not necessarily be accepted."[2] Although *Sun-tzu* does have the line "some lords' orders need not necessarily be accepted" (Book 8, "The Nine Adaptations," pp. 75–76), this does not have the qualifier "when commanders are commissioned an army," which makes a world of difference.

In Book 8 the assumption is that one is facing the enemy; the response is demonstrated very clearly in Book 10, "Terrain," that "when the ways for battle are definitely victorious, even if the lord orders no battle, the battle may still be waged; when the ways for battle are not victorious, even if the lord orders a battle, the battle may still not be waged" (p. 92), which means that the sole determining factor here is whether it will bring victory over the enemy. (See also the introduction to Appendix 2.)

According to this record, though, as soon as "commanders are commissioned an

---

[2]This line is missing in the Linyi text, so the *Shiji* was used to amend it, but in Appendix 2 is the same line, with *shou* (to be accepted) reading *xing* (to be carried out).

army," they have the power to "not necessarily accept some lords' orders." With this qualifier, political authorities become locked outside any military camp. Thus, the day that a commander is appointed is also the day that the country's sovereignty is sundered, and the fear arises that military power will overturn the government. No place in *Sun-tzu* conveys even the slightest hint of this absurd suggestion.

Such a rationalization as this record gives ought to have originated in the middle Warring States Period (475–221 B.C.).[3] From the above observations we can plainly demonstrate that this record's story about Sun Wu was no more than a popular Warring States Period legend and should not be considered historical. However, over many thousands of years the belief that "when commanders are commissioned an army, some lords' orders need not necessarily be accepted" has, at least in China, grievously caused interminable tragedies.

---

[3] *Sun Bin bingfa* has the line "a lord's orders do not enter the military camp" (*xia*, "Jiangde," p. 109). Also, the *Sima fa* says, "Regulations of the country do not enter the army" (*shang*, "Tianzi zhi yi," pp. 3a and 4a). Their intimation is that a country's governing stops outside a military camp.

TEXT

. . . [The King of Wu visited Sun-tzu] at his guest house . . . *

Sun-tzu said, "Forces are for advantages, not for amusement. Forces are for . . . not a game. My lord asks me with regard to amusement and games. A reply from this foreign guest would be inconvenient."

Helü [the King of Wu] said, "I lack knowledge. It is inconvenient to pursue advantages, and [justice] . . . "

. . . Sun-tzu said, "As my lord wishes. Using the nobles is permissible. Using the humble is permissible. Using women is permissible. Try [placing] men on the right [and] try [placing] women on the left . . . "

. . . [Helü] said, "I would prefer to use women."

Sun-tzu said, "One is apprehensive of using women. Please allow me to substitute [men] . . . "

. . . [Helü said,] " . . . fear, what could be regretted?"

Sun-tzu said, "Then allow me to request the palace [ladies] . . . to the rear-left of the capital city, inside the royal hunting preserve. Divide them into two arrays . . . "

. . . [Sun-tzu] said, "If the training of the arrays is not finished, [they are] not yet ready for your review. When finished, . . . *ye*. My lord will wait in the belvedere. I . . . will request your pleasure at noon . . . *"

The lord said, "Agreed."

Sun-tzu appointed his charioteer as [commandant] . . . [appointed his] adjutant as the training officer, . . . *

. . . [Sun-tzu] . . . ladies and asked them, "Do you know where your right hand is?"

[The ladies answered,] "[We know] it."

"Do you know where your chest is?"

[They] answered, "[We] know it."

"Do you know where your back is?"

[They] answered, "[We] know it." . . . *

" . . . If an order is issued and there are those who do not obey, they will be punished . . . *"

. . . [The orders were announced three times and] explained in detail five times, [then] the drums [sounded and they were ordered] to advance. The ladies became unruly [and started to laugh] . . . gongs [sounded and ordered] them to kneel. Again [the orders were] announced three times [and] explained in detail five times, [then] the drums [sounded and they were ordered] to advance. The ladies became unruly [and started to] laugh. Thrice [the orders were] announced three times and explained in detail five times, but [the] orders could not be carried out.

Sun-tzu called over his commandant and training officer, telling them, "The military rules are: do not order [what the troops] do not understand, [otherwise this] is the fault of the lord and the commanders; an issued order which has already been announced and explained [but is not carried out] is the fault of the troop-lieutenants. The military rules are: rewards and merits [should] start with the lower ranks; punishments [should begin with the higher ranks] [Note: Sun Wu then ordered the execution of two concubines of Helü] . . . "

. . . [The King of Wu said,] " . . . request their pardon."

Sun-tzu said, "The lord . . . [when commanders are commissioned an army, some lords' orders need not necessarily be accepted] [Note: below it says that with the two concubines' execution, all of the palace ladies were frightened and became totally obedient, so the arrays were fully trained] . . . lead them to form a circle, [and] the circle fits a compass; lead them to form a square, [and] the square fits a ruler . . . "

. . . Helü for six days could not [put] himself [at ease] . . .

. . . Sun-tzu bowed again and stood, saying, " . . . * This is ingrained training and the way of being a commander. The people . . . nothing is more important than power. When power is recognized by the legions, strictness is recognized by the officers, and the armies trust and obey their commanders' power, their enemy will be surpassed."

. . . it is used . . . obtained. If in . . . the thirteen books [of Sun-tzu] . . .

. . . [1]3 books disclose the doctrine and explain [how to] succeed; indeed, [one] will learn . . . *

APPENDIX 6

QUERIES ON THE NINE ZONES

INTRODUCTION

This record appertains to Book 11, "The Nine Zones"; it concerns questions the King of Wu asked Sun Wu on the use of each zone's specific nature in military operations, with Sun Wu providing solutions for each of the difficulties encountered.

The descriptions of the nine zones in this record are not identical to the ones in the text of *Sun-tzu*, so they could not have been personally given by Sun Wu; however, they do have definite reference value. Because some of Cao Cao's annotations adopted the same perspectives as this record, we can propose that this record was written very early.

Several editions exist of this record; we follow the one by (Song) He Yanxi.[1]

[1]Other than He's edition, ones by Zhang Yu and Bi Yixun are also available, but, except for the fact that they are not as detailed as He's, there are few differences. The editions of He and Zhang were collected in the Song Dynasty *Sunzi shiyijia zhu,* while Bi's edition is included in his *Sunzi xulu.*

One other version is called *Sun Wu binglue wenda* (Sun Wu and the King of Wu's Questions and Answers on Military Strategy), which was edited into a separate volume. An annotation was added to Zhang's notes on each type of zone (attributed to "Culai *xiansheng,*" possibly of the Ming Dynasty); after each zone in Zhang's edition is He's edited text. The editor is given as "Dachunzhen, with the title of *cishi* of Xinyang"; the place name and official position suggest that he might have lived in the Song Dynasty.

TEXT

The King of Wu asked Sun Wu, "In separated zones, soldiers are concerned about their homes and cannot conduct battle; then we can only steadfastly defend our fortifications. If the enemy besieges our small towns and appropriates our fields, inhibits our collection of firewood, and blockades our main routes, awaiting our vulnerability and then suddenly launching attacks, what then should be done?"

[Sun] Wu said, "When the enemy deeply penetrates our city areas and has many of our towns to their rear, their soldiers make the army their home, their will is united, and they are easily devoted to battle. Our troops within the fortifications are accustomed to living easily and lack the will to die; if used in battle arrays, they will not be reliable, and if used in battle, they will not obtain victory. We then should assemble the people and legions to store up provisions and valuables, to protect the fortifications, and to guard in the barriers, [and] send out light troops to cut off their supply lines. Their challenges will have no response, their deliveries will not arrive, and the fields will have nothing to appropriate. Their armies will be fatigued and starved. And, by taking the opportunity to lure them, we will then be able to succeed.

"If we want to conduct a battle, then we must certainly take advantage of the balance of strengths, adapt barriers, and set ambushes. If there are no specific barriers, then we should shroud ourselves in the weather's darkness, shades, and mists, emerge to their surprise, and attack their laxity; we will be able to succeed."

The King of Wu asked Sun Wu, "We approach susceptible zones and have barely entered the enemy's territory. Our warriors and soldiers wish to turn back, it is hard to advance and easy to retreat, no barriers support our backs, and the armies are frightened. The field marshal wants to advance, but the warriors and soldiers desire retreat, so the superiors and the subordinates are of two different minds. Enemies set defenses within their fortifications, prepare their chariots and cavalries well, and are either blockading our front or attacking our rear; what then should be done?"

Sun Wu said, "When armies approach a susceptible zone and the warriors and soldiers are not yet unified, deep penetration is the first consideration, not battle. So, do not go near their major cities, do not take their main routes, set smoke screens and deceptions that show our departure. Then, select tough cavalries to march in first with their gags on. Appropriate their cattle, horses, and livestock. As soon as the armies see these exploits, they will not be frightened. Send a detachment of our finest soldiers to furtively lay ambushes. If the enemy comes, strike without hesitation. If the enemy does not come, then leave the ambush positions and depart."

Sun Wu also said, "When the armies enter enemy territory, the enemies steadfastly defend their fortifications and refuse to battle. The warriors and soldiers are eager to return home, but a retreat is difficult: this is called a susceptible zone.[2] We should select tough forces to lay ambushes on the main routes; if when we retreat the enemies pursue us, strike them."

The King of Wu asked Sun Wu, "If enemies approach first, occupy tactical positions, maintain superiority, hone their weapons, drill their soldiers, and either make an emergence or conduct a defense against our unexpected actions, what then should be done?"

[Sun] Wu said, "The principle for contended zones is that the first to occupy them possesses superiority. If the enemy obtains these sites, be sure not to attack them. Pull out to make a false retreat toward what the enemy cares about with raised banners and sounding drums; drag firewood to raise clouds of dust; confuse the enemy's ears and eyes. Send our finest soldiers to furtively lay ambushes, and the enemy will have to come to the rescue. What they want, we give; what they do not want, we take: this is the way to outrival the enemy. If we approach such a site first and the enemy exercises such a method, select our elite soldiers to firmly defend this site and light troops to pursue the enemy, sending a detachment of forces to lay ambushes at barriers. If the enemy turns around to fight, our ambush forces will rise up from the sides. This is the way for complete victory."

The King of Wu asked Sun Wu, "In a dually traversable zone I want to blockade the enemy and make it unable to come; we must order our border fortifications to ready their defenses, completely cut off their transport routes, and strengthen the protection of narrow paths. But, if we do not have these ready first, then the enemy has preparedness, so they are able to come, but we are unable to go over. Also, if both sides' troops are equivalent, what then should be done?"

[2]"This is called a susceptible zone" is most likely an erroneous amendation.

[Sun] Wu said, "Since we cannot go over but they can come, we will dispatch troops to hide and make our defenses easy and lax to show our inability. As soon as the enemy approaches, lay ambushes, hide long weapons,[3] and emerge to their surprise. This will succeed."

The King of Wu asked Sun Wu, "With key traffic zones, one must arrive first. If our journey is long and we also set out late, then even with swift chariots and fleet horses we will be unable to arrive there before the enemy; what then should be done?"

[Sun] Wu said, "A lord's [zone] converges with many other places and its roads reach to all directions. Also, we and the enemy are equally matched and other countries are on the sideline. What is meant by 'first' is that we must first present precious gifts and send fast envoys to make allegiances with these lateral countries, establishing intimate friendships and granting reciprocal favors. Even if our forces are delayed, the majority already belongs to us. When we have the aid of the majority and the enemy loses its federations, all our feudal allies will form pincer actions and launch an attack synchronized with the thunder of drums. The enemy will frighten and be unsure of how to defend."

The King of Wu asked Sun Wu, "If I lead my forces in deeply penetration of the dominant zones, many important places will be passed by and the supply line will thus be blocked. Suppose that I wish to retreat, but their combat power is insurmountable. I want to appropriate the enemy's provisions and maintain my forces without loss; what then should be done?"

[Sun] Wu said, "Generally, when halting in a dominant zone, the warriors and soldiers display their courage easily. If transport has been cut, conduct appropriations to maintain food supplies. When the lower ranks obtain food and goods, all must present these to the superiors. Reward those who make more contributions, and the warriors and soldiers will drop their desire to withdraw. If we want to pull out, guard

---

[3]"To hide long weapons" in the Chinese text reads "*yinlu.*" Previous scholars have believed that this meant "to hide in a hut," which is problematic with regard to the character *lu*. The *Zhouli* mentions the position of *luren*, the duty of which was to make long weapons (vol. 41, "*Dongguan*" [*Shisanjing*, p. 2002]). We therefore know that *lu* here actually indicates "long weapons."

with deep moats and high fortresses to show the enemy we intend to stay. When the enemy raises the alarm on the main routes, secretly clear the trails to strategic sites, then order an advance with light chariots and muffled gags. Use oxen and horses as lures. If the enemy emerges, sound drums and pursue them. Furtively hide warriors and cut through the enemy. Cooperate from within and without. Their defeat can be predicted."

The King of Wu asked Sun Wu, "If I enter a compartmentalized zone, it will be difficult to cross routes through these mountains, rivers, and obstacles; after the long march, soldiers will be exhausted. The enemy is at our front and ambushes lie at our back. They encamp to our left and conduct defenses to our right, and also have fine chariots and tough cavalries to obstruct our narrow paths; what then should be done?"

[Sun] Wu said, "First advance light chariots about ten miles away from our army, make a stand against the enemy, and conduct joint operations within the obstacles, or dispatch toward their left, or dispatch toward their right. The chief commander makes a complete inspection, then rushes through their gaps with all of us concentrating on where it is equidistant to all points. When we are fatigued, then halt [for defensive actions]."

The King of Wu asked Sun Wu, "If I enter a surrounded zone, strong enemies will be to the front and both difficult terrains and hindrances to the back; enemies will have cut our supply lines. The conditions compel us to escape; enemies sound their drums and shout but do not advance in order to test our ability. What then should be done?"

[Sun] Wu said, "The appropriate way to handle a surrounded zone is to block its openings to show that it is an inextricable position. The soldiers will make the army their home, the will of all the troops is thus united, and the armies' strengths will be combined. Cease cooking hot food for a number of days; no fire or smoke may be seen. Intentionally appear disorderly and unruly, of few men and weak. When the enemies find us like this, their defenses will be careless. Then, encourage our warriors and soldiers, build up their morale, lay our finest soldiers for ambush in barriers to both the left and right, and then emerge with the sounding of drums. If the enemy makes a stand, conduct a swift assault to crush them. We will fight in their front and rear, or launch pincer attacks."

[The King of Wu] again asked, "If the enemy is surrounded by us but lays ambushes, has made impenetrable plans, shows us opportunities, confuses us with their flags, and is embroiled in apparent confusion, their intentions will be difficult to discern; what then?"

[Sun] Wu said, "Have a thousand soldiers bear battle standards and spread out to occupy the important trails. Send light forces to issue challenges. Set battle arrays but do not engage them. Entangle them but do not withdraw. This is the method for defeating their stratagems."

The King of Wu asked Sun Wu, "If my troops pass over the border, encamp in enemy territory, and the enemy approaches en masse, surrounding us many times over, and we want to break through but every side is blocked, and we want to exhort our warriors and encourage the legions into devoting their lives to breaking this besetment, what then should be done?"

[Sun] Wu said, "Show our defenses with deep moats and high fortresses. Remain calm and take no action to hide our abilities. Make an announcement to our armies and show these desperate circumstances. Slaughter the oxen and burn the carts to feed our warriors. Set fire to all the provisions, fill in the wells, bank up the stoves, shear hair, relinquish hats, and abandon all hope for survival. Commanders harbor no other plans; the warriors have the will to die. Therefore, fortify armor and sharpen blades, unify spirit and merge strengths. Make flanking attacks and charge forward with thundering drums and shouts; the enemy will frighten and not know how to withstand us. Send elite troops to advance separately in a swift attack on the enemy's rear. This is the abandonment of exits for survival. So it is said, 'With difficulty, lack of deliberations leads to desperation; with desperation, lack of battles leads to destruction.'"

The King of Wu [again] asked, "If we are to beset the enemy, how can it be done?"

[Sun] Wu said, "Those in steep mountains and precipitous gorges that are difficult to pass through are called desperate foes. The tactic for attacking them is to lay ambush soldiers, hide long weapons, and open exits to show them the path of escape. As soon as their desire for survival emerges, they no longer have the will to fight. If we take this chance to attack them, even if they be hordes, they certainly will be destroyed.

"In military strategy it also notes, 'If the enemy is in a lethal zone, their warriors and soldiers will be courageous. When we want to strike them, go with and not against them. Furtively guard superiority. Definitely provide an exit. Dispatch fine cavalries to blockade important paths. Send light forces to advance and lure them. Set battle arrays, but do not engage them. This is the method for defeating their stratagems.' "

DYNASTIC CHRONOLOGY OF CHINA

Xia .... 2205–1767 B.C.

Shang .... 1766–1123 B.C.

Western Zhou .... 1122–771 B.C.

Eastern Zhou .... 770–221 B.C.

    Spring and Autumn Period .... 770–404 B.C.

    Warring States Period .... 403–221 B.C.

Qin .... 221–207 B.C.

Han .... 206 B.C.–A.D. 220

    Western Han .... 206 B.C.–A.D. 24

    Eastern Han 25–220

Three Kingdoms 220–280

Western Jin 265–316

Eastern Jin 317–420

Southern and Northern Dynasties 420–589

Sui 581–618

Tang 618–907

Five Dynasties 907–960

Song 960–1280

    Northern Song 961–1127

    Southern Song 1128–1280

Liao 926–1125

Western Xia 1038–1227

Kin 1115–1234

Yuan 1281–1368

Ming 1368–1644

Qing 1644–1911

BIBLIOGRAPHY

SUN-TZU

Bi Yixun (Qing). *Sunzi xulu.* (*Dainange congshu* compendium.) Taipei, n.d.

Cao Cao (Han). *Weiwudi zhu, Sunzi.* (*Pingjingguan congshu* compendium.) Taipei, n.d. Cao's annotations in this version surpass the *Shiyijia zhu* version insofar as readability is concerned; however, some discrepancies exist in the content.

Chen Jiuxue. *Qizi bingfa.* Taipei, 1979.

Da Chunzhen (Song), ed.; Mr. Culai, *xunjie. Sun Wu binglue.* Taipei, 1963.

Giles, Lionel, trans. *Sun Tzu: On the Art of War.* London, 1910.

Griffith, Samuel B., trans. *Sun Tzu: The Art of War.* Oxford, 1971.

Guo Huaruo. *Sunzi jinyi.* Shanghai, 1973.

Hattori Chiharu. *Sonshi hyohō kōkai.* Beijing, 1987.

He Shoufa (Ming). *Sunzi yinzhu.* (in *Zhongguo bingxue daxi.*) Taipei, 1957. (Referred to as the *Yinzhu.*)

Ji Tianbao (Song), ed. *Shiyijia zhu Sunzi.* Taipei, n.d. Transcribed and repaired copy of the original Song Shaoxi reign (c. 1190–95) edition. National Central Library (Taipei) collection. (Referred to as the *Shiyijia* version.)

This book uses (Han) Cao Cao's annotated edition as its foundation and adds to it the annotations of (Liang) Mengshi; (Tang) Du You, Li Quan, Du Mu, Chen Hao, and Jia Lin; and (Song) Mei Yaochen, Wang Xi, He Yanxi (generally called ''Heshi''), and Zhang Yu.

Kanetani Osamu. *Sonshi.* Tokyo, 1964.

Linyi text versions:
  a. *Yinqueshan Hanmu zhujian ''Sunzi bingfa.''* Typeset ed. Beijing, 1976.
  b. *Yinqueshan Hanmu zhujian ''Sunzi bingfa.''* String-bound ed. Beijing, 1975.
  c. Copy in the Chinese Military Science Academy collection. (Reproduction in Hattori Chiharu, *Sonshi hyohō kōkai.*)
  This is the earliest edition of *Sun-tzu*, dating from about twenty-one hundred years ago (see Introduction). Because of the considerable damage suffered over the years by the bamboo slats in an ancient Han tomb, what remains of the Linyi text is only about one third of the Song Dynasty versions, but it nonetheless cannot be overlooked in determining the correct text of *Sun-tzu*.
  The above three copies compiled by various scholars are more or less the

same; although very slight differences exist among them, none is of great import. We mainly have used copy (a) and referred to it as the Linyi text.

Li Riyu. *Sunzi bingfa xinyanjiu.* Taipei, 1956.

Liu Ying (Ming). *Wujing qishu zhijie.* Taipei, 1972.

Sakurada Tei, criticism and annotations. *Kobun Sonshi seibun.* (Japanese-transmitted version referred to as the Sakurada version.)

    a. Wood-block ed., appended to Hattori Chiharu, *Sonshi hyohō kōkai.*

    b. Typeset ed., appended to Satō Kenji, *Sonshi no shisōshi no kenkyu.*

        The special characteristic of this version's text is its similarity to the *Wujing* version; more discrepancies exist between it and the *Shiyijia* version. Also notable are the occasional alterations clearly made by later generations.

Satō Kenji. *Sonshi no shisōshi no kenkyu.* Tokyo, 1962.

Sun Xingyan (Qing) and Wu Renji, *jiao. Sunzi shijia zhu.* (*Sibu beiyao* compendium.) Taipei, 1968. (Referred to as the *Shijia* version.)

        This book is a revised edition of the *Shiyijia* version. Sun and Wu felt that (Tang) Du You "had never actually annotated *Sun-tzu,*" so they edited the *Shiyijia zhu* (Eleven Annotations) down to the *Shijia zhu* (Ten Annotations). However, since Du You often quoted Cao Cao's annotations and was more complete, and also because he used such other ancient annotations as those of Wang Ling and Mengshi, they retained Du You's text in their edition.

Wujing qishu. Taipei, 1971. Facsimile of a Southern Song ed. (Referred to as the *Wujing* version.)

        Seven strategic classics handed down

from the Han Dynasty were compiled for an imperial edition in the third year of the Northern Song Yuanfeng reign (1080): *Sun-tzu, Wuzi, Sima fa, Li Weigong wendui, Weiliaozi, Sanlue,* and *Liutao.* This became the government's official military textbook. Although the original book is no longer extant, this Southern Song edition is a surviving copy.

Wu Jiulong et al. *Sunzi jiaoshi.* Beijing, 1990.

Yang Bingan. *Sunzi huijian.* Henan, 1986.

Zhao Benxue (Ming). *Sunzi shu jiaojie yinlei.* Taipei, 1970.

Zheng Youxian (Song). *Sunzi yishuo.* (*Dainage* compendium.) Taipei, n.d.

CLASSICS

Author unknown (Zhou). *Sima fa.* (*Wujing qishu* compendium.) Taipei, 1971.

Ban Gu (Han). *Baihutong delun.* (*Gujin yishi* compendium.) Taipei, 1969. (Referred to as *Baihutong.*)

Chen Li (Qing). *Gongyang yishu.* (*Huang Qing jingjie xubian* compendium.) Taipei, n.d.

Guo Moruo et al. *Guanzi jijiao.* Tokyo, 1981.

Hao Yixing (Qing). *Erya yishu.* Taipei, 1980. Facsimile of an 1865 ed.

He Yan (Wei), *jijie;* (Liang) Huang Kan, *yishu. Lunyu jijie yishu.* Taipei, 1963.

Jingfa. Mawangdui silk text. (*Boshu zhujian* compendium.) Taipei, 1976.

Liang Qixiong. *Xunzi jianshi.* (Selected Interpretations of *Xunzi.*) Taipei, 1979.

———. *Xunzi jianshi.* (Simplified Interpretations of *Xunzi.*) Taipei, 1975.

Li Jing (Tang). *Li Weigong wendui.* (*Wujing qishu* compendium.) Taipei, 1971.

Ma Ruizhen (Qing). *Mao Shi zhuanjian tongshi.* (*Huang Qing jingjie* compendium.) Taipei, n.d.

Shisanjing zhushu. Kyoto, 1971. (Qing) Ruan Yuan, *jiaokan.*

Du Yu (Jin), *zhu;* (Tang) Kong Yingda, *zhengyi. Chunqui Zuozhuan zhengyi.* (Referred to as the *Zuozhuan.*)

Fan Ning (Jin), *jijie;* (Tang) Yang Shixun, *shu. Chunqiu Guliang zhuan zhushu.* (Referred to as the *Guliang zhuan.*)

Guo Pu (Han), *zhu;* (Song) Xing Bing, *shu. Erya zhushu.* (Referred to as the *Erya.*)

He Xiu (Han), *zhu;* (Tang) Xu Yan, *shu. Chunqiu Gongyangzhuan zhushu.* (Referred to as the *Gongyangzhuan.*)

He Yan (Wei), *zhu;* (Song) Xing Bing, *shu. Lunyu zhushu.* (Referred to as the *Lunyu.*)

Kong Anguo (Han), *zhuan;* (Tang) Kong Yingda, *zhengyi. Shangshu zhengyi.* (Referred to as the *Shujing.*)

Mao Heng (Han), *zhuan;* (Han) Zheng Xuan, *qian;* (Tang) Kong Yingda *zhengyi. Mao Shi zhengyi.* (Referred to as the *Shijing.*)

Wang Bi (Wei), (Wei) Han Kangbo, *zhu;* (Tang) Kong Yingda, *zhengyi. Zhou Yi zhengyi.* (Referred to as the *Yijing.*)

Xuanzong emperor (Tang), *zhu;* (Song) Xing Bing, *shu. Xiaojing zhushu.* (Referred to as the *Xiaojing.*)

Zhao Qi (Han), *zhu;* (Song) Sun Shi, *shu. Mengzi zhushu.* (Referred to as the *Mengzi.*)

Zheng Xuan (Han), *zhu;* (Tang) Kong Yingda, *zhengyi. Liji zhengyi.* (Referred to as the *Liji.*)

———; (Tang) Jia Gongyan, *shu. Yili zhushu.* (referred to as *Yili.*)

———. *Zhouli zhushu.* (referred to as the *Zhouli.*)

Sibu beiyao. Taipei.

Deng Xi (Zhou). *Deng Xizi.* 1970.

Dong Zhongshu (Han). *Chunqiu fanlu.* 1968.

Guo Xiang (Jin), *zhu. Zhuangzi.* 1980.

Liu An (Han); (Eastern Han) Gao You, *zhu. Huainanzi.* 1974.

Lü Buwei (Qin). *Lüshi Chunqiu.* 1979.

Lu Dian (Song), *zhu. Heguanzi.* 1970.

Wang Bi (Jin). *Laozi.* 1980.

Wang Fu (Han), *xuan;* (Qing) Wang Jipei, *jian. Qianfulun.* 1971.

Yang Jing (Tang), *zhu. Xunzi.* 1968.

Sun Xingyan (Qing). *Zhou Yi jijie.* Shanghai, 1988.

Sun Yirang (Qing). *Zhouli zhengyi.* Beijing, 1987.

Takezoe Kokou. *Sashi kaishen.* Taipei, 1961.

Wang Fu (Han), *xuan. Qianfulun.* (*Baizi quanshu* ed.) Zhejiang, 1984.

Wang Pinzhen (Qing). *Dadai Liji jiegu.* Taipei, 1974. (Referred to as the the *Dadai Liji.*)

Weiliao (Warring States). *Weiliaozi.* (*Wujing qishu* compendium.) Taipei, 1971.

Wei Zheng (Tang) et al. *Zhuzi zhiyao.* (Separate ed. created out of *Qunshu zhiyao,* vols. 31–50.) Taipei, 1979.

Wu Qi (Zhou). *Wuzi.* Taipei, 1971. Facsimile of Song ed. of the *Wujing qishu.*

Xinbian "Zhuzi jicheng." Taipei, 1983.

Sun Yirang (Qing). *Mozi jiangu.* (Referred to as the *Mozi.*)

Wang Xianqian (Qing), *jiegu. Xunzi jijie.*

———, *jijie. Zhuangzi jijie.*

Wang Xianshen (Qing). *Hanfeizi jijie.* (Referred to as the *Hanfeizi.*)

Yi Zhizhang (Tang), *zhu;* (Qing) Dai Wang, *jiaozheng. Guanzi jiaozheng.* (Referred to as the *Guanzi.*)

Yang Bojun. *Chunqiu Zuozhuan zhu.* Rev. ed. Beijing, 1990.

Yinqueshan Hanmu zhujian zhengli xiaozu, ed. *Sun Bin bingfa*. Beijing, 1975.

Zhang Zhan (Jin), *zhu. Liezi*. Taipei, 1960. Facsimile of the Tieqintongjianlou ed.

Zhang Zhichun, ed.; Cao Jiada, *jiaoding. Zhuzi jinghualu*. Taipei, 1970. (Originally published with Zhang Chunyi incorrectly listed as author.)

Zhao Rui (Tang). *Changduanjing*. (*Hanhai congshu* compendium.) Taipei, 1972.

———, *xuan*; (Qing) Zhou Guangye, *jiao. Changduanjing*. Taipei, 1977.

Zheng Xuan (Han), *zhu. Lunyu zhu*. (*Han Wei yishu chao* compendium; included in Wang Mo, ed., *Zengdi Han Wei congshu*.) Taipei, 1983.

Zhu Shiche. *Shangjunshu jiegu dingben*. Taipei, 1966. (Referred to as the *Shangjunshu*.)

Zhu Xi (Song). *Zhouyi benyi*. Taipei, 1975. Reprint of the Southern Song Wu Ge ed.

———. *Lunyu jizhu*. Taipei, 1974.

HISTORY

Ban Gu (Han). *Han shu*. (*Bainaben* compendium.) Taipei, 1981.

Capon, Edmund. *Qin Shihuang: Terracotta Warriors and Horses*. Victoria, Australia, 1983.

Chiang Wei-kuo et al. *History of Wars in China*. Rev. ed. Taipei, 1981.

Du Zhengsheng. *Zhoudai chengbang*. Rev. ed. Taipei, 1979.

Fan Ye (Liu Song); (Tang) Li Xian, *zhu. Hou Han shu*. (*Bainaben* compendium.) Taipei, 1981.

Gu Zuyu (Qing). *Dushi fangyu jiyao*. Taipei, 1981.

Hsu, Cho-Yun. *Xi Zhou shi*. Taipei, 1984.

Liu Xiang (Han), *ji;* (Eastern Han) Gao You, *zhu. Zhanguoce*. Taipei, 1975.

Ouyang Xiu (Song) et al. *Xin Tang shu*. (*Bainaben* compendium.) Taipei, 1981.

Qian Zai. "Suixian chutu Zhanguo Zenghou yimu qiqi tanpian." *Gugong wenwu yuekan*, vol. 9, no. 12, 1992 (Taipei).

"Shandong Linyi Jinqueshan jiuhao Hanmu de fajue." *Wenshi jilin*, fifth collection. Taipei, 1981.

Shandongsheng bowuguan Linyi wenwuzu. "Shandong Linyi Xi Hanmu faxian 'Sunzi bingfa' he 'Sun Bin bingfa' deng zhujian de jianbao." *Kaogu*, no. 2, 1974.

Sima Guang (Han) et al. *Zizhi tongjian*. Taipei, 1972.

Sima Qian (Han). *Shiji*. (*Bainaben* compendium.) Taipei, 1981.

Taizong emperor (Tang). *Jin shu*. (*Bainaben* compendium.) Taipei, 1981.

Wenwu kaogu gongzuo sanshinian, 1949–1979. Beijing, 1979.

Wu Luo. *Zhongguo duliangheng shi*. Taipei, 1981.

Yang Hong. *Zhongguo gubingqi luncong*. Taipei, n.d.

Ying Shao (Han). *Fengsu tongyi*. (*Sibu beiyao* compendium.) Taipei, 1976.

Yokoda Yiko. *Senkokusaku seikai*. Taipei, 1976.

Yuan Zhongyi. *Qing Shihuang bingmayong yanjiu*. Beijing, 1990.

Yuejueshu. Taipei, 1967. Tieruyiguan manuscript. (The *Yuejueshu* is a compilation of pre-Qin historical accounts compiled and amended during the Han Dynasty, as has been shown by previous scholars.)

Yuejueshu. (*Zengding Han Wei congshu* compendium.) Taipei, 1983.

Zhanguoce. Mawangdui silk text. (*Boshu zhujian* compendium.) Taipei, 1976.

Zhao Ye (Han). *Wu Yue Chunqiu.* Taipei, 1967. Facsimile of a Ming Hongzhi ed.

Zhongguo junshishi bianxiezu. *Zhongguo junshishi,* vol. 2, "Binglue" *shang.* Beijing, 1986.

Zhongguo lishi ditu, vol. 1. Taipei, 1980.

Zhu Youzeng. *Yi Zhou shu jixun jiaoshi.* Taipei, 1971. (Referred to as the *Yi Zhou shu.*)

Zuo Qiuming (Spring and Autumn), *xuan;* (Wu) Wei Zhao, *zhu. Guoyu.* (*Sibu beiyao* compendium.) Taipei, 1968.

LANGUAGE

Cihai. Shanghai, 1989.

Ciyuan. Rev. ed. Shanghai, 1983.

Dai Tong (Song). *Liushugu.* (*Siku quanshu* compendium.) China, 1781.

Huilin (Tang). *Yiqiejing yinyi.* (*Haishanxianguan congshu* compendium.) Taipei, n.d.

Liu Xi (Han), *xuan;* (Qing) Wang Xianqian, *xuanji. Shiming shuzheng bu.* Shanghai, 1984. (Referred to as the *Shiming.*)

Lu Deming (Tang). *Jingdian shiwen.* Taipei, 1980. Facsimile of the Baojingtang ed.

Ma Xulun. *Shuowen jiezi liushu shuzheng.* Taipei, 1975. (Author's name missing on this ed.)

Pei Xuehai. *Gushu xuzi jishi.* Taipei, 1975.

Qi Peirong. *Xunguxue gailun.* Taipei, n.d.

Wang Li. *Gu Hanyu tonglun.* Hong Kong, 1976.

———. *Wang Li wenji.* Series I. Shandong, 1984.

Wang Shumin. *Gushu xuzi xinyi.* Taipei, 1978.

Wang Yinzhi. *Jingzhuan shici.* Hong Kong, 1975.

Wang Yun (Qing). *Shuowen shili.* Taipei, 1969.

Wu Changying (Qing). *Jingci yanshi.* Taipei, 1975.

Xuanying (Tang). *Yiqiejing yinyi.* Taipei, 1973.

Xu Shen (Han); (Qing) Duan Yucai, *zhu. Shuowen jiezi zhu.* Taipei, 1980.

———; (Song) Xu Xuan, *ding. Shuowen jiezi.* Beijing, 1965. (Qing) Chen Changzhi wood-block ed.

Yang Bojun, Xu Ti. *Chunqiu Zuozhuan cidian.* Beijing, 1985.

Yang Shuda. *Ciquan.* Taipei, 1977.

Zhang Binlin. *Wenshi.* (*Zhangshi congshu* compendium.) Taipei, 1983.

Zhang Shunhui. *Shuowen jiezi yuezhu.* Taipei, 1984.

Zhang Yi (Wei), *xuan;* (Qing) Wang Niansun, *shuzheng. Guangya shuzheng.* (*Sibu beiyao* compendium.) Taipei, 1970. (Referred to as the *Guangya.*)

Zhou Fagao. *Hanzi gujin yinhui.* Hong Kong, 1979.

———. *Zhongguo gudai yufa.* "Zaojubian," *shang.* Taipei, 1972.

Zhu Junsheng. *Shuowen tongxun dingsheng.* Taipei, 1975.

GENERAL WORKS

Cheng Dachang (Song). *Yanfanlu.* Taipei, 1984.

Chen Li (Qing). *Dongshu dushuji.* (*Huang Qing jingjie* compendium.) Taipei, n.d.

Chen Pan. *Han Jin yijian zhixiao.* Taipei, 1975.

Du You (Tang). *Tongdian.* Taipei, 1964.

Guo Maoqian (Liu Song). *Yuefu shiji.* Taipei, 1970.

Gu Yanwu (Ming). *Rizhilu.* Taipei, 1981.

Huang Zhen (Song). *Huangshi richao.* Taipei, 1984.

Hu Yuanyi. *Shisong jingshi wenlu.* (*Dingchou congbian* compendium.) Taipei, n.d.

Jiang Nan. *Xuepu yuli.* (*Yihai zhuchen* compendium.) Taipei, n.d.

Jiao Xun (Qing). *Qunjing gongshitu.* (*Huang Qing jingjie xubian* compendium.) Taipei, n.d.

Li Fang (Song) et al. *Taiping yulan.* Kyoto, 1980.

Ling Yangzao (Qing). *Lishuobian.* Taipei, 1963.

Liu Xie (Liang). *Wenxin diaolong.* Taipei, 1979.

Luo Zhenyu. *Luo Xuetang xiansheng quanji,* VI. Taipei, 1976.

Qian Daxin (Qing). *Shijiazai Yangxinlu.* Taipei, 1977. (Referred to as the *Yangxinlu.*)

Sun Yirang (Qing). *Zhayi.* Taipei, n.d.

Wang Men-ou. *Zouyan yishuokao.* Taipei, 1966.

Wang Niansun (Qing). *Dushi zazhi.* Taipei, 1972.

Wang Yinzhi (Qing). *Jingyi shuwen.* Taipei, 1975.

Wang Zhong (Qing). *Shuxue.* (*Sibu beiyao* compendium.) Taipei, 1971.

Xiao Tong (Liang; the prince Zhaoming), ed.; (Tang) Li Shan et al., *zhu. Wenxuan.* Taipei, 1977.

Yang Shuda. *Jiweiju dushuji.* Beijing, 1962.

———. *Jiweiju jiawenshuo.* Shanghai, 1986.

Ye Shi (Song). *Xixue jiyan xumu.* (*Huang Qing jingjie xubian* compendium.) Taipei, n.d. (Referred to as the *Xixue jiyan.*)

Yu Chang (Qing). *Xiangcao xujiaoshu.* Taipei, 1985.

Yu Shengwu. *Zhuzi xinzheng.* Taipei, 1970.

Yu Shinan (Sui), *xuan;* (Qing) Kong Guangtao, *jiaozhu. Beitang shuchao.* Taipei, 1974.

Yu Yue (Qing). *Zhuzi pingyi.* (*Zhuzi jicheng* compendium.) Taipei, 1983.

———. *Zhuzi pingyi bulu.* Taipei, 1978.

Zhu Xi (Song). *Chuci jizhu.* Taipei, 1956. (Referred to as the *Chuci.*)

INDEX

actions
  cohesive, 99
  design, 69
  dynamic, 50, 160
  enemy, 82–84
  ensnaring, 50, 160
  flexible, 57
  follow-up, 97
  manipulation through, 62
  offensive, 99–100
  regular and irregular, 57–58
  risks, 70
  surprise, 52, 72
adaptations
  four (apocrypha), 262–263
  methods in dominant and
    susceptible zones, 201
  nine, 75–78, 200–204
  variable situations, 68
administration, pre-Qin, local
    units, 192n
advance
  clandestine, 82
  enemy desire to, 83
  partial, as a lure, 213–214
  superior, 64
  swift, 102, 232
advantages
  armed contention for, 69–70
  enticement using, 40
  obtainment, 44–45, 46–67
  perception, 76
  practical, 24
  purpose of strategy, 23
  risks in an operation to gain,
    70

taking action in accordance
    with, 96
  weighting balances, 40
agents, 112–115
  activities, nature, 113
  agents-in-place, 112, 113,
    114, 250
  double, 249n
  enemy, 114, 252
  execution of, 114, 252
  hidden provocation, 112, 113,
    115, 250
  mobile informants, 112, 113,
    115
  moles, 112, 113
  turned, 112, 113, 114–115,
    249
allies
  feudal lords, 203–204
  handling, 77
  securing, 71, 103, 190, 235–
    236, 277
  uniting, 75, 201
ambush, 82, 276–277, 278, 279
armed conflict
  capability of waging, 43, 148
  conduction, 39–41
  court reckonings, 41, 141–143
  logistics, 43, 144–147
  using "few" and "many," 65,
    182–183
armed contention, 69–74, 188–
    199
  advantages and disadvantages,
    69–71, 189
  conduct, 71–74

armor, 43, 46, 70, 145–147
  laced corselets, 43, 145–147
  mail, 147n
  pre-Qin, 146–147
army
  advance, 190
  annexation, 48
  camp, 70, 189
  cohesion, damage to, 51
  disruption, 51, 161
  failure, cause, 78
  gate, misinterpretation, 188
  maneuvers, see maneuvers
  matériel, 38, 128, 130–131
  operations, guides for, 115,
    253
  positioning, 79
  relationship with agents, 113,
    251
army organization
  buqu system, 129–131, 171
  division into three armies,
    190
  pre-Qin, 129, 171–172
attack, 49, 50, 63, 97, 109, 180
  decisive, 41, 56
  defeatability, 53, 165
  elite soldiers, do not, 74, 196
  fire, 107–110, 241–244
  flank, 82, 279
  for deficiency, 54, 165–166
  frontal, 74, 196
  pre-Qin signals, 72, 194n
  using few against many, 64–
    65, 182–183
  weaknesses, 41, 139–140

barbed terrain, 88, 218
battle, 55, 92, 96, 168, 169, 170, 202
  avoidance, 48
  await, 62, 179
  chariot, 46–47, 133, 154
  environmental factors and, 109
  launching, 65–66, 184
  pause in, enemy desire, 85
  preparation, enemy, 83
  ratios of us and the enemy, 50, 64–65, 158–160, 182–183
  rigid, 68
  risk, 52, 162
  synchronized power, 171
  of those sophisticated at strategy, 55, 167
  terrain, unusable, 93
  of Xiao, 178
  see also those sophisticated at battle
battle arrays, 73, 98–99, 141n
  buqu, see army organization
  chariots in, 145n
  close mutual support, 98–99
  cohesion, 99
  commanding, 59, 72, 73, 194–195
  deploying, 55, 83, 145n, 212, 218, 267–268, 279, 280
  effective, rules for, 265
  flanks, 188
  front, rear, left, and right, 66, 184
  perpendicular, 265–266
  well-ordered, 96, 191n, 225
battle standards, switching, 46
  use, 46n, 72, 172, 188n, 193–194, 279
  wobbling, 85
Beitang shuchao (Yu Shinan), 173n, 186n, 194n, 216n
benevolence
  definition of dao, 124
  misinterpretation of ren, 251
  requisite for commander cultivation, 38, 125
  uniting soldiers through, 86, 216, 270

bing
  misinterpreted as "war," 121
  pre-Qin definitions, 121n, 132n
  weapons, extended to mean soldiers or forces, 132n, 146n
  see military affairs
Bi Yixun (Qing), 237n, 274n
blockade
  by the enemy, 275
  city, 49
  the enemy, 276–277
  important paths, 279
  openings, 102

camp
  abandonment, 84
  bringing, 70, 189
  enemy, 242
  setting, 83, 213
Cao Cao (Eastern Han, 155–220; annotator in the Shiyijia), 76n, 119n, 120n, 125, 126n, 128, 129, 133, 135, 136, 138, 140n, 144, 145, 153n, 154, 157n, 158, 159–160, 161n, 163, 166, 171–172, 173, 176, 177, 180n, 200, 203, 205, 206, 207, 209–210, 212n, 216, 218, 221–223, 224, 226, 229, 230, 232, 234, 235, 237n, 238, 239, 240, 241, 242n, 246, 262, 274
Cao Kuai (Spring and Autumn Period, seventh century B.C.), 169, 227, 228n
capability
  establishment of, 57
  hiding, 40, 137
  military systems, 37, 39
  strategic, 158n
  to subjugate eyes and ears, 100, 230–231
  troop, 60–61
  to wage armed conflict, 43, 148
Changduanjing (Zhao Rui), 185n, 214n, 215n, 220n, 222n, 229n, 233n, 251n

chariots
  battles, 46–47, 133, 154
  damaged, 46
  leather-armored, 43, 145
  light, 83, 145n
  movement, 83
  swift, 43, 145
Chen Hao (Tang; annotator in the Shiyijia), 119n, 134n, 217n, 242n
Chen Li (Qing, 1809–1869; author of Gongyang yishu), 191n
Chen Li (Qing, 1810–1882; author of Dongshu dushuji), 129n
Chen Shu (father of Sun Wu), 17, 19, 26–27n, 29n
circuitous as direct, the means of, 69, 72, 193
cities
  besieged, 49, 75, 157, 262, 264
  blockade, 49, 158
  enemy, occupation of, 104, 236
  occupation without siege, 49
citizenry, finances, 45, 111, 150–152
  definition, 152
cohesion, 52, 99
collapse
  economic, 150n, 152
  forces, 90
combat power, 57–61, 171–178
  balanced, 89, 90, 158n
  creation, 40, 59, 135–136
  description in the five classics, 192n
  development, 226
  enemy, obstructing, 96
  exercise of, 57–58, 60
  of forces, not immutable, 68, 186–187
  insurmountable enemy, 277
  lack of, 221
  principles for applying, 59
  relationship with troop capability and situation, 60–61

and a restrained release of
   force, 59–60
command
   of armies, concerns in, 100
   art of, 92
   battle arrays, 59
   duty of, 100
   enemy, inferior, 84–85
   flexible, 58
   forceful, 59, 104–105
   requisite capabilities, 101
   signal orders and, 72
   skill of, 100
   systems, effectual, 57
   way of, 99
   see also those sophisticated at
      command
commander
   accepting a lord's orders, 75,
      92, 270–271, 273
   appointment, 39–40, 133–135
   aptitude, 76
   candidate, 135
   capable, 39, 52, 56, 132
      character traits, harmful,
         77–78
   combat, four requisites, 66–67
   concerns for personal gain,
      111–112
   cultivation, 38, 230
   definition, 134–136
   duty, 39, 47, 92
   enemy, 114, 264
   ethic, 92
   Guardian of the people's lives,
      47, 154–155
   loyalty, 50–51
   obeying political goals, 109
   perception of soldiers, 92
   rage, 49
   spearhead of a force, 91, 219
   wise, 46
commandership, 37, 38, 125
commanding armies, concerns,
   99–100, 230
compartmentalized zone, 95,
   200, 201
   action, 75, 95, 102, 278
   definition, 95, 223–242
conflict
   advancing for, 111, 248

control in, 55
dominating superiority, 66–
   68
financial hardships during,
   45–46
flexibility in, 61
groundwork, 77
situations, 40, 48–49, 65–66
Confucius (Spring and Autumn
   Period, 480 or 479–551
   B.C.), 15, 27n, 28n, 121n,
   156n, 195n, 209n, 214n,
   244n
conscription, 43, 44, 45, 111,
   150
   labor, 192n
constellations
   alignment with the moon,
      108, 243
   influence on weather
      aberrations, 127n
   location of various, 108n
   White Tiger, 177n
contended zone, 94
   action, 95, 102, 232–233
   definition, 94
control, 53–56, 67, 163–170
   of forces, not immutable, 68,
      186–187
   imperceptible, 67
   strategy, 53
   superiority in war, 55–56
   victory, 54–55
country
   advancing out of, 111, 248
   annexing, 48, 157
   annihilated, 110, 247
   and commanders, 47, 50, 92,
      154–156
   comprehensive security
      strategy, 37
   damage to capacity, 44
   definition, 122
   enemy, overthrowing, 104,
      236
   entire, 47, 155–156
   feudal concept, 155–156
   financial hardships caused by
      war, 45–46, 111, 150–152
   military capability, 37
   military outlays, 260

vital political concerns, 37,
   121–122
court departments, 105, 239
court's reckonings, 41, 120n,
   141–142
cyclic natural occurrences, 37,
   38, 39, 127–128
   perception of, 93, 219

Dadai Liji (wang Pingzhen),
   133n, 145n, 152n, 192n
Dai Tong (Song), 123n, 185n,
   237n
daifu, 16, 26n
   territories, 153, 172n
dao
   "leadership," 124
   "means," 137
   misinterpretations, 124n,
      128–129n, 241
   read *shou*, 130, 219n
   see also leadership; way
deception
   tactical capability, 60
   types, 40
   and unconventional means,
      136–137
   see also unconventional means
defeat, 55, 120
   assurance of, 40
   caused by operational
      detriments, 92
   controller of, 55, 168
   definite, 92
defeatability, 53, 164–165
defender, 97, 158n, 226
defense
   concrete, 268
   conduction, 54, 276
   depth of, 221, 265
   design, 54
   functions, 53, 165–166
   markets and, 152n
   superior, 63, 64, 180–181
   unconventional means, 41
   understanding, 53–54
defensive measures, 109, 245
Deng Xizi, 229n
destruction
   of a country, etc., 48, 259
   enemy allied support, 104

destruction *(cont.)*
  lethal zones, 95, 224
  restrained release of force, 59,
    176–177
  way of, 37
diplomacy, 95, 102, 224, 233
diplomatic relations, enemy, 49
directions
  cardinal, 205n, 207
  optimum, 267
disadvantage
  armed contention, 69–71
  strategic adaptations, 76–77
discipline
  commander cultivation, 38,
    125
  disorder and, 60, 73
  enemy, loss of, 85
  internalized, 39, 86–87, 216–
    217, 270
  lack of, 92, 219, 221
disorder
  await enemy, 73
  of soldiers, 85, 215
  unconventional means, 41,
    60, 137–138
dominant zone, 94, 201
  action, 95, 102, 277–278
  definition, 95, 101, 221
domination
  of the enemy, 62, 66, 161n
  of enemy actions, 60
  over enemy people and
    terrain, 71–72
  of enemy strength, 64
  of safe terrain, 206
  of situation, 168
dually transversable zone, 94
  action, 95, 102, 233
  definition, 94
Duan Yucai (Qing, 1735–1815),
    see Shuowen
duty
  command, 100
  commander, 39, 47, 90, 91,
    111–112
  of court departments, 105,
    239
  daifu, 26n
  official, 38, 128, 130
  of officials, 152n

shirking, 215
of spearhead forces
  commander, 91–92, 219
Du Mu (Tang, 803–852;
  annotator in the *Shiyijia*),
  119, 120n, 124n, 133n,
  137, 140n, 142, 160, 161n,
  183, 192n, 203–204, 205n,
  206, 210, 212, 217n, 226,
  239, 241n, 243n, 244n,
  245n, 250
Du You (Tang, 735–812;
  annotator in the *Shiyijia*),
  119n, 127n, 183, 190n,
  208n, 219n, 233n, 241n,
  250n, 251n, 252n
Du Yu (Jin, 222–284), 133n,
  137n, 140n, 141n, 158n,
  189n, 212n

economy, 45, 150–152
  pre-Qin China, 125n
enemy, 62–63, 71, 72, 95, 106,
  180, 225
  actions, 60, 82–83
  adapting to, 68
  agents, 113, 114, 249,
    252
  burdens, shifting, 44–45
  defeat, 49, 53, 55, 78
  defeatability, 64–67
  domination, 64, 66, 73
  entrapping, 59–60
  handling, 46, 62–63, 67,
    137
  hidden, 82, 211–212
  inferiorities, 41, 56
  intention, 49
  many, 64, 66, 182–183
  perception, 52, 92–93, 111–
    112
  potential for harm, 73–74
  preparations for battle, 83
  reactions in encounters, 83,
    108
  soldiers, kindness toward
    captured, 47, 154
  studying, 79, 82–86, 105,
    237–238
  territory, 71–72, 275–276,
    279

weaken, 40
well-prepared, 96
Erya (Guo Pu), 123n, 144n,
  153n, 163n, 175n, 190n,
  193n, 200n, 215n, 225n,
  227n, 248n
Erya yishu (Hao Yixing), 175n

failure
  of army, cause, 78
  of enemy, existence of victory
    in, 53
  perception, 39, 42, 133
fatigue
  await, 73
  enemy, 84, 214
  unconventional means, 41
Fengsu tongyi (Ying Shao), 155n
feudal state
  definition, 155–156
  misinterpretation for *guo*, 122n
field marshal
  in susceptible zone, 275
  misinterpretation for
    shangjiang, 190
fire
  attacks, 107–110, 241–247
  invading like, 71, 191
five
  colors, 58, 174, 265
  factors in the control of
    victory, 55–56
  spheres, 37–38, 39n
  tastes, 58, 174
  these, 37, 38, 52, 122–123, 131
  tones, 58, 174
flags, switching, 46
  use, 46n, 72, 172
  well-ordered, 73
  wobbling, 85
flexibility
  to actual needs, 108
  in control, 67
  key to combat power, 61
  in tactics, 67–68
  in troop use, 52
  unpredictable, 136n
foes
  desperate, 74, 85, 197, 214–
    215
  hidden, 82

force, restrained release, 59, 176–177
forces
  combat power, 68, 186–187
  employment, 97–99, 104
  enemy, 74, 82, 86, 196, 212–215
  hazards and benefits of using, 44, 149–50
  missions, 71
  nature, 96–97, 103, 225, 233–234
  of overlord, 103, 234–235
  principles for applying (*bingfa*), 25n
  prize victory, 47
  sizes, ratios, 50, 158–160
  victorious and losing, 55–56
  see also fundamentals in using forces
fundamentals
  in armed contention, 72
  in employing legions, 72, 193–194
  for planning an offense, 50
  in using forces, 43, 48, 50, 69, 73–74, 75, 77, 94, 146, 197–99

Gao You (Han), 126n, 148n, 155n, 181n, 225n, 251n
generals, 38, 131–132, 134n
geographical factors, 37
  adaptations, 39
  definition, 38, 125
  perception, 93, 219
gold
  expenditure, 43, 148
  pre-Qin measurement, 148
Gongyangzhuan (He Xiu), 140n, 141n, 191n, 232n
gorge-path terrain, 88, 89, 218, 234
grammar, ancient sentence patterns, 121n, 126n
Guangya (Zhang Yi), 123n, 126n, 130n, 132n, 140n, 146n, 158n, 161n, 175n, 176n, 189n, 191n, 196n, 203n, 211n, 234n, 245n

Guangzi jijiao (Guo Moruo), 130n
Guanzi (Yi Zhizhang), 120n, 123n, 125n, 127n, 129–130n, 148n, 149n, 151n, 153n, 171n, 174n, 179n, 192n, 194n, 195n, 216, 217n, 228n, 235n
guerrilla warfare, 32n
Guliang zhuan (Fan Ning), 28n, 158n, 159n
Guoyu (Zuo Qiuming), 124n, 135n, 145n, 152n, 190n, 216n, 229n, 236n, 242n, 244n
Guo Xiang (Jin), 124n, 215n
Gu Yanwu (Ming, 1613–1682), 147, 238n

Hanfeizi (Wang Xianshen), 136n, 188n, 221
Han shu (Ban Gu), 129n, 165n
Hao Yixing (Qing, 1757–1825), 175n
harm, 51, 161, 262
  enemy potential for, 73–74
hazards
  elimination, 44, 46–47
  knowing, 44, 149
  laying, 62, 180n
heartland, 45, 259
  definition, 45n
heavens, 90, 125n, 218
  endless as, 58
  highest reaches of, 54, 165–167
Heguanzi (Lu Dian), 128n, 175n, 228n
Helü, the King of Wu, 18–19, 26n, 27n, 30–31n, 32n, 66n, 134n, 135, 227n
  queries (apocrypha), 257–261, 274–280
  tested Sun Wu's military abilities (apocrypha), 30–31n, 269–273
He Shoufa, 134n
He Xiu (Han, 129–182), 140n, 141n, 191n, 232n
He Yanxi (Song; annotator in the *Shiyijia*), 119n, 274

Hou Han shu (Fan Ye), 142n, 165n
Huainanzi (Liu An), 128n, 132n, 194n, 216n
Huang Kan (Liang), 182n, 214n
Huang Zhen (Song, 1213–1280), 136
Huilin (Tang), 131n, 177n

impenetrability, 54
  absolute, 63
  scheming in, 100, 230
infantry, 83, 133
inferiority, 62–68, 179–187
  occurrence, 65
  striking enemy, 41, 56, 57, 68, 186
information
  agent obtainment, 114, 249
  leaked, 114, 252
intelligence work
  influence on military actions, 115
  necessity, 112
  reliance on outstanding, 52
invader, 97, 226
invasion, 71–72, 103–104, 105–106
irregular actions, 58, 82, 173, 174

Jia Gongyan (Tang), 122n, 146n, 189n, 238n
Jia Kui (Han, 30–101), 33n, 120n, 124n, 145n, 146n, 148n
Jia Lin (Tang; annotator in the *Shiyijia*), 119n, 157, 209–211, 213n, 222n, 240n, 241
Jiao Xun (Qing, 1763–1820), 122n, 142n
Jingdian shiwen (Lu Deming), 124n, 133n, 207n, 211n
Jingfa, see Mawangdui silk texts
Jin shu, 206n
judgment
  correct, 51, 65–66, 108
  suppressing, 100, 231
Junzheng, 72, 197n, 198

key traffic zone, 94
  action, 75, 95, 102, 224
  definition, 95, 101, 201, 223
Kong Anguo (Western Han),
  33n, 162n, 230n
Kong Yingda (Tang, 574–648),
  123n, 126n, 127n, 130n,
  132n, 136n, 141n, 146n,
  158n, 174n, 189n, 192n,
  203n, 212n, 218n, 226n,
  229n, 234n, 247n, 250n

Laozi (Wang Bi), 130n, 230–
  231n
leadership, 38, 124, 125–126,
  132
  cultivation of, 55
  definition, 37, 124, 125–126
  enemy, lack of, 81
  establishment, 86–87
lethal land, 37, 38
lethal terrain, 67, 206, 268
lethal zone, 94, 201
  action, 75, 95, 102, 279–280
  definition, 95, 102, 224
Liezi (Zhang Zhan), 186n, 209n
Li Jing (Tang; 571–649), 172n
Liji (Zheng Xuan), 26n, 28n,
  33n, 128n, 129n, 130n,
  133n, 136n, 141n, 142n,
  147n, 149n, 155n, 162n,
  165n, 168n, 171n, 174n,
  185n, 192n, 226n, 229n,
  246n, 247n
Linyi text, 15, 21, 119n, 120,
  123, 126, 128, 132, 135n,
  138, 147, 148, 149n, 150n,
  151, 153, 154n, 157, 161,
  163, 164, 165, 166, 167,
  168, 169, 172, 174, 175,
  177, 179, 180, 181, 182,
  183, 184, 186, 187, 190,
  193, 195, 196, 197, 198,
  200, 201, 202, 206, 208,
  209, 211, 212, 213, 214,
  215, 216, 217n, 218n,
  221, 222, 223, 224, 225,
  226, 227, 228, 231, 232,
  233, 235, 236, 237, 238n,
  239, 241, 242, 243, 244,

246, 247, 248, 249, 250,
  251, 252, 253, 256, 269n,
  270n
Li Quan (Tang; annotator in the
  Shiyijia), 119n, 136–137,
  139, 142, 153n, 160n,
  185n, 212n, 213n, 215n,
  234, 241n, 250
Li Shan (Tang, d. 689), 124n,
  126n, 127n, 129n, 142n,
  148n, 186n, 239n
Liu Xi (Han), 163n
Liu Ying (Ming), 134n, 197–
  198
Li Weigong wendui (Li Jing),
  172n, 178n, 196n
lords
  agent actions, knowledge,
  115, 252–253
  arrogant, 261
  capable, 126n
  enlightened, 109, 110, 112,
  185, 246
  feudal, 203, 204, 222, 224,
  233n, 257, 259
  harm armies, 51, 161
  leadership ability, 38, 132
  modest, 261
  orders, 69, 75–76, 92, 135,
  202, 262–264, 270–271,
  273
  other, 44, 51, 71, 77, 100,
  103, 203
  overlord, *see* overlord
  surnames and, 152n
  to not intervene, 52
lowlands, 81, 205n, 211, 265–
  266
Lu Deming (Tang, 556–627),
  133n, 178n, 207n, 211n
Lunyu (He An), 121n, 140n,
  148n, 156n, 182n, 195n,
  208n, 214n, 244n
Lunyu zhu (Zheng Xuan), 140n
Lüshi Chungiu (Lü Buwei), 126n,
  128n, 140n, 155n, 225n,
  251n

maneuvers, 63, 71
  advantageous, 103

army, 81, 211
  troop, 79–87, 205–217
Mao Heng (Han), 33n, 176n,
  208n, 213n, 231n, 236n
Ma Rong (Han, 79–166), 122n,
  209n
Ma Ruichen (Qing, 1782–1853),
  191n
mastery, covert, 112, 249–250
matériel and supplies
  management, 38, 128, 131
  burning, 107
  risks caused by loss of, 70
Ma Xulun, 126n
Mawangdui silk texts
  Jingfa, 148–149n, 244n, 246
  Zhanguoce, 140n, 149n
Mei Yaochen (Song, 1002–1060;
  annotator in the *Shiyijia*),
  119n, 134n, 208n, 210,
  218, 237n, 243n, 245n, 250
Mencius (Warring States, 372–
  289 B.C.), 156n, 251
  see also Mengzi
Mengshi (Liang; annotator in
  the *Shiyijia*), 119n, 126n,
  127n, 134n, 223
Mengzi (Zhao Qi), 130n, 156n,
  223n, 235n, 248n, 249n
methodical swiftness, 44, 149
miles, pre-Qin measurement,
  147
military actions
  costs, 111
  hazards, 44
military affairs, 123, 125n, 128n,
  131, 140, 142, 143, 155,
  172, 187
  definition, 121
  precepts for, 115, 253
  Sun-tzu, guide for, 15
  and surveying, 119
  vital political concerns, 37,
  121
military operations, 109, 132n,
  274
  causes for "many" and "few"
  in, 65
  joint, 222
  key to, 139

need for effectiveness and
    brevity, 44, 47
terrain, 267
unconventional means, 40,
    136–137
mission
    achievement of, 105, 112,
        238, 246
    expeditionary, 136
mobilization, regulations, 38,
    128, 130
mobilizing for armed conflict,
    43–47, 144–156
    definition, 144
moon, 54, 58, 68, 127n, 128n,
    263
    aligned with constellations,
        108, 243
    influence on weather
        aberrations, 127n
morale
    depression of, 41, 73, 85, 138,
        194–196
    handling of enemy, 73
    high, 46, 138, 261
mountain forests, 71, 81, 95,
    103, 201, 222n, 223–224
Mozi (Sun Yirang), 28n, 235n,
    242n

nature, 68
    of agent activities, 113
    of forces, 96, 103, 225, 233–
        234
    of logs and rocks, 60–61
    of victory, 53
numbers, pre-Qin definitions
    the four or five, 234–235
    hundred, 162
    nine, 166–167n, 200
    three, 189–190, 223
    thrice, 150

obedience
    ingrained, 217, 270
    internalized, 98
    loss of troop, 85
    of people, 86–87
obstacled terrain, 88, 89, 234
obstacles, 71, 81, 91, 95, 103,

201, 211, 212n, 222n, 223–
    224, 278
offense
    conduction, 54, 97–103
    government coordination,
        105–106
    planning, 48–52, 157–162
    understanding, 53–54
officers, fear of soldiers, 85,
    215
operation
    basic principles, 71
    conduction, 45–47
    of fires, 107
    in offense, 97–103
    joint, 84, 105, 213, 222, 239–
        240
    requirements, 71
    risks, 70
    six detriments, 90–91
    wariness of enemy, 108
orders
    adaptation of, 104
    carrying out, 39
    countermanding those of a
        lord, 31n, 75–76, 92, 135,
        202, 262–264, 270–271,
        273
    in employing forces, 104
    ingrained execution of, 87,
        217, 270
    troop discipline, 39
organization and squad training,
    57, 171–172
overlord, 103–104, 234–235

passable terrain, 88
passes
    difficult to forge, 95, 222n,
        223–224
    sunder, 105, 238
Pei Xuehai, 149n, 165n, 166n,
    194n, 236n, 240n, 244n
people
    engaged in battle, 56, 169–
        170
    obedience, 37, 86, 126–127
    ruled, 71
    strong, 39, 132
    united, 72

of Yue and Wu, 99
    see also citizenry
perception, 52, 93, 161, 195
    of battles, 65–66, 184
    definition, 161
    of victory, 51
peripheral sites, 80, 206–207
pincer movement, 82, 212
plans, 75, 97, 100
    enemy, 49
policy, 104, 105, 236
political concerns, 37, 121–122,
    134
position on heights, 80, 205–
    206
positions, 101, 221
    inextricable, 97, 98, 102, 201,
        226, 232
    undefeatable, 55
power, 56, 169, 177
    mental, 49
    military, 246
    military, enemy, 49
    pre-Qin definitions, 135
    superior, 103–104
    see also combat power
preparedness
    awaiting unpreparedness
        with, 52, 53, 62, 140
    enemy, 276
    existence of victory in, 53
    in fire attacks, 108
    pre-Qin period, definition, 120
protraction, 44, 149
    avoidance, 49
    as opposed to victory, 47
provisions, 70
    burning, 107, 279
    collection, 97, 275, 277
    drayage, 43, 144, 150–151
    enemy, 45
    requisitioning additional, 44
psychology
    anticipated reactions, 99
    burnout, 85
    manipulation through, 62
    troop, 97–98

Qian Daxin (Qing, 1744–1813),
    124n

Qianfulun (Wang Fu), 155n, 165n
Qi Jiguang (Ming, 1528–1587), 134n
Qi state, 15–17, 19–20, 140n, 223, 228n, 248n, 253, 257
 dialect, ancient, 140n, 191n
 see also Sun Wu
 (*see* Map 2, p. 258)

regions, four major types, 79–80, 207
regular actions, 57, 58, 173, 174
remote terrain, 88, 89
restrained release of force, 59, 176–177
retreat, 72, 74, 83, 181–182, 234, 275, 276, 277
rewards, 216, 217
 adaptation, 104
 agent, 113
 conferring, 85, 236, 246, 273
 motivation, 46, 154
 and punishments, clarity, 39
rigidity, gaining, 99, 229
risk, 52, 162
 numerous deaths, 98, 227
rivers, 58, 79–80, 174, 207, 210, 278
Ruan Yuan (Qing, 1764–1849), 237n, 247n
rule(s), 37, 39, 55, 217, 265
 functions, 38, 128
 tactical, adherence to, 108
 there is a, 55, 168–169
 transcending, 104, 236

safe land, 37, 38
safe terrain, 67, 205–208
Sakurada version, 119n, 121, 126n, 139, 150n, 178, 196, 197, 198, 199, 201n, 212n, 213, 215, 235n, 249n, 250n, 251n
seasons and lunar periods, 38, 125, 127–128
security, 37–39, 47, 48, 92, 154
sense, 73, 194–195
separated zone, 94
 action, 95
 definition, 94, 102, 222–223

serpent at Mount Heng, 98–99, 228
severable zone, action, 75
 definition, 101, 201
Shangjunshu (Zhu Shiche), 144n, 216
Shiji (Sima Qian), 28n, 29n, 30n, 31n, 32n, 120n, 141n, 148n, 155n, 158n, 174n, 222–223, 227n, 231, 267, 269n, 270n
Shijia (*Sunzi shijia zhu*, Sun Xingyan and Wu Renji), 28n, 29n, 33n, 119n, 123n, 126n, 139n, 150n, 155n, 157n, 173n, 176n, 180, 185n, 194n, 201n, 202n, 205n, 208n, 211n, 212n, 215n, 217n, 219n, 224n, 233n, 241n, 243n, 248n
Shijing (Mao Heng), 123n, 127n, 152n, 176n, 191–192n, 208n, 213n, 231n, 236n, 250n
Shiyijia (*Shiyijia zhu Sunzi*, Ji Tiaobao), 25n, 119n, 120n, 121n, 126n, 139, 150n, 161, 169, 178, 180, 192n, 194n, 196n, 198n, 200, 201, 202, 205n, 211, 212n, 213, 215, 218, 219, 220, 223, 224, 227, 231, 235, 238n, 240n, 241n, 251, 252, 256, 274n
Shujing (*Shangshu zhengyi*, Kong Anguo), 127n, 162n, 171–172n, 177n, 191n, 192n, 218n, 230n
Shuowen (*Shuowen jiezi*, Xu Shen), 120n, 123n, 124n, 126n, 128n, 130n, 132, 135n, 142n, 144n, 147n, 148n, 153n, 157n, 161n, 163n, 167n, 168n, 172n, 175n, 176n, 178n, 181n, 182n, 183n, 185n, 188n, 192n, 196n, 203n, 204n, 205n, 206n, 209n, 212n, 213n, 216n, 218n, 222n, 223n, 227n, 229n, 230n,

231n, 236n, 239n, 245n, 246n, 248n, 249n
Shuowen tongxun dingsheng (Zhu Junsheng), 161n, 177n, 225n, 231n, 233n
signals
 and designations, 57, 179
 orders, 72, 193–194
Sima Biao (Jin), 129n
Sima fa (author unknown, Zhou), 271n
Sima Qian (Western Han, 145–86 B.C.), 29n, 31n
Sima Zhen (Tang), 155n
situation
 ambiguous, 85
 conflict, 40
 grasp of one's, 52
 relationship with combat power and troop capability, 60–61
soldiers, 39, 60, 90, 92–93, 96, 133, 178
 bond with, 86
 dangers of overindulgence, 92, 219
 elite enemy, 74, 196
 enemy, care of, 47, 154
 will to fight, 104–105
 see also forces; infantry; troops
speed, in offensive strategy, 96
stalemated terrain, 88, 89
stratagems, 75, 96, 97, 279, 280
strategic adaptations, 75–76
strategic zones
 six varieties, 88–90, 101–102
 nine types, 94–96
strategy
 commander aptitude regarding, 76
 commander duty, 39
 conduction, 50–52
 designing, 43
 offensive, 48–50, 94–97, 158n
 political, 109, 246
 security, 37, 48
 successful, 41
 war, 184
strength
 balance of, 54
 cataclysmic flood, 59, 135, 175

concentrate, 86, 238
contrasts in, 57, 173
domination of enemy, 64
exhausted, 44
full expression, 99
gaining through victory, 46
handling enemy, 73
shortcomings in, causes, 65
striking enemy, 41
strike
  decisive, 41, 57
  of raptors, 59, 176–177
Sun Bin (Warring States, fourth
  century B.C.), 25n, 135n,
  139n, 169, 217n
Sun Bin bingfa (*The Strategic
  Doctrine of Sun Bin*,
  Yinqueshan Hanmu zhujian
  zhengli xiaozu), 33n, 121n,
  135n, 139n, 158n, 164n,
  169n, 175n, 176n, 194n,
  217n, 235n, 242, 262n,
  271n
Sun-tzu, *see* Sun Wu
Sun Wu
  author of *Sun-tzu*, 15
  biography, 15, 17–20, 25–32n,
    66n, 227n
  family, 15–17, 20, 27–28n,
    29n
  influence on *Sun Bin bingfa*,
    139n
  and Mencius, 251
  native of Qi, 15, 29n, 129,
    140n, 191n, 232n
  precept, 23, 185
  writings, 25n, 33n
  see also Chen Shu; Helü; Qi
    state; Wu state
Sun Wu binglue wenda, 274n
Sun Xingyan (Qing, 1753–
  1818), 22, 25n, 28n, 29n,
  119, 123n, 135n, 150n,
  155n, 157n, 173, 176,
  180, 201n, 202n, 208n,
  211, 212n, 214n, 215n,
  217n, 219n, 224n, 243n,
  251n
Sun Yirang (Qing, 1848–1908),
  131n, 190n, 242n, 246n,
  251n

superiority, 66, 97, 205–206,
  276, 280
  control of, in war, 55–56
  establishment, 40
  and inferiority, 62–68, 179–
    187
superior powers, 103–104
superstition, 98, 227
suppleness, 99, 229
supplies, 46, 70, 128
  vehicle and armor, 43, 145
support
  allied, 103
  commander, 51
  enemy, 104
  mutual, 66, 98–99, 184
supremacy, 73
surprise
  actions, 72
  emergence, 41, 63, 139, 180,
    275, 277
  flank attacks, 82
  offense, 97, 106
surrounded zone, 94
  action, 75, 96, 102, 278–279
  definition, 95, 101, 201
surveying, 37–42, 119, 143
  national security or
    possibilities for victory, 37
  pre-Qin definitions, 119–120
surveys, 140
  advantages, 40
  commander obeyance, 39–40,
    133–135, 202
  verification through, 37, 38,
    123
susceptible zone, 94
  action, 95, 102, 201, 232,
    275–276
  definition, 94, 101
swamp, 71, 80, 95, 103, 201,
  222n, 223–224
synchronization
  in employing forces, 104
  inability of feudal lords, 222
  restrained power, 177

tactical capability, for entrapping
  the enemy, 59–60
tactics, 58, 67–68, 226
  basic tactical doctrine, 73

individual requirements,
  108
rigid, 68
in *Sun Bin bingfa*, 164n
tricks, 82
Taiping yulan (Li Fang), 139n,
  147n, 150n, 151n, 155n,
  157n, 180n, 185n, 192n,
  194n, 206n, 208n, 209n,
  214n, 215n, 216n, 217n,
  219n, 236n, 240n, 243n,
  247n, 248n, 250n, 251n,
  252n
taxes
  heavy, 45, 150
  pre-Qin, 150n, 153n, 259–61
terrain, 88–93, 164, 218–220
  advantages, 71, 80, 99, 103
  four major regions, 79–80
  gigantic coops, 81, 209, 210
  gigantic pits, 81, 209, 210
  gigantic prisons, 81, 209, 210
  gigantic rifts, 81, 209, 210–
    211
  gigantic traps, 81, 209, 210
  hills and banks, 81
  nine zones, 94–99
  principle for, 99, 229
  reinforcement for forces, 91
  searching and guarding, 81
  severed ravines, 81, 209–210
  six zones, 88–90, 101–102
  superiority, 205–206
  II (apocrypha), 267–268
  unstable for battle, 93
  water conforms to, 68, 186
  see also specific headings
those sophisticated
  at attack, 54, 63
  at battle, 59, 60, 62, 96, 161n,
    167, 225
  at command, 64, 182
  at commanding battle arrays,
    98, 228
  at creating irregular actions,
    58, 173
  at defense, 54, 63, 181
  at strategy, 53, 54, 55, 164,
    167
those who weigh victory, 56,
  169

Tongdian (Du You), 150n, 151n, 157n, 185n, 192n, 194n, 206n, 208n, 214n, 215n, 217n, 220n, 233n, 243n, 251n, 252n
topography, 71, 103
training, 86
  quality, 39
  squad, 57, 60, 171–172
troop capability
  relationship with combat power and situation, 60–61
  requirement for combat power, 59
troops, 178n
  ambush, definition, 212
  cause of country's impoverishment, 45, 150–151
  designations, 172
  discipline, 39
  enemy bivouacking, 83
  face mortality, 102
  motivation, 46
  perilously caught, 105
  preparation for combat, 98
  raising, 43, 111, 145
  surrounded organized enemy, 74, 196
  use, flexibility in, 52

unconventional means, 40–41, 136–137
unconventional warfare, 40n
undefeatability, 53, 164, 165

variations
  handling enemy, 73
  in irregular and regular actions, 58
victory, 39, 41, 42, 46, 47, 51, 52, 53, 54, 56, 86, 92–93, 140, 167, 169, 206, 226
  achievement, 48, 168, 187, 217
  attainment, 48, 55
  can be grasped, 66, 183, 184
  complete, 54, 93, 166, 220, 276
  contending for, 111, 248
  definite, 92

determination, 53, 55, 67, 185
  of a force, 68, 186
  military, achievement of political goals following, 109, 245–246
  perception, 39, 52, 92, 93, 133
  prediction, 41, 141–143
  surrendering, 51, 161
  unorthodox, 55, 167
  ways for battle, 92, 262, 270
vital political concerns, 37, 121, 122, 134

Wang Bi (Jin), 130n, 231n
Wang Fu (Eastern Han), 165
Wang Jipei (Qing), 155n
Wang Li, 121n, 123n
Wang Niansun (Qing, 1744–1832), 123n, 130, 159, 173n, 191n, 208n, 211n, 239n, 245n
Wang Pinzhen (Qing), 147n, 192n
Wang Xi (Song; annotator in the *Shiyijia*), 119n, 134n, 136n, 151n, 172, 174n, 209n, 210, 211, 252n
Wang Xianqian (Qing, 1842–1917), 131n, 135n, 163n, 215n
Wang Yinzhi (Qing, 1766–1834), 121n, 146n, 185n, 189n, 190n, 195n, 207n, 236n, 240n, 243n, 245n
Wang Yun (Qing, 1784–1854), 189n
Wang Zhong (Qing, 1744–1794), 166n, 223n
war, 141
  logistical burdens, 144
  misinterpretation for *bing*, 121
  pre-Qin euphemisms, 141n
  should never be lightly initiated, 110
  strategy, 184
  see also armed conflict; battles; military affairs
way
  of command, 99

of existence and destruction, 37
of safeguarding the country and securing the army, 110
weakness
  attack enemy, 41, 139–140
  deception, 60
weapons
  bing, 121n
  burning, 107, 241n
  dull, 44
  incendiary, 242n
  long, hiding, 277
  quality, 39, 132
weather
  aberrations, 38n, 127
  for attack fires, 107–108, 242
  using as a shroud, 275
Weiliao (Warring States), 25n
Weiliaozi, 152n
Wei Zhao (Three Kingdoms, 204–273), 124n, 135n, 145n, 152n, 216n, 229n, 236n, 242n, 244n
Wenxuan (Xiao Tong), 124n, 126n, 127n, 129n, 142n, 148n, 174n, 186n, 209n, 228n, 239n
Wenzi jilue, 131n
winds, 71, 109, 127n, 191, 244
  in attack fires, 108, 242
  gales of, 108, 228–229, 243
withdrawal, 51, 64, 84, 89, 134, 181–182, 213–214, 234
Wu Changying (Qing), 150n, 183n
Wujing (Wujing qishu), 119n, 121n, 126n, 139, 149n, 150n, 161, 169, 178, 180, 194n, 196, 197, 198, 200, 201, 202, 211, 212n, 213, 215, 218, 219, 223–224, 231, 235, 238, 251, 252
Wu Renji (Qing), *see* Sun Xingyan
Wu Shidao (Yuan, 1283–1344), 146n
Wu state, 17–20, 25n, 26n, 27n, 29n, 31n, 32n, 33n, 66, 99
  location, 259

see also Helü; Sun Wu (*see* Map 2, p. 258)
Wu Yue Chunqiu (Zhao Ye), 269n
Wuzi (Wu Qi), 141n

Xiaojing (*Xiaojing zhushu*, Xuanzong emperor), 126n
Xing Bing (Song, 932–1010), 123n, 148n, 153n, 193n, 195n
Xin Tang shu (Ouyang Xiu et al.), 29n
Xuanying (Tang), 120n, 126n, 182n
Xuanzong (Tang emperor), 126n
Xu Han shu (Sima Biao), 129n
Xun Ying, General (Warring States), 33n
Xunzi (Yang Bing), 122, 123n, 124n, 126n, 130n, 131n, 135n, 139n, 140n, 155n, 163n, 171n, 175n, 192n, 202, 211n, 235n, 237n, 245n, 250n
Xu Shen (Eastern Han, 30–124), 163n, 196n

Yang Bojun, 28n, 29n, 30n, 121n, 122n, 140n
Yang Jing (Tang), 122n, 123n, 126n, 130n, 139n, 140n, 155n, 163n, 171n, 237n, 245n
Yang Shuda (1885–1956), 121n, 133n, 150n, 166n, 167n,

185n, 188n, 243n, 245n, 248n
Yan Yannian (Han), 239n
Yellow Emperor
attack on the Red Emperor (apocrypha), 265–266
victory of, 80, 207
Ye Shi (Song), 31n
Yu Fan (Three Kingdoms, 164–233), 135n
Yu Shengwu, 211n, 231n, 248n
Yu Xingwu, 140n
Yu Yue (Qing, 1821–1906), 126n, 128n, 130n, 215n

Zhang Pen version, 198–199
Zhanguoce (Liu Xiang), 131n, 140n, 141n, 146n, 147n, 149n, 181n, 203n, 228n, 247
Zhang Yu (Song; annotator in the *Shiyijia*), 119n, 134n, 136, 137, 142, 150n, 178n, 190, 192n, 206n, 208n, 210–211, 212n, 217n, 222n, 235, 242, 243n, 245n, 250, 252n, 274n
Zhang Zhan (Jin), 186n
Zhao Benxue (Ming), 134n, 139, 144, 200, 208n, 212, 213, 219n, 224n, 231n
Zhao Chongkuo (Western Han, 137–52 B.C.), 165
Zhao Qi (Han), 130n, 223n, 249n

Zheng Xuan (Han, 127–200), 33n, 120n, 127n, 129n, 130n, 136n, 140n, 145n, 146n, 147n, 149n, 152n, 153n, 155n, 162, 165, 168n, 171n, 172n, 174n, 175n, 185n, 208n, 226n, 231n, 238n, 246n, 251n
Zheng Youxian (Song), 173, 185n
Zhou Fagao, 123n, 185n
Zhou Guangye (Qing), 233n
Zhouli (*Zhouli zhushu*, Zheng Xuan), 28n, 120n, 122n, 129n, 131n, 133n, 145n, 146n, 153n, 155n, 172n, 188n, 189n, 192n, 231n, 238n, 251n, 277n
Zhuangzi (Guo Xiang), 124n, 178n, 211n, 215n
Zhuan Zhu (Warring States), 227
Zhu Junsheng, 161n, 177n, 225n, 231n
Zhu Shiche, 144n
Zhu Xi (Song, 1130–1200), 144n, 237n
Zizhi tongjian (Sima Guang et al.), 147n, 158n
Zuozhuan (Du Yu), 29n, 30n, 32n, 33n, 121n, 122n, 123n, 126n, 132n, 133n, 137n, 138n, 140n, 141n, 142n, 146n, 155n, 158n, 169n, 189n, 191n, 195n, 203n, 212n, 235n, 247n